REVISION W[

Constitutional Law:
THE MACHINERY OF GOVERNMENT

Third Edition

OLD BAILEY PRESS

OLD BAILEY PRESS
at Holborn College, Woolwich Road,
Charlton, London, SE7 8LN

First published 1997
Third edition 2002

ISBN 1 85836 460 4

British Library Cataloguing-in-Publication.

A CIP Catalogue record for this book is available from the British Library.

Printed and bound in Great Britain.

Contents

Acknowledgements

Some questions used are taken or adapted from past University of London LLB (External) Degree examination papers and our thanks are extended to the University of London for their kind permission to use and publish the questions.

Caveat

The answers given are not approved or sanctioned by the University of London and are entirely our responsibility.

They are not intended as 'Model Answers', but rather as Suggested Solutions.

The answers have two fundamental purposes, namely:

a) to provide a detailed example of a suggested solution to an examination question; and

b) to assist students with their research into the subject and to further their understanding and appreciation of the subject.

Introduction

This Revision WorkBook has been designed specifically for those studying constitutional law to undergraduate level. Its coverage is not confined to any one syllabus, but embraces all the major constitutional law topics to be found in university examinations.

Each chapter contains a brief introduction explaining the scope and overall content of the topic covered in that chapter. There follows, in each case, a list of key points which will assist the student in studying and memorising essential material with which the student should be familiar in order to fully understand the topic.

Additionally in each chapter there is a key cases and statutes section which lists the most relevant cases and statutory provisions applicable to the topic in question. These are intended as an aid to revision, providing the student with a concise list of materials from which to begin revision.

Each chapter ends with several typical examination questions, together with general comments, skeleton solutions and suggested solutions. Wherever possible, the questions are drawn from University of London external constitutional law papers, with recent questions being included where possible. However, it is inevitable that, in compiling a list of questions by topic order rather than chronologically, not only do the same questions crop up over and over again in different guises, but there are gaps where questions have never been set at all.

Undoubtedly, the main feature of this Revision WorkBook is the inclusion of as many past examination questions as possible. While the use of past questions as a revision aid is certainly not new, it is hoped that the combination of actual past questions from the University of London LLB external course and specially written questions, where there are gaps in examination coverage, will be of assistance to students in achieving a thorough and systematic revision of the subject.

Careful use of the Revision WorkBook should enhance the student's understanding of constitutional law and, hopefully, enable you to deal with as wide a range of subject matter as anyone might find in a constitutional law examination, while at the same time allowing you to practise examination techniques while working through the book.

Studying Constitutional Law

Constitutional law is a vast subject covering a variety of topics ranging from the structure and organisation of government to civil liberties. Examiners must be selective in the areas they choose to examine and students should pay regard to their particular syllabus and the emphasis placed on each topic. By and large however the subject divides into two areas – the characteristics of the British Constitution and civil liberties. If your syllabus includes judicial review of administrative action you should also refer to the *Administrative Law Revision WorkBook*, published by Old Bailey Press.

The first part of any syllabus – usually the characteristics of the British Constitution – demands a background knowledge of British history and politics. This can cause problems for students who do not have any interest or knowledge of this area and overseas students in particular can experience difficulty here. To place the subject in its proper context requires some background reading – Maitland's *A Constitutional History of England* is authoritative – and knowledge gleaned from keeping abreast of current affairs is vital. In addition there are several good introductory works which help students. In terms of the examination this area can unsettle students simply because there is an absence of legal authority for the points they make. The questions are often discursive demanding the discussion of an issue and the presentation of a point of view. A well-read student who can present the salient points with authority will achieve good marks – the student who 'waffles' will not. Examples are important eg answer to a question on conventions demands an explanation of the part played by convention in our constitution backed by examples of conventions in operation.

The second part of the syllabus will deal with civil liberties. Again this is an extensive area and examiners are often selective. Police powers may appear in some syllabuses, citizenship and immigration in others. It is important to appreciate that what liberties are enjoyed in the United Kingdom are residual and the part played by the European Convention on Human Rights as enacted in the Human Rights Act 1998 must be understood. The subject matter is topical, statute and case law are important. Questions can be either essay or problem. Problem questions, for example on public order or police powers, require students to apply the relevant statute and case law to the facts given, remembering again to take care to advise the client.

In essence constitutional law, like all legal subjects, requires students to present arguments in a precise, reasoned and authoritative manner.

Revision and Examination Technique

Revision Technique

Planning a revision timetable

In planning your revision timetable make sure you do not finish the syllabus too early. You should avoid leaving revision so late that you have to 'cram' – but constant revision of the same topic leads to stagnation.

Plan ahead, however, and try to make your plans increasingly detailed as you approach the examination date.

Allocate enough time for each topic to be studied. But note that it is better to devise a realistic timetable, to which you have a reasonable chance of keeping, rather than a wildly optimistic schedule which you will probably abandon at the first opportunity!

The syllabus and its topics

One of your first tasks when you began your course was to ensure that you thoroughly understood your syllabus. Check now to see if you can write down the topics it comprises from memory. You will see that the chapters of this WorkBook are each devoted to a syllabus topic. This will help you decide which are the key chapters relative to your revision programme, though you should allow some time for glancing through the other chapters.

The topic and its key points

Again working from memory, analyse what you consider to be the key points of any topic that you have selected for particular revision. Seeing what you can recall, unaided, will help you to understand and firmly memorise the concepts involved.

Using the WorkBook

Relevant questions are provided for each topic in this book. Naturally, as typical examples of examination questions, they do not normally relate to one topic only. But the questions in each chapter will relate to the subject matter of the chapter to a degree. You can choose your method of consulting the questions and solutions, but here are some suggestions (strategies 1–3). Each of them pre-supposes that you have read through the author's notes on key points and key cases and statutes, and any other preliminary matter, at the beginning of the chapter. Once again, you now need to practise working from memory, for that is the challenge you are preparing yourself for. As a rule of procedure constantly test yourself once revision starts, both orally and in writing.

Strategy 1

Strategy 1 is planned for the purpose of quick revision. First read your chosen question carefully and then jot down in abbreviated notes what you consider to be the main points at issue. Similarly, note the cases and statutes that occur to you as being relevant for citation purposes. Allow yourself sufficient time to cover what you feel to be relevant. Then study the author's skeleton solution and skim-read the suggested solution to see how they compare with your notes. When comparing consider carefully what the author has included (and concluded) and see whether that agrees with what you have written. Consider the points of variation also. Have you recognised the key issues? How relevant have you been? It is possible, of course, that you have referred to a recent case that is relevant, but which had not been reported when the WorkBook was prepared.

Strategy 2

Strategy 2 requires a nucleus of three hours in which to practise writing a set of examination answers in a limited time-span.

Select a number of questions (as many as are normally set in your subject in the examination you are studying for), each from a different chapter in the WorkBook, without consulting the solutions. Find a place to write where you will not be disturbed and try to arrange not to be interrupted for three hours. Write your solutions in the time allowed, noting any time needed to make up if you are interrupted.

After a rest, compare your answers with the suggested solutions in the WorkBook. There will be considerable variation in style, of course, but the bare facts should not be too dissimilar. Evaluate your answer critically. Be 'searching', but develop a positive approach to deciding how you would tackle each question on another occasion.

Strategy 3

You are unlikely to be able to do more than one three hour examination, but occasionally set yourself a single question. Vary the 'time allowed' by imagining it to be one of the questions that you must answer in three hours and allow yourself a limited preparation and writing time. Try one question that you feel to be difficult and an easier question on another occasion, for example.

Misuse of suggested solutions

Don't try to learn by rote. In particular, don't try to reproduce the suggested solutions by heart. Learn to express the basic concepts in your own words.

Keeping up-to-date

Keep up-to-date. While examiners do not require familiarity with changes in the law during the three months prior to the examination, it obviously creates a good impression if you can show you are acquainted with any recent changes. Make a habit of looking through one of the leading journals – *Modern Law Review, Law Quarterly Review* or the *New Law Journal*, for example – and cumulative indices to law reports, such as the *All England Law Reports* or *Weekly Law Reports*, or indeed the daily law reports in *The Times*. The *Law Society's Gazette* and the *Legal Executive Journal* are helpful sources, plus any specialist journal(s) for the subject you are studying. In particular, for company law, the *Company Lawyer* is the best source of the most recent cases, most of which will be supplied with an excellent summary.

Examination Skills

Examiners are human too!

The process of answering an examination question involves a communication between you and the person who set it. If you were speaking face to face with the person, you would choose your verbal points and arguments carefully in your reply. When writing, it is all too easy to forget the human being who is awaiting the reply and simply write out what one knows in the area of the subject! Bear in mind it is a person whose question you are responding to, throughout your essay. This will help you to avoid being irrelevant or long-winded.

The essay question

Candidates are sometimes tempted to choose to answer essay questions because they 'seem' easier. But the examiner is looking for thoughtful work and will not give good marks for superficial answers.

The essay-type of question may be either purely factual, in asking you to explain the meaning of a certain doctrine or principle, or it may ask you to discuss a certain proposition, usually derived from a quotation. In either case, the approach to the answer is the same. A clear programme must be devised to give the examiner the meaning or significance of the doctrine, principle or proposition and its origin in common law, equity or statute, and cases which illustrate its application to the branch of law concerned. Essay questions offer a good way to obtain marks if you have thought carefully about a topic, since it is up to you to impose the structure (unlike the problem questions where the problem imposes its own structure). You are then free to speculate and show imagination.

The problem question

The problem-type question requires a different approach. You may well be asked to advise a client or merely discuss the problems raised in the question. In either case, the most important factor is to take great care in reading the question. By its nature, the question will be longer than the essay-type question and you will have a number of facts to digest. Time spent in analysing the question may well save time later, when you are endeavouring to impress on the examiner the considerable extent of your basic legal knowledge. The quantity of knowledge is itself a trap and you must always keep within the boundaries of the question in hand. It is very tempting to show the examiner the extent of your knowledge of your subject, but if this is outside the question, it is time lost and no marks earned. It is inevitable that some areas which you have studied and revised will not be the subject of questions, but under no circumstances attempt to adapt a question to a stronger area of knowledge at the expense of relevance.

When you are satisfied that you have grasped the full significance of the problem-type question, set out the fundamental principles involved.

You will then go on to identify the fundamental problem (or problems) posed by the question. This should be followed by a consideration of the law which is relevant to the problem. The source of the law, together with the cases which will be of assistance in solving the problem, must then be considered in detail.

Very good problem questions are quite likely to have alternative answers, and in advising a party you should be aware that alternative arguments may be available. Each stage of your answer, in this case, will be based on the argument or arguments considered in the previous stage, forming a conditional sequence.

If, however, you only identify one fundamental problem, do not waste time worrying that you cannot think of an alternative – there may very well be only that one answer.

The examiner will then wish to see how you use your legal knowledge to formulate a case and how you apply that formula to the problem which is the subject of the question. It is this positive approach which can make answering a problem question a high mark earner for the student who has fully understood the question and clearly argued their case on the established law.

Examination checklist

a) Read the instructions at the head of the examination carefully. While last-minute changes are unlikely – such as the introduction of a compulsory question or an increase in the number of questions asked – it has been known to happen.

b) Read the questions carefully. Analyse problem questions – work out what the examiner wants.

c) Plan your answer before you start to write.

d) Check that you understand the rubric before you start to write. Do not 'discuss', for example, if you are specifically asked to 'compare and contrast'.

e) Answer the correct number of questions. If you fail to answer one out of four questions set you lose 25 per cent of your marks!

Style and structure

Try to be clear and concise. Fundamentally this amounts to using paragraphs to denote the sections of your essay, and writing simple, straightforward sentences as much as possible. The sentence you have just read has 22 words – when a sentence reaches 50 words it becomes difficult for a reader to follow.

Do not be inhibited by the word 'structure' (traditionally defined as giving an essay a beginning, a middle and an end). A good structure will be the natural consequence of setting out your arguments and the supporting evidence in a logical order. Set the scene briefly in your opening paragraph. Provide a clear conclusion in your final paragraph.

Table of Cases

Table of Statutes and Other Materials

Chapter 1

The Nature and Sources of Constitutional Law

1.1   **Introduction**

1.2   **Key points**

1.3   **Key cases and statutes**

1.4   **Questions and suggested solutions**

1.1 Introduction

Constitutions define political authority and the basis for the exercise of political authority. They regulate the relationships of the principal organs of government – legislature, executive and judiciary – to each other and define their functions. A constitution is essentially a framework of rules that makes up the system whereby a state is governed.

In most modern states these rules are contained in a single document which may or may not incorporate a Bill of Rights. The Bill of Rights will normally provide citizens with guarantees regarding the protection of certain civil liberties. Such constitutions are subject to judicial interpretation in the sense that the courts can assess the legality of legislative measures by reference to the constitutional document. The United Kingdom has no written constitution as such, although some of the sources of the constitution are to be found in written form, such as statute and common law. Other key sources of constitutional law, however, are clearly unwritten – such as custom and convention. Whilst conventions undoubtedly play an important part in the United Kingdom they cannot be enforced in the courts.

The constitution of the United Kingdom has evolved over centuries and the 'rules' of constitutional behaviour are not contained in any single document. A point of comparison can be made with the USA where, following the American War of Independence, a written document was prepared, which established fundamental constitutional principles and safeguarded the rights of citizens.

1.2 Key points

Written and unwritten constitutions

The term 'written constitution' is used in relation to those countries with a single document (or a group of documents) that contains the basic rules and to which reference can be made to test whether or not the organs of government are acting 'constitutionally'. By contrast, under an 'unwritten constitution' no such document exists and the rules have to be established from the ordinary laws of the land.

Flexible and rigid constitutions

Most countries with a written constitution require some special procedure before constitutional changes can be effected – for example a referendum or a two-thirds majority of the elected chamber. In this sense the constitution is 'entrenched'. Flexible constitutions are so described because constitutional change can be achieved by the same procedure as changes in laws generally. This is the position in the United Kingdom.

Other classifications

A system of government which is accountable to the people is described as democratic government. constitutions define the way in which a government is to be responsible and the way in which it is elected.

Federal states are those states in which regions enjoy autonomous law-making power – such as the United States. Unitary states are those in which power is focused on central government. The United Kingdom has a unitary system of government in that the United Kingdom Parliament at Westminster is the supreme law-making body. Some power has been devolved to the regions, such as the creation of the Scottish Parliament under the Scotland Act 1998, and the Welsh Assembly under the Government of Wales Act 1998, but neither are sovereign legislatures in their own right.

The head of state can vary in form. It may be a monarch, a president or a chairman. The extent of their powers is defined by the constitution so that, for example, while the President of the USA enjoys significant powers, the President of the Republic of Ireland enjoys a position analogous to our own monarch – that is to say most of their executive powers are exercised by ministers.

A constitution is in a sense a 'higher' form of law. It is the basis upon which all other laws derive their validity and force. However, it remains valid only for as long as those subject to it accept its rules as binding.

Aspects of the United Kingdom constitution

The United Kingdom Parliament is sovereign. There is no limit on the competence of Parliament to enact legislation (subject to the constitutional implications of membership of the European Union). Furthermore, constitutional changes can be achieved by ordinary legislation, ie a simple majority in each house of Parliament and the Royal Assent.

The legislature of the United Kingdom comprises the House of Lords and the House of Commons – a bi-cameral system. The House of Lords remains (for the time being) an unelected chamber, although reforms introduced by the House of Lords Act 1999 resulted in the removal of the hereditary peers.

The Head of State is the Queen but the role of the monarch is largely ceremonial and circumscribed by convention. Residual powers of the Crown are in fact exercised by the government.

Government is democratic, ie membership of the House of Commons is dependent on elections and the government is ultimately accountable to the electorate. The electoral system used for general elections in the UK – 'first past the post' – as opposed to any form of proportional representation arouses occasional political controversy.

In the absence of a written constitution there is a greater dependence on the government's respect for the rule of law as there is no clear line on what is constitutionally legitimate.

Some argue that the United Kingdom needs a written constitution in order to more effectively protect the individual rights of citizens. Parliament has responded by giving statutory force to the European Convention on Human Rights via the Human Rights Act 1998.

Sources of the constitution

Because the United Kingdom has an unwritten constitution its sources are to be found in the general law, ie statute and precedent, and in practices that have become firmly established over time, ie conventions. In addition, the United Kingdom's membership of the European Union has important constitutional implications.

Statute

There are many statutes which relate either to the system of government or to the rights of the citizens. Identifying statutes of constitutional significance can be difficult. Major examples are: the Bill of Rights 1689 which laid down the foundations of the modern constitution; the Act of Settlement 1700 which provided for the succession to the throne; the Act of Union 1706 which united the Parliaments of England and Scotland; the European Communities Act 1972 by which the United Kingdom acceded to the Treaty of Rome; and the Human Rights Act 1998 which effected the incorporation of the European Convention on Human Rights into domestic law.

Case law

Through the development of the common law the courts can establish important rules relating to the powers of the various organs of government: *Entick* v *Carrington* (1765) 19 St Tr 1030; *Council for Civil Service Unions* v *Minister for the Civil Service* [1984] 3 All ER 935. Similarly, through the interpretation of statutory provisions.

Community law

The United Kingdom became a member of the European Communities from 1 January 1973: see European Communities Act 1972. As a consequence Community law takes precedence over domestic law: see *Costa* v *ENEL* [1964] ECR 585. The main sources of Community law are:

a) The treaties – provisions directly applicable in United Kingdom courts.

b) Regulations – these are directly applicable in United Kingdom courts.

c) Directives – Community objectives which must be complied with.

d) Decisions of the European Court of Justice on European law – these will be applied by the courts in the United Kingdom.

The royal prerogative

These are residual powers, privileges and immunities belonging to the Crown, such as the power to: declare war, enter into treaty obligations, issue passports, recognise foreign governments, and maintain domestic law and order. The courts will review the exercise of these powers to the extent that the subject matter is 'justiciable'.

The European Convention on Human Rights

With the enactment of the Human Rights Act 1998 the European Convention on Human Rights has (in part) been incorporated into the domestic law of the United Kingdom. The Act came into effect fully in October 2000. Decisions of the European Court of Human Rights are effectively binding on domestic courts as regards the interpretation of relevant Convention provisions, although the courts will have to give precedence to domestic legislation if it cannot be interpreted so as to comply with the ECHR.

Conventions

Definition: Conventions are 'rules of constitutional behaviour which are considered to be binding by and upon those who operate the constitution but which are not enforced by the law courts – nor by the presiding officers of the Houses of Parliament.' (Dicey)

Some examples of conventions relating to the monarchy:

a) The sovereign should act on the advice of her ministers.

b) The sovereign should ask the leader who commands a majority in the House of Commons to form a government.

c) The sovereign should dissolve Parliament at the request of the Prime Minister.

d) The sovereign should not refuse the royal assent.

Some examples of conventions relating to the executive:

a) Ministers are collectively and individually responsible to Parliament.

b) Ministers must be members of the House of Commons or House of Lords.

c) The government must resign if it loses the confidence of the Commons.

Some examples of conventions relating to Parliament:

a) Public expenditure measures must originate in the House of Commons.

b) The House of Lords ought ultimately to defer to the will of the House of Commons.

Some examples of conventions relating to the judiciary:

a) A judge's professional conduct should not be questioned in either House except on a motion for dismissal.

b) A judge should not be active in party politics.

The importance of conventions

The aim of conventional rules is the smooth working of government. See Sir Ivor Jennings who suggested a three-part text for recognising a valid convention: Is there a precedent?; Do those who operate the constitution accept that the convention is binding? Is there a good political reason for the convention?

The conventional wisdom is that the conventions of ministerial and collective responsibility help to ensure the accountability of the executive – the extent to which this theory is matched by reality is considered further in Chapter 8. The failure to observe constitutional conventions can have significant political repercussions, eg the refusal of a government to resign on losing the confidence of the House of Commons. Such repercussions are dependent on the perceived importance of the conventional rule. Rules of political practice do change and conventions can change accordingly. This gives the constitution flexibility.

Conventions and the courts

Conventions are not enforceable in the courts because they are not rules of law: see *Madzimbamuto* v *Lardner-Burke* [1969] 1 AC 645. The courts do, however, recognise the existence of conventions: see *Attorney-General* v *Jonathan Cape* [1976] QB 752 and *Re Amendment of the Constitution of Canada* (1982) 125 DLR (3d) 1.

1.3 Key cases and statutes

- *Amendment of the Constitution of Canada, Re* (1982) 125 DLR (3d) 1 (Canadian Supreme Court)
  How courts identify conventions

- *Attorney-General* v *Jonathan Cape Ltd* [1976] QB 752 (CA)
  Court recognising importance of convention

- *Carltona Ltd* v *Commissioner of Works* [1943] 2 All ER 560 (CA)
  Convention of ministerial responsibility

- Act of Settlement 1700 – determines union of England and Scotland

- Bill of Rights 1689 – legal basis for parliamentary sovereignty

- European Communities Act 1972 – transfers sovereignty to the European Community institutions

- Statute of Westminster 1931 – limits sovereignty over dominions

1.4 Questions and suggested solutions

QUESTION ONE

Sir Ivor Jennings states that as between constitutional conventions and rules of law 'there is no distinction of substance or nature'. Do you agree?

University of London LLB Examination
(for External Students) Constitutional Law June 1995 Q2

General Comment

This is a brief question that requires students to write all they know about the relationship between conventions and straightforward legal rules. Care must be taken to define the terms used in the question before launching into an answer, or the use of examples. The comparative importance of different types of conventions and legal rules should be explored. The temptation to be prolix in answering must be avoided. The structure of an answer to this type of brief question is all-important to the marks that will be ultimately awarded.

Skeleton Solution

Take issue with the detail of Jennings' statement – explain the terms 'conventions' and 'rules of law' – discuss enforcement of each – conventions: Queen in Parliament – examples of conventions in state opening of Parliament – the rule of law – distinction between constitutional legal rules and ordinary legal rules – conclusion.

Suggested Solution

Ivor Jennings is perhaps being disingenuous when he states that there is no distinction between constitutional conventions and rules of law in nature, but perceptive when he states that there is no distinction in substance. A rule of law is not a term of art necessarily. Legal rules, if they are to be taken as the same thing, can be said to be either statutory or common law. Where a rule is created by statute it has been approved by the Queen in Parliament or passed by a system of delegated legislation. Such a rule occupies a very particular place derived from the sovereignty of Parliament. Common-law rules are created by the courts and are similarly susceptible to definition in the decisions of the judiciary. The way in which legal rules are reformed is clearly understood: the decision of a superior court that the rule is to be changed settles the question.

However, conventions are considerably less certain than rules of law. Conventions are understood ways of behaviour rather than explicit rules. It is not possible to know from one day to the next whether or not a convention retains the same level of authority as it did the day before. It is only possible to understand the importance of conventions by their observance over time. The state opening of Parliament, for example, is an event which is loaded with convention. The role of the bargemaster in carrying the Cap of Indulgence and the Sword of State to the Palace of Westminster is a matter of convention dating from the days of Henry VIII, but it is not such an important rule that its abolition would cause a constitutional crisis. The convention that the Queen must assent to any Bill before it becomes law is a more significant legal rule because it controls the validity of legislation.

Another aspect of conventions is that they are not observable in the same way as legal rules, and they are not horizontally equal. Some conventions are more important than others, as indicated above. The delineation of legal rules is more certain. Statutes are given effect over common-law rules, but the two codes are able to interact in a way that is controlled by the practices of the courts and the legal profession.

The rule of law, in Dicey's sense, is a different perspective on the concept of 'rules of law'. This is in itself a convention which underpins the understanding of democratic political systems. Law in this sense is placed at the centre of the orientation of political arrangements. It is also a convention that the principle that no one is above the law will be respected. However, this is a convention which is typically honoured more in the breach than the observance. It is unclear when the rule of law is broken in most circumstances because it is such an elastic rule, which seeks to guide behaviour rather than impose punishment for its breach. The fact that a convention may be breached without certainty as to whether or not it has been breached creates a very large difference from legal rules where, usually, not only is breach clear but the means of redress or punishment are set out or ascertainable.

Therefore, the nature of the rules of law and the constitutional conventions are very different. However, there is some similarity in their significance. With reference to the convention that the Queen in Parliament passes Bills into Acts of Parliament by signing the royal assent, it is possible to say that when this convention is altered it would constitute a very great alteration in British constitutional arrangements. Therefore, one might conclude that there had been a significant change in the constitutional arrangements of the United Kingdom as a result. Similarly, where it is clear that there has been an alteration in a piece of legislation, or a change in the common law by a superior court, there would be a change in the framework of the legal system within the United Kingdom. Many such changes in legal rules would, of course, not be of similar importance to the constitutional alteration caused by the end of the convention surrounding the Queen in Parliament. However, measures such as the House of Lords Act 1999 (ending the hereditary basis for membership) or the Human Rights Act 1998 (effecting the incorporation of the European Convention on Human Rights) would be regarded as statutes of 'constitutional significance'. Therefore, it is possible to say that there are occasions where the alteration of a legal rule or a constitutional convention would be of similar importance and that, in those circumstances, there is no distinction in substance between the two.

QUESTION TWO

Discuss the nature and effect of the constitutional conventions which regulate the public conduct of the Sovereign as Head of State in the United Kingdom.

University of London LLB Examination
(for External Students) Constitutional Law June 1996 Q2

General Comment

This question is not simply concerned with the narrow range of issues surrounding the monarch as Head of State. It requires an examination of the quasi-legal rules that have built up as a result of the United Kingdom having a constitutional monarchy.

An understanding of the term 'convention(s)' is required. The candidate should also be able to discuss such issues as the appointment and dismissal of the Prime Minister and the related issue of the dissolution of Parliament. Historical examples are necessary when dealing with the influence of conventions upon the role of the monarchy. Also some knowledge of the 1975 Australian constitutional crisis would be useful.

Skeleton Solution

Definition of conventions – royal assent to Bills – apportionment of ministers and the Prime Minister – dissolution of Parliament – conclusion.

Suggested Solution

Constitutional conventions have been described by Dicey (*Law of the Constitution* (10th edn, 1959)) as 'understandings, habits or practices – which are not in reality laws at all since they are not enforced by the courts'. They do, however, make sense of the constitution, and in the words of Sir Ivor Jennings (*The Law and the Constitution* (1959)) 'they provide the flesh which clothes the dry bones of the law; they make the legal constitution work'.

This is particularly true of the role of the monarch. The powers of the Head of State are limited by convention, and in the majority of cases the functions of the monarch have passed into the hands of other actors of the constitution or else the monarch has no discretion on how to act. This is correct, for example, at the basic level of how statutes come into existence. When a Bill has passed both House of Parliament (the Parliament Acts 1911–1949 notwithstanding) the monarch is obliged to give it royal assent, or so the convention would indicate. The position is, however, slightly clouded when one looks at past events in constitutional history. The classic textbook example is that of Queen Anne in 1708 refusing to give her assent to the Scottish Militia Bill, thus seeming to indicate that the monarch is not obliged by convention to assent to each and every Bill. The facts are, however, somewhat more opaque in that not only did her ministers not object, but in fact they rather approved of this course of action. In more recent times the issue was resurrected over the question of Home Rule for Ireland in the period of 1912–14. In April 1912 the Liberal government introduced a Home Rule Bill in the House of Commons, and to avoid the nineteenth-century precedent of the Bill being rejected by the House of Lords stated that they would, if necessary, utilise the Parliament Act 1911 to bypass the House of Lords' veto. The proposed legislation aroused strong opposition amongst the Ulster Protestant community and their supporters, the Conservative Unionists. The King (George V) had the theoretical power to thwart the progress of the Bill by insisting that an election be held before the legislation was passed or by refusing to assent to the Bill. A memorandum was in fact prepared by the King to Prime Minister Asquith but it was never sent because the outbreak of the 1914–18 war. The memorandum indicated that there might be occasions on which the King would be justified in refusing to assent to legislation. When this would occur is not completely clear, but the memorandum indicated that the Crown would only adopt this course of action if it would have the effect of diffusing a crisis. It is doubtful whether in today's political climate the monarch would contemplate such an action, even if proposed legislation would have the effect of abolishing the UK's position as a sovereign state (for instance, proposed legislation to join a federal European Union).

The sovereign (Queen Elizabeth II) has the theoretical power to appoint whoever she wishes as a minister, and she could in theory appoint somebody outside Parliament. In fact her power is regulated by convention, and ministerial appointments are made on the advice of the Prime Minister in relation to individuals who either sit in Parliament (meaning both Houses) or whom it is proposed will sit in Parliament by means of either a successful by-election or an elevation to the peerage. Such a constitutional arrangement does not generate controversy; in greater dispute is the sovereign's power to appoint a Prime Minister.

The Prime Minister (PM) is appointed from the contestants who are able to command an overall majority in the House of Commons. This does not normally present a problem, since because of the workings of the electoral system one party usually commands an overall majority in the House of Commons and it is usually the leader of that party who then becomes PM.

Problems may arise if, for instance, an incumbent PM resigns. In the two leading political parties, Conservative and Labour, a method of electing the next leader is provided for. This was not always the case, and up to 1964 the Conservative Party leader used to 'emerge', which could theoretically leave the monarch with an area of discretion. In 1923, when the Conservative PM Bonar Law resigned, the Conservative Lord Curzon was put forward as his successor, but George V thought it appropriate to appoint the Conservative commoner Baldwin as the Labour Party was unrepresented in the Lords and the King was of the opinion that it would be inappropriate to appoint a peer as PM.

Such an event is unlikely to occur again, but in more recent history the question as to who should be PM was raised again. In February 1974 the election result proved inconclusive as no one party had an overall majority. The incumbent PM, Edward Heath (as he then was), only resigned after spending three days trying to construct a coalition government. The Queen waited until the situation sorted itself out and then called for the main opposition leader, Harold Wilson, to form a government. The possibility of such events repeating themselves would, of course, be more likely if electoral reform is introduced and overall majority governments cease to be the norm. The role of the monarch in this area would be highlighted and the Queen would be able to exercise a discretionary function.

Of more constitutional significance is the role of the monarch in the dissolution or non-dissolution of Parliament. Whether or not Parliament is dissolved is not in fact governed by convention (contrary to popular belief). The request as to the dissolution of Parliament is made, since November 1918, by the PM. The Queen could in theory refuse to grant a dissolution, although this is not likely, particularly as the PM would probably then resign. The converse is also true, and the monarch could insist upon a dissolution of Parliament if the government of the day was planning controversial and unprecedented legislation. The example of George V in the decade before the 1914–18 war is a precedent for such action. Before George V would create the required number of Liberal peers to effect the passage of the Parliament Act 1911 he insisted upon the dissolution of Parliament and an election. This power is still vested in the monarch and it is correct to describe it as a personal prerogative rather than a conventional practice.

A more recent instance of this power of the monarch, and also the role of the monarch in appointing a PM, arose in Australia in 1975. The Governor-General of Australia represents the Queen and enjoys the power and privileges of the Head of State. As a result of an impasse between the House of Representatives and the Senate, the government was denied its financial support. In order to break the deadlock the

Governor-General, Sir John Kerr, dismissed PM Gough Whitlam and called in the opposition leader as PM upon condition that he then requested a dissolution of Parliament. There would appear, however, to be no reason to suppose that the Governor-General, exercising the royal prerogative, could not insist upon a dissolution of Parliament.

The public conduct of the sovereign is largely determined by the operation of conventions. Although they are not laws, conventions are regarded by the sovereign as obligatory. Many matters, particularly relating to foreign affairs, such as the signing of treaties, are done in the name of the sovereign; they are not, however, associated with the public conduct of the sovereign. Those that are, such as the appointment of the Prime Minister, leave the sovereign with little discretion as to how to act. If an unpopular, in the eyes of Parliament, individual were to be appointed PM he or she would be unable to obtain a vote of confidence. It is the application of conventions that prevents the sovereign from becoming embroiled in political controversy and preserves the institution in a symbolic role.

QUESTION THREE

'While an unwritten constitution has the merit of flexibility, this flexibility is purchased at the expense of individual rights.'

Critically assess this statement.

University of London LLB Examination
(for External Students) Constitutional Law June 1997 Q2

General Comment

The question calls for an explanation of what is meant by a flexible constitution and how this can undermine individual rights. Comparison needs to be drawn with a rigid (written) constitution with entrenched rights. Finally, some thought needs to be given to how rights might be better protected under a flexible constitution.

Skeleton Solution

Explanation of unwritten constitution – how does it provide flexibility? – how does this flexibility undermine individual rights? – absence of entrenchment – failure of the common law to develop certain rights – proposals for incorporation of the European Convention on Human Rights.

Suggested Solution

The British constitution is usually classified as flexible in nature. This means that it is not fixed and can be changed relatively easily. The thrust of the quotation under consideration is, therefore, that any rights provided by such a constitution are, of necessity, vulnerable because they too can be changed or removed just as easily. The primary reason why the British constitution is classified as unwritten is the absence of any document laying down the basic rules within which the legislature, judiciary and executive must operate. By contrast, the American constitution provides perhaps the best known example of a written constitution. Unlike the British constitution where, in theory, Parliament is sovereign and can make and unmake laws as it pleases, in the American constitution the legislature has to operate within the limits laid down by the written constitution. It is also subject to the controls exercised by the judiciary, for example where legislation is declared 'unconstitutional' by the Supreme Court. To ensure that they are not at the mercy of any particular political administration, the rights laid down in the American constitution are entrenched, meaning that the constitution can only be altered if two-thirds of Congress and three-quarters of the individual state legislatures agree to a proposed change. Hence, any change is likely to be a long, drawn-out business, with ample opportunity for lobbying and debate.

In the British constitution even the most basic civil rights currently provided for by statute, such as the right to vote, can (in theory) be removed by a simple majority in Parliament in favour of a Bill having such effect. There is no written constitution limiting the power of Parliament, and the role of the judiciary is (in theory) to give effect to the will of Parliament as expressed in primary legislation. Other aspects of constitutional practice are found in conventions, such as ministerial responsibility, collective responsibility and the 'Salisbury Convention', whereby the House of Lords will not block the passage of legislation passed by the House of Commons that reflects a manifesto commitment upon which the government was elected. Again conventions are flexible because they emerge, develop and disappear according to current political practice. They are treated like rules but do not have the force of law. Although conventions tend to be concerned with the operation of central government, rather than individual rights, they can have an indirect bearing on the rights of the subject.

In the British constitution individual rights can also be developed by the judges at common law, the theory being that the common law is there to supply the omission of the legislature. Again this has the merit of flexibility, the courts being able to respond to new situations or threats as the case may be, but the decisions of the courts have no special status that offers these precedents protection from subsequent change by the legislature, or even the judges themselves. The doctrine of parliamentary sovereignty means that Parliament can legislate to nullify the effect of any court decision it disagrees with or finds inconvenient. The enactment of the War Damages Act 1965 reversing the effect of the House of Lords' decision in *Burmah Oil* v *Lord Advocate* [1965] AC 75 is a well known example of this power being used. Neither should it be assumed that the courts are necessarily always willing to recognise the existence of rights at common law. In *Malone* v *Metropolitan Police Commissioner* [1979] Ch 344 the court refused to grant the plaintiff a declaration that his right to privacy was being violated by the police tapping his telephone line – the fact that such a right was enshrined in art 8 of the European Convention on Human Rights did not persuade the court at that time that the common law provided such a right.

Arguably things have moved on, however. The Labour government elected in May 1997 committed itself to the incorporation of the European Convention on Human Rights into English law, and the Human Rights Act 1998 duly came into force in October 2000. Under the Act any person who is a 'victim' (in the sense that their Convention rights have been breached by a public body) can to bring an action, or apply for judicial review, against a public body, claiming a remedy. If a court finds that there has been a violation it can grant an appropriate remedy. If the court cannot interpret domestic legislation so as to ensure compatibility with the Convention it can grant a declaration of incompatibility to the effect that a particular statutory provision offends against the Convention. It will then be for the appropriate minister to introduce amending legislation by means of a fast-track method. This compromise is interesting because it does not affect in any way the notion of parliamentary sovereignty, nor does it affect the flexibility of the constitution. Instead it assumes that political pressure will ensure the passage of the necessary amending legislation. Similarly, ministers will still be free to introduce legislation into the House of Commons that contravenes the Convention, but will be required to make a statement to this effect. Again, the political repercussions of such a move are such that compliance with the Convention can probably be achieved without recourse to any major constitutional reforms.

It is also significant that the courts have started to develop at common law the notion that certain statutes are special, in the sense that they can be regarded as constitutional. Examples include the European Communities Act 1972, the Human Rights Act 1998 and the Bill of Rights 1689. The view taken by the judges is that constitutional statutes cannot be impliedly repealed by later legislation. The rights set forth in such statutes can only be abrogated by the express wording in later legislation. As Laws LJ observed in *Thoburn* v *Sunderland City Council* (2002) The Times 22 February, this development regarding constitutional statutes gives the benefits of a written constitution in which fundamental rights are accorded special respect, but also preserves the sovereignty of the legislature and the flexibility of the United Kingdom's uncodified constitution. It operates on the basis that the courts, in interpreting statutes, will pay more or less deference to the legislature according to the subject in hand.

QUESTION FOUR

Consider the view that the United Kingdom needed a 'new constitution for a new century'.

Adapted from University of London LLB Examination
(for External Students) Constitutional Law June 1999 Q1

General Comment

This should be an attractive question for most candidates as it offers the opportunity to select examples from across the syllabus and to offer a personal interpretation of current trends in constitutional law. The important thing is that candidates should have something to say – an argument or viewpoint to put forward. The question requires more than a mere recital of what the characteristics of the United Kingdom constitution are.

Skeleton Solution

Explain the nature of the current constitution – analyse the apparent failing of current arrangements – provide specific examples – review the changes made following the 1997 election – have they gone far enough? – what would wholesale reform involve? – is it necessary? – conclusion.

Suggested Solution

The statement under consideration invites comment on the proposition that, at the end of the twentieth century, the United Kingdom's constitution was lacking in several respects as regards what would be needed for it to function effectively in the twenty-first century. A proper examination of this view first requires an assessment of the constitution that the United Kingdom had in the last few years of the last century. Most would classify it as unwritten on the basis that there was no single document or group of documents providing a law of the constitution delimiting the powers of the legislature, executive and judiciary. It was unitary, in the sense that Parliament, sitting at Westminster, was the only body competent to legislate for the whole of the United Kingdom. Flexible, in the sense that all law in the United Kingdom, including laws relating to 'constitutional' issues, were enacted, repealed or amended by the Queen in Parliament using the same procedure, ie changes can be effected by ordinary legislation. The constitution was based on parliamentary sovereignty – subject to the constraints imposed by membership of the European Union, Parliament was empowered to make or unmake any law. There was no limit to Parliament's competence to legislate. The United Kingdom had a constitutional monarchy in which the Queen was the Head of State and succession to the throne was hereditary. Although the monarch retained many of the legal powers of government, by convention these powers were exercised in her name by her ministers. It was a bicameralist legislature, ie composed of the House of Lords and the House of Commons. It was a democracy based on responsible government – membership of the House of Commons was determined by the outcome of a general election, based on universal adult suffrage, conducted at least once every five years. The government was drawn from the political party that had the majority of seats in the House of Commons and ministers of the government were answerable to Parliament for the activities of their departments.

It will be immediately apparent that many key features of the constitution remain unchanged. In some areas, however, the Labour government elected in May 1997 has fulfilled its promises of constitutional reform – particularly in areas such as human rights, devolution and in respect of the House of Lords. The question under consideration, however, suggests that more radical change is needed. Is this the case? What are the perceived failings of the current arrangements?

It is argued that it is anachronistic for a modern constitution to remain largely unwritten. The adoption of a written constitution would result in a more secure protection for individual rights, would ensure that the legislature was truly subject to the rule of law, rather than being able to dispense with it, and would secure a more effective separation of powers between the branches of government. Some contend that Parliament at Westminster cannot effectively represent the regions of the United Kingdom and that more power should be devolved to the regions and local government revitalised. Those with republican tendencies would argue that a modern constitution should not have the holder of a hereditary title as its Head of State. The House of Lords is seen by many as an undemocratic body in the sense that its members are not answerable to the electorate and as such it should play no part in the passage of legislation. The democratic credentials of the House of Commons might not bear close scrutiny if one examines the actual operation of the 'first past the post' system for electing its members. The variable geometry of the electoral process often results in the party that wins the election securing a disproportionate number of seats in the House of Commons, at the expense of marginal parties. A government with a huge majority in the House of Commons is perhaps less sensitive to the dictates of responsible government, the legislature being effectively under the control of the Cabinet. Power is vested in the House of Commons – in the majority party – with the executive grouping of that majority party.

As indicated above, the European Convention on Human Rights has been incorporated into domestic law with the enactment of the Human Rights Act 1998. This is not the same as adopting a written constitution to protect fundamental rights, but it does go some way to effectively entrenching these rights in the constitution. It is true that the Human Rights Act 1998 could be repealed by any future Parliament on a simple majority vote, but politically this is unlikely. Legislation could be enacted that conflicted with the rights protected by the 1998 Act, but a minister would be required to bring this fact to the attention of the House of Commons when presenting a Bill that was designed to achieve this outcome – in effect he would have to invite the Commons to ignore the Human Rights Act. Devolution in Scotland and Wales has been effected through the Scotland Act 1998 and the Government of Wales Act 1998. London now has an elected assembly for the first time since 1985, headed by a mayor. Other changes are likely to take longer and be more difficult. Reform of the voting system for general elections has been considered by the Jenkins Commission, but there is no evidence to suggest that any changes will be introduced in the foreseeable future. Proportional representation has been introduced for the elections for MEPs. The House of Lords Act 1999 has abolished the rights of hereditary peers to sit and vote in the House of Lords – those remaining do so as life peers. Debate continues as to how the composition of the House of Lords should be determined in future.

Given the timescale involved these are fairly major changes and it could be said that, compared with the situation pre-1997, the United Kingdom does have a constitution for the twenty-first century that is new in many respects. Closer examination reveals, however, that the constitutional fundamentals remain unchanged. The monarch remains the Head of State and no major political party has been willing to seriously espouse republican ideas. Power has been devolved to the regions, but the Welsh Assembly and Scottish Parliament are not independent sovereign legislatures. As has been illustrated by events in Northern Ireland, Westminster has the ultimate say in terms of what the regional assemblies can do – they are all subordinate to Westminster. The House of Lords reforms are misconceived, not because the hereditary principle should have been retained, but because the debate has been about membership rather than what the House of Lords should have as its functions.

We therefore enter the twenty-first century with a constitution that is still fundamentally unwritten, has only a tenuous adherence to the doctrine of the separation of powers, and is one in which power is heavily concentrated in the hands of a few senior members of the executive. What more could be done? A truly new constitution would involve a constitutional resettlement. The adoption of a written constitution would place the legislature firmly within clear legal limits, place prerogative power on a statutory basis with the ultimate power in the hands of the judges and secure a clear demarcation between the three branches of government. The American constitution is often cited as the paradigm. If this scheme were to be adopted it would be possible for legislation enacted by the legislature to be struck down as 'unconstitutional' by the Law Lords acting as a Supreme Court.

The American model has its attractions. Rights could be entrenched – ie no change unless, for example, two-thirds of the legislature vote in favour – but such constitutional safeguards come at a price. The rate of progress if changes are sought can be painfully slow and one has to ask if the ultimate power in a constitution should rest with the elected legislature or the unelected judiciary.

In conclusion, it is submitted that there is no popular clamour for a fundamental change in the United Kingdom's constitutional arrangements. Issues such as the banning of foxhunting with hounds or the repeal of 'clause 28' seem to excite much more passion. Other changes are made on a more pragmatic basis, such as the introduction of freedom of information legislation, registration for political parties and new anti-terrorist legislation. In reality if there is a 'new' constitution it is one being forged via the European Union, as it moves from a body concerned with economic harmonisation to one concerned with greater social convergence. Once economic sovereignty passes out of the hands of the United Kingdom government, as will surely happen in the event of monetary union, constitutional changes will follow.

QUESTION FIVE

Consider the view that the United Kingdom should now adopt for itself a written constitution.

University of London LLB Examination
(for External Students) Constitutional Law June 1998 Q1

General Comment

The question calls for an explanation of what is meant by a written constitution and why the adoption of such a constitution might be considered necessary. Candidates need to address the implicit assumption that the United Kingdom constitution is unwritten – there are many written sources. A consideration of the costs and benefits of an unwritten constitution is required, as is an explanation of what would have to be changed to make a written constitution effective. Be prepared to express your own preferences supported by reasons.

Skeleton Solution

Challenge the assumption that the constitution is unwritten – review sources – comment on weakness – explain what a real written constitution involves – compare with USA – look at advantages of conventions – consider the impact of EU law and ECHR – summarise on whether any change needed.

Suggested Solution

The statement under consideration has within it an implicit assumption that the United Kingdom lacks a written constitution. Perhaps this point should be tackled first. The United Kingdom is unusual in not having a written constitution in the sense of a single document, or collection of documents, comprising the basic rules for the conduct of government. The term 'rules for the conduct of government' is used to refer to those principles that the courts will recognise as being enshrined in law, and thus enforceable in a court of law. In the United Kingdom there are, in fact, two such sources of law, legislation and case law or common law.

Of the two, legislation is the most important source of constitutional law, in the sense that the courts, in accordance with the doctrine of parliamentary sovereignty, will always give precedence to a statutory provision in favour of the common law. There are many major statutes of constitutional significance, and examples include: the Magna Carta 1215; Petition of Rights 1628; Bill of Rights 1689; Act of Settlement 1700; Act of Union with Scotland 1706; Parliament Acts 1911 and 1949; Statute of Westminster 1931; Crown Proceedings Act 1947; the European Communities Act 1972; Scotland Act 1998; and the Human Rights Act 1998. Community law also increasingly provides an important body of written law of constitutional significance, dealing with economic and social rights.

Some principles of constitutional law are enshrined in common law, ie the decisions of judges. Under the doctrine of precedent, decisions of the superior courts are binding on all courts below, thus enabling a body of case law to be built up. Important rules of constitutional law may be found in many judicial decisions. For example, the case of *Entick* v *Carrington* (1765) 19 St Tr 1030 determined that general search warrants were illegal; in *Council of Civil Service Unions* v *Minister for the Civil Service* [1985] AC 374 the

House of Lords determined the circumstances in which an exercise of prerogative power would be reviewable by the courts.

Given that there are these written sources of constitutional law, why should any change be necessary? One weakness is that, under the doctrine of parliamentary sovereignty, those statutes providing for basic constitutional rights have no special status. They are not entrenched in anyway. Any Parliament could vote to repeal those measures by a simple majority of one. As will be explained below this is not the hallmark of a strong written constitution. Similarly with the common law. Judges can only adjudicate upon real cases that are litigated, hence the opportunity to develop the law on certain aspects of individual rights and freedoms, or ministerial or police powers may arise infrequently. Further, Parliament can legislate to nullify any ruling by the courts as the dramatic reversal of the decision in *Burmah Oil* v *Lord Advocate* [1965] AC 75 by the enactment of the War Damages Act 1965 illustrates.

When people talk of a written constitution they normally have in mind the sort of model to be found in the American constitution. This operates on the basis that there are three branches of government, each with different spheres of operation, each with powers to act as a check and balance on the other. The key point is that each branch of the government is subordinate to a written document, referred to as the constitution, setting out the powers and functions of the judiciary, legislature and executive. Each branch of government must operate within the limits on its powers laid down in the constitution. In this sense it is possible for legislation enacted by the legislature to be struck down as 'unconstitutional' by the Supreme Court. To ensure that they are not at the mercy of any particular political administration, the rights laid down in the American constitution are entrenched, meaning that the constitution can only be altered if two-thirds of Congress and three-quarters of the individual state legislatures agree to a proposed change. Hence, any change is likely to be a long, drawn-out business, with ample opportunity for lobbying and debate. The argument goes that, as a result, individual rights are much better safeguarded under such a constitution. In theory this is undoubtedly the case. In practice these rights are secured at a cost – the delay and difficulty in making sensible amendments. The problems experienced by those seeking to amend the constitutional right to bear arms in the United States is testament to that. The system also puts immense power into the hands of those appointed to the Supreme Court – judges who are appointed, not elected.

Not only is the United Kingdom constitution different in the status accorded to written rules, but many key aspects of its constitution are based on non-legal rules known as conventions – often defined as rules of constitutional behaviour which are considered to be binding by and upon those who operate the constitution but which are not enforced by the law courts nor by the presiding officers in the Houses of Parliament. Examples include the convention that: the sovereign must not exercise (on her own initiative) her legal right to refuse to assent to Bills which have passed through both Houses of Parliament; the government shall be headed by a Prime Minister and the Prime Minister shall choose a Cabinet of ministers to lead the government; the sovereign shall appoint as Prime Minister the leader of the party with the majority of seats in the House of Commons; the Prime Minister and the Chancellor of the Exchequer must be members of the House of Commons; ministers are collectively and individually responsible to Parliament; the government must resign or advise a dissolution of Parliament if it loses the confidence of the House of Commons; ministers must be members of the House of Commons or the House of Lords.

It could be argued that these are all such important rules that they ought to be enshrined in law. The riposte might be that leaving them as they are allows them to be amended easily and gradually through practice. Also, if they are obeyed as if they were laws, why do they need to be enshrined in law, assuming that they could be adequately defined? Further, conventions allow discretion and can be waived if the particular circumstances make this desirable. Most conventions concern matters of a political nature. Their non-legal nature thus helps to keep the judiciary and the courts out of politics and political controversy.

For the United Kingdom to adopt a written constitution based on the American model would involve a constitutional revolution, making Parliament a subordinate body and handing over ultimate power to the Law Lords. This might appeal to those with a desire to see 'tidier' constitutional arrangements, but where is the compelling evidence that such changes are needed? Where are the widespread abuses of individual rights and unconstitutional practices?

It is submitted that wider political changes may make the debate about the adoption of a written constitution otiose. As the United Kingdom becomes more deeply embedded in the European Union the laws and procedures of the EU increasingly provide a backdrop that comes to resemble a written constitution. Another key development is the incorporation of the European Convention on Human Rights into English law by means of the Human Rights Act 1998. Under the Act any person who is a 'victim' may to bring an action, or apply for judicial review, against a public body, claiming a remedy because his or her Convention rights have been violated. If a court finds that a particular statutory provision cannot be interpreted so as to operate in conformity with the requirements of the Convention a declaration of incompatibility can be granted. It will then be for the appropriate minister to introduce amending legislation by means of a fast-track method. This compromise is interesting because it does not affect in anyway the notion of parliamentary sovereignty, nor does it affect the flexibility of the unwritten constitution. Instead it assumes that political pressure will ensure the passage of the necessary amending legislation. Similarly, ministers will still be free to introduce into the House of Commons legislation that contravenes the Convention, but will be required to make a statement to this effect. This major change has been achieved without recourse to any major constitutional reforms.

In summary, therefore, it is submitted that the adoption of a written constitution would not greatly improve constitutional arrangements within the United Kingdom. It would introduce rigidity and perhaps hand too much power to the judiciary at the expense of the democratically elected legislature. Increasingly EU law and the jurisprudence of the European Convention on Human Rights is combining to provide citizens with more flexible and effective safeguards than could be provided by a written constitution. Further, as Laws LJ observed in *Thoburn v Sunderland City Council* (2002) The Times 22 February, the courts are well able to vary the stringency with which they approach the task of statutory interpretation depending on the subject matter in hand. If a measure purports to abrogate basic rights it will be subject to close judicial scrutiny. In that sense only the clearest possible wording in a statute would persuade the judges that basic rights were being taken away by legislation – how could a written constitution provide more protection if a government was truly that despotic?

Chapter 2

Constitutional Principles: The Separation of Powers and the Rule of Law

2.1   Introduction

2.2   Key points

2.3   Key cases and statutes

2.4   Questions and suggested solutions

2.1 Introduction

Whilst the United Kingdom may lack a written constitution in the formal sense, it does display two crucial features associated with constitutionalism, namely some adherence to the doctrine of the separation of powers and a commitment to a culture of the rule of law. The doctrine of the separation of powers provides that there should be three distinct sectors of government: the legislature to make the law; the executive to put it into effect; and the judiciary to adjudicate upon disputes regarding the application of the law. Further, the doctrine provides that there ought to be some system of checks and balances whereby each arm of government can exercise some control over the other. The doctrine of parliamentary sovereignty considered in Chapter 3 means that, in theory, the legislature has ultimate power within the United Kingdom constitution – although this does not mean that they system of checks and balances is fatally flawed. Regard should also be had to the extent to which the legislature is subject to popular democratic control. The doctrine of the rule of law has several facets, but in simple terms it means that no body is above the law, that the law applies to all equally, and that the law is certain and consistent, not arbitrary. Again there are many ways in which the United Kingdom constitution fails to satisfy all of these requirements, but essentially there is a culture of respect for the law. Crucially, the judiciary, through the use of the judicial review procedure, can exercise control over members of the executive and, where necessary, strike down their decisions as unlawful.

2.2 Key points

The separation of powers

As outlined above, the three basic and essential organs of state are legislative, executive and judicial. With a view to avoiding the potential for an autocratic and tyrannical form of government it has been considered theoretically desirable for the functions to be kept separate. In 1748 the French jurist Montesquieu developed the doctrine of the separation of powers which argues the need for checks and balances to exist between the three. It is a useful concept for analysing the nature of our parliamentary democracy.

Legislature and executive

There is a significant overlap. Ministers head departments of state. The government initiates legislation and has the controlling voice in Parliament. Ministers and local authorities have a limited law-making function through delegated legislation.

Executive and judiciary

The Lord Chancellor heads the judiciary, presides in the House of Lords and has a seat in Cabinet. Judges are appointed by the Lord Chancellor or by the Queen on the advice of the Lord Chancellor. The judiciary control the executive authorities from exceeding their powers: see *Associated Provincial Picture Houses Ltd* v *Wednesbury Corporation* [1948] 1 KB 223.

Judiciary and legislature

A degree of separation exists: House of Commons Disqualification Act 1975. Judges do, however, to a certain extent make law: see *Shaw* v *Director of Public Prosecutions* [1962] AC 220.

Within our constitution Parliament is supreme and the courts cannot challenge an Act of Parliament. In many countries with written constitutions the courts can challenge an act of the legislature as unconstitutional: see *Pickin* v *British Railways Board* [1974] AC 765. Following the enactment of the Human Rights Act 1998, however, the judges in the higher courts do have the power to issue declarations of incompatibility where it is found to be impossible to interpret a statute so as to ensure its conformity with the European Convention on Human Rights. This is a relatively weak form of check and balance as the declaration has no coercive effect.

The United Kingdom's membership of the European Union obliges it to legislate in a way that is consistent with European law. In theory, however, Parliament could repeal the European Communities Act 1972, so any loss of sovereignty is limited and partial.

The rule of law

The rule of law is a somewhat abstract concept based on the principle that government must be seen to be legitimate – in the sense that it is impartial, fair and obeyed even when disagreed with. Dicey expressed this in terms of the following propositions:

No man is punishable except for a distinct breach of the law and then only in the ordinary courts and in the manner prescribed by law. This is contrasted with arbitrary and discretionary power. Governments in the twenty-first century do enjoy wide discretionary powers – welfare benefits, public health, sentencing policy etc. Wide arbitrary powers are avoided and attempts made to ensure accountability.

No one is above the law and everyone should be subject to the jurisdiction of the ordinary courts: *Entick* v *Carrington* (1765) 19 St Tr 1030. Disputes between government and citizen are settled in the ordinary courts. But note the part played by administrative tribunals. Whilst the courts cannot challenge an Act of Parliament, they will review administrative action. Note also the fact of parliamentary supremacy and the wide powers of governmental officials. See *R* v *Inland Revenue Commissioners, ex parte Rossminster Ltd* [1980] 1 All ER 80.

Principles of constitutional law are contained in judicial decisions that serve to ensure that individual liberties are protected. This is contrasted with the position in countries with a written constitution where a single document seeks to establish citizens' rights and places reliance on the judiciary to develop laws that protect liberties. The extent to which civil liberties in the United Kingdom are protected in the absence of an entrenched Bill of Rights remains a matter of debate, although the incorporation of the European Convention on Human Rights by means of the Human Rights Act 1998 goes some way to meeting these concerns.

2.3 Key cases and statutes

- *Council of Civil Service Unions* v *Minister for the Civil Service* [1985] AC 374; [1984] 3 All ER 935 (HL)
  Courts willing to review prerogative power if justiciable

- *Duport Steels Ltd* v *Sirs* [1980] 1 WLR 142; [1980] 1 All ER 529 (HL)
  Judicial recognition of the importance of the doctrine of the separation of powers

- *Entick* v *Carrington* (1765) 19 St Tr 1030
  Legal justification required for executive action – rule of law

- *M* v *Home Office* [1993] 3 WLR 433; [1993] 3 All ER 537 (HL)
  Executive bound by the rule of law and judicial remedies)

- *Malone* v *Metropolitan Police Commissioner* [1979] Ch 344
  Courts refusing to make new law

- *McGonnell* v *United Kingdom* (2000) The Times 22 February (ECHR)
  Query whether the Lord Chancellor's role is tenable

- *Pickin* v *British Railways Board* [1974] AC 765 (HL)
  Courts refuse to question what the legislature does

- *R* v *Secretary of State for the Home Department, ex parte Pierson* [1997] 3 WLR 492; [1997] 3 All ER 577 (HL)
  Principle of legality – legislature not above the law

- *R* v *Secretary of State for the Home Department, ex parte Simms* [1999] 3 All ER 400 (HL)
  Principle of legality – legislature not above the law

- *Shaw* v *Director of Public Prosecutions* [1962] AC 220 (HL)
  Courts willing to discover new common law offences

- Bill of Rights 1689 – parliamentary privileges

- House of Commons Disqualification Act 1975 – limits executive and judicial membership of the House of Commons

2.4 Questions and suggested solutions

QUESTION ONE

In what respects does the British constitution conform to, or contradict, the doctrine of separation of powers?

University of London LLB Examination
(for External Students) Constitutional Law June 1996 Q1

General Comment

The question involves an understanding of the basic structure and workings of the British constitution. The candidate should be familiar with what is meant by the doctrine of separation of powers and how this idea is put into practice in the context of the unwritten constitution of the United Kingdom. This will also involve an appreciation of the workings of conventions and the role of important 'actors' in the constitution.

Skeleton Solution

Definition of the doctrine – its strict application in other constitutional jurisdictions, eg the US – relevance to the UK; the Westminster model – the comments of Bagehot – the role and functions of the Attorney-General, Lord Chancellor, the Law Lords – in contradistinction, the independence of the judiciary, Act of Settlement, House of Commons Disqualification Act 1975 and the judiciary – the status of the Crown – conclusion.

Suggested Solution

The doctrine of separation of powers divides the workings of a constitution into three distinct branches. These are the legislature, the executive and the judiciary. The legislature passes the laws, the executive puts them into practice and the judiciary interprets them. The 'highpoint' of this doctrine is to be found in the works of the eighteenth century philosopher Montesquieu. In this book *The Spirit of the Laws*, published in 1748, the author advances the view that the best foundation for individual liberty and good governance is to separate the three branches of government. The three branches of government will have distinct functions and none will be powerful enough to dominate the others. Montesquieu wrongly believed that this formula applied to the England of his time, but the theory served to influence the founding fathers of the American constitution, which does apply the doctrine in practice. A member of the United States Congress is forbidden, for example, to be a member of the United States government: art 1, s6.

How, then, is this doctrine relevant to the UK? First, the United Kingdom constitution is characterised by the blending of the executive and the legislature. It is unusual, as a result of constitutional conventional practice, for a member of the executive not to be a member of the legislature. If the government of the day wishes to bring in an outsider – a non-professional politician – into government then that individual must be found a seat in the legislature, either in the House of Commons through election or in the House of Lords through ennoblement. Walter Bagehot in his classical work *The English Constitution* (1867) describes the constitution as displaying 'the close union, the nearly complete fusion of the executive and legislative powers'.

He then went on to argue that the fusion takes place in the Cabinet, a body which he graphically described as 'a combining committee – a hyphen which joins a buckle which fastens the legislative part of the state to the executive part of the state. In its origin it belongs to the one, in its functions it belongs to another.'

The Cabinet and government only come into existence because the majority of the legislature wish it so, but, as Bagehot points out, the Cabinet (and now the Prime Minister) may request a dissolution of Parliament and 'annihilate the legislature'. In contrast, the United States' President cannot dissolve the Congress, nor is his existence dependent upon a majority in the legislature. The amalgamation of the executive and the legislature and the answerability of the executive to the legislature, demonstrated in Question Time, is one of the fundamental characteristics of the Westminster model of government.

The role and functions of particular offices in government display this amalgamation of the branches of government. The Attorney-General has a function as a quasi-judicial officer of the Crown. In this role he decides in a limited number of offences and cases whether or not to initiate a prosecution. In this he is answerable to Parliament – usually the House of Commons – and may in theory be removed by them in a vote of no confidence. The Attorney-General is a member of the government, although not a member of the Cabinet, a convention which resulted from the alleged pressure which was placed upon the then Attorney-General, Sir Patrick Hastings, who withdrew a prosecuting against J R Campbell, acting editor of a Communist paper, for 'incitement to mutiny'. The Attorney-General does take into account the views of the Cabinet when performing his functions, but he is not bound by the views of the Cabinet or Prime Minister. When Lord Denning, in an inventive phase, tried to make the Attorney-General answerable to the courts, this was firmly repudiated by the House of Lords in *Gouriet* v *Union of Post Office Workers* [1977] 3 All ER 70. Similarly, the Divisional Court in *R* v *Solicitor-General, ex parte Taylor* (1995) The Times 14 August reiterated that the Attorney-General, or the Solicitor-General acting on his behalf, is not amenable to judicial review of his official decisions.

It is with the office of Lord Chancellor that the absence of separation of powers is most marked. The Lord Chancellor is a member not only of the government but also of the Cabinet. He is chosen by the Prime Minister, and previous Lord Chancellors, such as Lord Hailsham, have had an active political career before ascending to the office. Indeed, Lord Hailsham once ran for the leadership of the Conservative Party. The Lord Chancellor has important administrative functions to perform in connection with the judiciary and is responsible for law reform, some of which may be politically controversial, as with Lord Mackay's proposed reform of the divorce laws. The Lord Chancellor is also a judge and may preside over the Judicial Committee of the House of Lords. This office also entitles the holder to sit in the legislature (in the House of Lords), and the Lord Chancellor acts as Speaker of the upper chamber, performing a Janus-type role of acting as an umpire – although less active than the House of Commons Speaker – and participant. The Lord Chancellor is also instrumental in the appointment of members of the judiciary in practice and theory. Justices of the Peace (JPs) are appointed by the Lord Chancellor on the advice of local advisory committees. Without the benefit of an advisory committee he appoints, for instance, High Court judges, circuit judges and recorders. He also has the power to remove members of the judiciary below the status of superior court judges.

While an adherence to the doctrine of separation of powers would imply the disconnection of the judiciary and the legislature this is not found with regard to the role of the Lords of Appeal in Ordinary. The Law Lords can and do play a part in the proceedings of the upper chamber, and while it used to be correct to say that they avoided politically controversial issues, this is not now strictly the case. The response of Lord Taylor, the then Lord Chief Justice, in 1996 to the Home Secretary's proposed reform of sentencing casts doubt over the previously accepted view.

Considering the above discussion then how may Lord Diplock accurately state that 'the British constitution is firmly based upon the separation of powers' (see *Duport Steel* v *Sirs* [1980] 1 WLR 152)? Presumably what is meant by this statement is the adherence to the concept of the independence of the judiciary. The Act of Settlement 1700 provided that the superior court judges should hold office upon 'good behaviour' rather than the 'King's pleasure' as had been the case. The independence of the judiciary and the inability of the executive to remove them is one of the hallmarks of the separation of powers. Since 1700 superior court judges can only be removed by the Crown on an address presented to it by both Houses of Parliament. It has to be said, however, that circuit judges and recorders may be removed from office by the Lord Chancellor for 'inability or misbehaviour'.

Also, in accordance with the separation of the judiciary from the legislature and the executive is the statutory prohibition of full time members of the judiciary from the House of Commons: House of Commons Disqualification Act 1975.

All of the above, of course, is based upon the conventional (in the technical sense) role of the monarchy. While the Queen is forbidden to enter the House of Commons this is of little or no practical significance as her ministers dominate the chamber. One may conclude that although under the Westminster model the theory of separation of powers is more honoured in the breach than the observance, nevertheless the adherence to the practice of the independence of the judiciary has meant that the courts may maintain an independent and separate existence from the law-makers.

QUESTION TWO

To what extent was Walter Bagehot correct in his assertion that the close fusion of the executive and the legislature represents the 'efficient secret' of the constitution?

University of London LLB Examination
(for External Students) Constitutional Law June 1997 Q3

General Comment

Essentially a question dealing with the separation of powers, but one that requires examination of a particular aspect, the relationship between the executive and the legislature. In particular consideration is required of the extent to which there is an overlap in the membership of these two branches of the constitution and the extent to which the legislature is able to perform its task of controlling and scrutinising the executive. The effectiveness of ministerial responsibility, select committees, parliamentary debates and questions needs to be considered.

Skeleton Solution

Identify the executive – identify the legislature – outline the doctrine of the separation of powers – how are the executive and legislature fused? – effectiveness of control mechanisms.

Suggested Solution

The executive comprises the Prime Minister, the Cabinet, others holding ministerial office, as well as the civil service and other administrative agencies. The legislature comprises the House of Commons, the House of Lords and, in a technical sense, the Privy Council.

The doctrine of the separation of powers provides that the three functions of government, namely legislative, executive and judicial, should be kept separate. The basis for this is the belief that concentrating more than one function in any one organ of government presents a threat to individual liberty (ie power should not be concentrated in one sector of government). It also holds that each branch of government should, to some extent, be able to limit the power exercised by the others. Hence, under the constitution of the United States the separation of powers manifests itself in a system of checks and balances whereby, for example, the Supreme Court can declare legislation to be 'unconstitutional'. Although the doctrine is not written into the British constitution, there being no written constitution to provide for this, it is undoubtedly the case that the separation of powers is, to some extent, a feature of the British constitution. For example, the judiciary has the power to declare actions of the executive (ie government ministers) unlawful: see *R v Secretary of State for the Home Department, ex parte Fire Brigades Union* [1995] 2 WLR 464. A key difference, however, between the British constitution and that of the United States is that, unlike Congress, Parliament at Westminster has (subject to the self-imposed restraints of EU membership) a legally unchallengeable right to make whatever laws it thinks right. The courts cannot declare an Act of Parliament to be unconstitutional, or in any way invalid. The most that the courts can do is grant interim relief in respect of legislation that appears to contravene Community law.

As Bagehot suggests the relationship between the legislature and executive is more complex. They are clearly not entirely separate branches of government. By convention the Prime Minister is now expected to be a member of the House of Common, as are his key ministers. Indeed this overlap is recognised in statute by s52(1) of the House of Commons Disqualification Act 1975, which limits the number of ministers who may sit in the House of Commons to 95. Second, there is an overlap in terms of functions. Members of the executive do legislate from time to time. An Act passed by Parliament will often empower the relevant minister to deal with detailed issues by means of statutory instrument. Ministers also have residual prerogative powers to legislate without the consent of Parliament by means of Orders in Council. By contrast, under the United States constitution, neither the President or members of his Cabinet can sit or vote in Congress. They have no direct power to initiate Bills, although the President can recommend legislation in his message to Congress. The President can veto legislation but can be overridden by a two-thirds vote in both Houses. Treaties are negotiated by the President, but must be approved by a two-thirds majority of the Senate

Given, therefore, that the British constitution fails to conform to the classical notion of the doctrine of separation of powers as regards the relationship between the executive and the judiciary, in what sense can the relationship be described as 'efficient'? First, there is the theory that the executive is accountable to the legislature (ie the House of Commons). The executive not only proposes the legislative programme to be considered by Parliament, but the responsible minister has to pilot the Bill through the House of Commons. This means that he has to maintain majority support in the legislature in order to ensure the passage of the legislation. If the government of the day were to lose a vote on a key piece of legislation, such as a Finance Bill, the convention is that it should resign, forcing a general election. Hence, in the most extreme case, the legislature can bring a government down. On a more day-to-day basis, having ministers in the House of Commons means that they can answer questions on the days when time is allocated for questions to ministers. They can also take part in debates, and can be asked to appear before select committees. The efficiency of the relationship between the executive and the legislature depends, however, on the extent to which these mechanisms work. Question Time in the House of Commons is seen by many critics as being merely ceremonial. Ministers will have been briefed on likely questions, and most take it as an opportunity to engage in political posturing or the manufacture of media 'soundbites'. This is particularly the case with Prime Minister's questions. Debates in the House of Commons will often be poorly attended, many MPs turning up simply to vote according to party allegiance. Select committees have perhaps been more successful in bringing ministers to account, although the rules are not entirely clear in terms of when a minister must appear or what questions he must answer.

Two issues are perhaps fundamental. Short of passing a resolution of 'no confidence' in a government, the legislature can only really perform its task of trying to control the executive if the doctrine of ministerial responsibility is upheld. Increasingly it would appear that the convention of ministerial resignation when things go wrong at a departmental level is disappearing. The Scott Report (1996) (inquiry into the 'Arms to Iraq' affair) revealed that the doctrine of ministerial responsibility had not operated effectively to ensure that the House of Commons was kept aware of changes in government policy regarding arms sales. Further, the usual mechanisms for enforcing ministerial responsibility, such as parliamentary questions and hearings of select committees, had not adduced accurate answers, with the result that members of the House were misled. Following a debate on the Scott Report in the House of Commons the Public Service Committee of the House of Commons launched an inquiry into ministerial responsibility, and in its report of 1996 concluded that ministerial responsibility in the modern constitution was less based on a convention of resignation in the wake of departmental failings, and more on keeping Parliament fully and accurately informed, of responding to questions asked in Parliament, whether as parliamentary questions or in front of select committees, and on resigning if found to have knowingly misled the House, ie where it was the minister's decision to lie.

The second issue is the size of a government's majority in the House of Commons. In simple terms a government with a large majority can normally be confident of getting its legislative programme through. A government with a slender majority has to pay far more attention to the views of individual MPs to head off rebellions that might result in defeat. Where a government has a large majority the role of the executive is more significant as regards its scrutiny of ministerial performance, rather than in challenging government policy.

In conclusion it would seem that Bagehot's observation is essentially correct, but does suggest a degree of complacency. The fusion of the executive and legislature in the British constitution does produce efficiencies, particularly in relation to accountability, but care has to be taken to assess whether those accountability mechanisms are in good working order.

QUESTION THREE

Why is judicial independence of special importance to the constitution of a free society? How is this principle recognised and guaranteed in British law and convention?

University of London LLB Examination
(for External Students) Constitutional Law June 1998 Q2

General Comment

The question requires an examination of judicial independence from a number of perspectives. These include independence in the sense of security of tenure; independence in the sense of impartiality; and independence in the sense of separation of powers. Of key significance is the relationship between the judiciary and the executive, prompting an explanation of judicial review and an assessment of its importance. It is also necessary to explain the safeguards that exist to protect the judiciary from removal from office and litigation. The *Pinochet* case provides a useful illustration, as does the incorporation of the European Convention on Human Rights.

Skeleton Solution

Explain significance of judicial impartiality – types of impartiality – the link with fundamental rights – explain the separation of powers – how this is achieved – role of the Lord Chancellor – scrutinise the links between judiciary and executive – highlight importance of judicial review – examine legal safeguards and against dismissal and bias – consider likely effect of ECHR incorporation.

Suggested Solution

Judicial independence is of special significance in a free society as it enables the judges to act as an independent control over the executive, most notably by means of exercising the power of judicial review. Independent judges are not fearful of being removed from office if they make decisions that the government of the day finds unpalatable. Without an independent judiciary the individual would be at the mercy of the organs of state power, unable to effectively challenge the actions of executive agencies such as ministers or police officers.

Judicial independence is also important in the sense that it requires judges to be above party politics in their decision-making. As Lord Diplock explained in *Duport Steels Ltd v Sirs* [1980] 1 WLR 142, were it otherwise it would endanger public confidence in the political impartiality of the judiciary, which is essential to the continuance of the rule of law.

Given the power vested in the legislature, and by extension, in the executive under the United Kingdom's political and constitutional arrangements, an independent judiciary is of especial importance when a government has a large majority in the House of Commons and is seeking to introduce radical changes.

Recent changes, such as the incorporation of the European Convention on Human Rights by means of the Human Rights Act 1998, will undoubtedly result in judges having to consider more politically sensitive cases, thus making it even more important that they maintain ideological impartiality. Some have suggested that, in light of this, it might be appropriate to create a Judicial Appointments Commission to vet prospective judges, with a view towards ensuring a balanced range of opinions, but there is little evidence that this change will be made.

How is this judicial independence recognised in the United Kingdom constitution? The glib answer would be to refer to the doctrine of the separation of powers, whereby the judiciary has its specific functions that it carries out independently of the other two branches of government. The reality, as is well known, is that the United Kingdom constitution adheres only loosely to the doctrine, preferring instead a pragmatic fusion of the branches of government and a system of legal and non-legal checks and balances.

The most glaring breach of the doctrine of the separation of powers regarding the judiciary and the executive is provided by the functions performed by the Lord Chancellor. He is a member of the executive as head of the Lord Chancellor's department and therefore a member of the Cabinet. He is also the head of the judiciary, entitled to preside over the House of Lords when it sits as a court. In this sense the Lord Chancellor could hardly be described as independent but this arrangement is usually defended as being 'pragmatic'. Problems could arise if, however, if the Lord Chancellor were to give judgment in a House Lords ruling regarding the legality of action taken by a fellow Cabinet minister.

The most significant control mechanism in terms of the relationship between the judiciary and the executive is the common law power of the High Court to review the legality of administrative action taken by executive agencies, such a s ministers, local authorities and other public bodies. A citizen with sufficient interest can apply for judicial review on the grounds that a public body has exceeded the limits of its powers, whether by acting unfairly or unreasonably. The same procedure could also be invoked by a person who alleges that he has been the victim of a breach of his Convention rights under the Human Rights Act 1998. The Divisional Court of the High Court can quash a decision of a public body on the basis that it has acted ultra vires (ie beyond its powers). By this means the citizen can seek some redress against the executive even in the absence of any express statutory right of appeal or other procedure for challenging its decisions. Key examples of the courts exercising this power of review include: *Council of Civil Service Unions* v *Minister for the Civil Service* [1985] AC 374 (prerogative power held to be reviewable by the courts); *Padfied* v *Minister of Agriculture, FIsheries and Food* [1968] AC 997 (minister's decision not to hold an inquiry unlawful due to the absence of any good reasons of not doing so); and *M* v *Home Office* [1992] 2 WLR 73 (remedies available against ministers of the Crown). The judges have been robust in their development of the power of judicial review and it is unlikely that they would countenance any attempt to whittle away at this right.

Judicial independence is guaranteed in the United Kingdom constitution (to the extent that that expression means anything in a constitution based on parliamentary sovereignty) in a number of ways. Although magistrates may be dismissed by the Lord Chancellor without cause and judges of inferior courts may be dismissed by the Lord Chancellor for incapacity or misbehaviour, judges of superior courts, ie the High Court, Court of Appeal and House of Lords, hold office during good behaviour subject to a power of removal by the Queen on an address to the Queen by both Houses of Parliament. This is provided for in the Act of Settlement 1700 as re-enacted in the Appellate Jurisdiction Act 1887 and the Supreme Court Act 1981.Under the House of Commons Disqualification Act 1975 holders of full-time judicial appointments are prohibited from membership of the House of Commons.

Judges also enjoy a degree of legal immunity. For example a judge cannot be subject to the law of defamation in relation to anything said in the course of court proceedings – this protection applies to all the judges no matter what their rank in the judicial hierarchy. It enables judges to express their views freely.

The rules of natural justice also operate to help ensure that judges determining issues are not only free from actual bias that undermine their independence, but also that the proceedings are free from any appearance of bias. If a judge has a financial interest related to an issue arising in the case before him he should not continue to preside. In *Dimes* v *Grand Junction Canal Proprietors* (1852) 3 HL Cas 759 the House of Lords struck out a decision made by the Lord Chancellor. It was shown that he had held shares in the canal company in his own right and as trustee but had continued to hear matters arising out of the litigation. Lord Campbell observed that it was of the utmost importance that the maxim that no man is to be a judge in his own cause should be held sacred. The rule against bias also operates in cases of non-pecuniary interest where there is a link between a judge and the parties appearing before him.

More recent cases illustrate that non-financial interest can also disqualify a judge from hearing a case, even where there is no suggestion that his interest might actually affect the exercise of judgment. In the House of Lords' ruling in *R* v *Bow Street Metropolitan Stipendiary Magistrate, ex parte Pinochet Ugarte (No 2)* [1999] 1 All ER 577 the House of Lords reconsidered one of its earlier hearings concerned with whether or not Pinochet enjoyed state immunity in respect of acts done whilst he held the position of head of state. The earlier decision was set aside because one of the Law Lords presiding over the first hearing was chairman and director of Amnesty International Charity Ltd. Amnesty had been one of the parties to the hearing. Lord Browne-Wilkinson explained that automatic disqualification of a decision-maker on grounds of bias was not limited to cases of pecuniary interest alone. The rule also applied where the adjudicator was a supporter of, or was connected with, a cause or interest group involved in the case before him. Lord Hoffmann was automatically disqualified because of his links.

Guarantees of judicial independence have been further strengthened by the European Convention on Human Rights being (partly) incorporated into domestic law. Article 6 provides for the right to a fair trial, including the right to a determination of civil and criminal matters by an independent and impartial tribunal. In *McGonnell* v *United*

Kingdom (2000) The Times 22 February the European Court of Human Rights held that constitutional arrangements on the island of Guernsey, whereby the Deputy Bailiff presided over the legislature that has enacted a law and the court that applied it, were in breach of the provisions of art 6. This ruling could create problems for any Lord Chancellor sitting in the House of Lords on a case concerning legislation enacted by a House of Lords that he was presiding over at the time.

QUESTION FOUR

'The Rule of Law is too vague a concept to be of practical relevance to an evaluation of the actions of Government.'

Discuss.

University of London LLB Examination
(for External Students) Constitutional Law June 1993 Q3

General Comment

This is a straightforward question largely requiring descriptive analysis. The challenge must be to make it as original and as critical as possible, with as many useful illustrations as possible, especially any of topical interest. It is important to give equal emphasis to each of Dicey's components of the Rule of Law; it is a common mistake, for example, to concentrate overmuch on equality under the law.

Skeleton Solution

Modern versions of the Rule of Law – the Declaration of Delhi 1959 – contrast with Dicey's nineteenth-century formula – the three elements and objectives of Dicey's Rule of Law – their influence in establishing safeguards against abuse of power – delegated legislation and tribunals – trades unions and security services – ministers of the Crown and *M* v *Home Office* – judicial review – conclusion.

Suggested Solution

Modern versions of the Rule of Law tend to be formulated in broad political language embracing concepts such as 'justice', the rights of man, fundamental freedoms etc. They tend to be too vague to serve as quality tests for the democratic behaviour of governments. An example is the Declaration of Delhi 1959:

'The Rule of Law means the principles, institutions and procedures, not always identical, but broadly similar, which the experience and tradition of lawyers in different countries of the world, often having themselves varying political structures and economic backgrounds, have shown to be important to protect the individual from arbitrary government and to enable him to enjoy the dignity of man.'

The absence of precise legalistic analysis from this Declaration probably allows various dictatorships around the world to claim that the Declaration has been transplanted, with modifications, into the soil of their constitution and legal system. The Rule of Law becomes a political concept made of clay to be moulded into the shape desired by the potter.

However, if one reverts to the classic, albeit largely discredited, theory of the Rule of Law as propounded by the Victorian Oxford Professor A V Dicey one finds a formal legal analysis which is at least capable of being used to measure the actions of government, and which even today is invoked from time to time to criticise abuses of power. It might well still be a political concept dressed up as law, but it is not as vague as the Declaration of Delhi or other modern variants.

Dicey contended that the Rule of Law has three essential elements:

a) that no one should be punished or lawfully made to suffer in body or goods except for a distinct breach of the law established in the ordinary legal manner before the ordinary courts of the land;

b) that no one should be above the law: that every person, whatever his rank or condition, should be subject to the ordinary law and answerable to the ordinary courts; and

c) that the general principles of the constitution, such as the right to personal liberty and the right of public meeting, are the result of judicial decisions and that so we have a judge-made constitution.

Dicey summed up the objective of those three elements as being 'the absolute supremacy or predominance of regular law as opposed to the influence of arbitrary power, and the exclusion of arbitrariness, of prerogative or even of wide discretionary authority on the part of government': from *Introduction to the Study of the Law of the Constitution* (1885).

Dicey's views proved immensely influential on thinking throughout the twentieth century in the British constitution. Element (a) lay behind Parliament's caution in setting up tribunals and in granting delegated law-making powers to ministers and others. Committees such as Donoughmore (1932) and Franks (1957) recommended safeguards against the risks of abuse of power by ministers, tribunals and inquiries, which, of necessity, had to operate in a fashion far removed from the due process of law administered by the ordinary courts of the land. Supervisory bodies such as Parliament's Committees on Statutory Instruments and the independent Council on Tribunals, as well as the relatively modern British phenomenon of ombudsmen (imported from Sweden), show how the British constitution has adapted to the social welfare needs of the twentieth century without losing sight of Diceyan concepts.

Element (b) of Dicey's theory, concerning equality under the law, was said to have been gravely weakened by certain power groups in society which were able to operate at times seemingly with utter contempt for the law, eg the mineworkers' union in the period of 1972–74 which flouted statutory income restraint legislation; trades unions generally in the period 1974–79; and the state security services where control and accountability seemed so minimal as to be virtually nonexistent until very recently. However, the 'Thatcher Years' of 1979–90 witnessed a reassertion of the rule of law over trades unions (it took a year-long miners' strike to end in failure to achieve it, in 1984) and steps were even taken to establish a statutory framework and system of parliamentary control for the security services, first with the home service, MI5, under the Security Service Act 1989 and then, during John Major's government, with the foreign service, MI6, under the Intelligence Services Act 1994. Even the long established common law immunities of the Crown, which sometimes seemed to put ministers above the law, suffered a blow with the historic decision that ministers, in their public capacity as Crown servants, could be made subject to the law of contempt of court, a decision which Sir William Wade QC hailed as a tremendous victory for the Rule of Law: *M v Home Office* [1993] 3 All ER 537.

Dicey's third element, which some have regarded as descriptive rather than normative in character, has also proven a useful weapon in the armoury of those who believe in vigorous judicial review of administrative action against an over-mighty executive. The rapid growth of principles of judicial review in the last 30 years is regarded by many senior judges as their most significant contribution to establishing constitutional restraints against abuse of power. Judicial review has indeed become a modern constitutional fundamental.

Dicey was against a Bill of Rights because he thought it would undermine parliamentary sovereignty, but in his day Parliament was not the executive-dominated institution that it is now. If he had lived to see the power of the whips and executive patronage Dicey may well have changed his view. The Human Rights Act 1998 can be seen as a measure that further bolsters the concept of the rule of law in so far as judges will use it as a basis for interpreting any legislation that impliedly interferes with or abrogates the fundamental rights of the individual citizen. Nothing can stop Parliament repealing the 1998 Act, but for as long as it is in force Parliament is presumed to legislate in a manner that is consistent with its provisions.

So Dicey's formula, far from being vague and transitory, has proven of solid and lasting value in influencing the development of controls over decision-makers and in bringing government back within the law.

QUESTION FIVE

'It must be conceded that the constitution of the United Kingdom deviates from a pure concept of separation of powers. Nevertheless the concept is respected and adequate safeguards exist to prevent abuse of power.'

Discuss.

University of London LLB Examination
(for External Students) Constitutional Law June 1993 Q1

General Comment

A straightforward question that calls for a clear narrative of the workings of the British constitution and the ways in which the democratic principle is upheld in a system without a rigid constitutional separation of powers. The challenge is to present the material in an original and lively way, because many average students will simply regurgitate large sections of traditional textbooks on this topic. Hence the suggested solution concentrates on a particular theme (the separation between law and politics) and very specialised illustrations, with no attempt to cover the entire (very wide) field of the distribution of power in modern British society. It is one approach; there are many others. It is a useful reminder that, for law exams, there are no 'model' answers, merely suggested approaches to solutions.

Skeleton Solution

Definition of Montesquieu's 'pure' concept of separation of powers – the British constitution and the overlapping of organs and functions – safeguards, illustrated by detailed discussion of one area: the separation of law and politics through constitutional conventions – application to the office of Lord Chancellor – do the particular conventions work? – the decision in *Pepper v Hart* and Lord Mackay's significant dissent – the courts and Parliament: Speaker Boothroyd's views and those of Lord Donaldson MR – alternatives to the conventional approach – difficulties in the American system of government.

Suggested Solution

The 'pure' concept of the separation of powers is that propounded by Montesquieu:

> 'The three main powers of government, namely, the legislative, executive and judicial, should be organically and functionally separated in order to avoid the risk of too much power being accumulated in one person or institution, ie the risk of tyranny': from *L'Esprit des Lois* (1748).

The theory proved of great influence in the drafting of the American constitution in 1787, but is clearly not strictly followed by the British constitution, which has developed in an unwritten, pragmatic fashion since the Norman Conquest of 1066. Today the three main organs of government can be found in one institution: Parliament. The functions of government are also shared, to take the most famous and obvious example: the Lord Chancellor, who combines the functions of judge, Cabinet minister and legislator in the House of Lords (where he also acts as Speaker).

Yet, as the assertion in question points out, respect is paid to the spirit of Montesquieu's theory, if not the letter of it. Safeguards have developed to minimise the risks of abuse of power from institutions such as Parliament and the Lord Chancellor. Whether they are adequate, however, is another matter, and one that has generated controversy among lawyers and politicians for generations.

Conventions of the constitution have assumed great importance in checking the exercise of power. Conventions are 'unwritten' guidelines designed to persuade decision makers to act fairly, responsibly, democratically and morally. For example, the holder of the office of Lord Chancellor will be expected, by convention, to separate his party political views from the views he must take when acting in the capacity as head of the judiciary, whether he is appointing judges or himself sitting as a judge to hear an appeal taken to the House of Lords.

It has been argued that conventions such as these are followed either because of the integrity and sense of honour of the office holder (an 'internal' limit) or because of the fear of the adverse political consequences of a breach of a fundamental convention (loss of reputation, removal from office, etc: an 'external' limit). A person who is appointed as Lord Chancellor is expected to command the confidence of the judiciary, the legal profession and the public generally when exercising judicial functions and hence the internal limit is more likely to operate in his case than with any other politician. Even the most passionate kinds of politician, eg Lord Hailsham, have been able to exercise dispassionate judgment when exercising those functions of the office of Lord Chancellor that require impartiality and independence from the executive.

Nevertheless the fear remains that, as a member of the Cabinet, the Lord Chancellor may be unable to separate his functions in the sophisticated and subtle manner which may be required. To take a recent example (and one is not questioning the integrity of Lord Mackay on this point) in the case of *Pepper* v *Hart* [1993] 1 All ER 42 six of the seven Law Lords (Lord Mackay LC dissenting) were prepared to allow access to Hansard for lawyers and judges when considering issues of statutory construction. Lord Mackay dissented solely on the ground that to permit such access would add greatly to the costs of litigation. One must be tempted to wonder whether his responsibility for public spending on the legal aid scheme (an executive, political responsibility) may have proved decisive in reaching this particular judgment, since none of the other Law Lords considered costs to be a major problem. If the Lord Chancellor were not permitted to sit as an appeal judge would the decision in this case have been unanimous if one of the other Law Lords had taken his place?

The curious point that emerges from the decision is that, in practical terms, Lord Mackay may be proved right, since use of Hansard has increased dramatically since that landmark decision and the impact on the costs of litigation is likely to be significant. This shows how a merger of powers and functions can be useful in (perhaps) influencing a decision and making it better informed than it otherwise would have been. Lord Mackay's judgment in *Pepper* v *Hart* reveals experience of empirical research that is lacking in the other judgments, which tend to rely heavily on abstract issues of principle.

The separation between law and politics is certainly regarded as a desirable objective in the British constitution, even if the two areas are not organically and functionally separated by rigid written rules. In the recent controversy over the legality of ratification of the Maastricht Treaty, the Commons Speaker, Betty Boothroyd, took the unusual step of reminding the courts not to get involved in politics when they came to exercise judicial review on the issue. In return, she said, Parliament and politicians respect the independence of the judiciary. This echoes part of a judgment given by Lord Donaldson MR in *R v HM Treasury, ex parte Smedley* [1985] 1 All ER 589 to the effect that, notwithstanding that the United Kingdom has no written constitution, it is a constitutional convention of the highest importance that the legislature and judiciary are separate and independent of one another. As he observed:

> 'It therefore behoves the courts to be ever sensitive to the paramount need to refrain from trespassing upon the province of Parliament ... I would hope and expect that Parliament would be similarly sensitive to the need to refrain from trespassing upon the province of the courts.'

What if the British pragmatic approach, based on convention, fails to work? The answer is probably a written constitution, with a Bill of Rights, providing for a compartment-alisation of organs and functions and a system of American style checks and balances. But the price may be high: less well informed decision-making and less efficient and effective government. The American experience of 'gridlock' between President and Congress in recent years is testimony to that risk.

Chapter 3

Constitutional Principles: The Sovereignty of Parliament

3.1   Introduction

3.2   Key points

3.3   Key cases and statutes

3.4   Questions and suggested solutions

3.1 Introduction

It is important to understand in outline the means by which Parliament's legislative supremacy came to be established, and to understand the ways in which the British constitution differs markedly from countries with a written constitution. The British constitution has evolved out of the long struggle between the Crown and Parliament that culminated, in 1689, with Parliament conclusively asserting its predominance over many of the powers previously exercised the Crown acting alone.

In countries with written constitutions there are normally express limits on the powers of the legislature. In addition, their courts may be able to rule on whether an act of the legislature is 'unconstitutional'. Notwithstanding the absence of any higher law in the United Kingdom that limits the power of the legislature there are clearly political limitations in terms of legislation that would be regarded as acceptable by the population at large. One must be careful not to equate sovereignty – the power to make any law – with effectiveness – the observance of the law by the people and indeed the judges.

3.2 Key points

The phrase 'the sovereignty of Parliament' is generally used to mean the absence of any legal restraint on the legislative powers of the United Kingdom Parliament. This absence of legal restraint has three aspects:

a) Parliament is legally competent to legislate on any subject matter, as evidenced by: the Act of Settlement 1700; His Majesty's Declaration of Abdication Act 1936; *Burmah Oil Co* v *Lord Advocate* [1965] AC 75 and the War Damage Act 1965; *Mortensen* v *Peters* 1906 14 SLT 227; the Parliament Acts 1911 and 1949; the Ireland Act 1949, s1(2); the Scotland Act 1998; and the Human Rights Act 1998.

b) No Parliament can bind its successors or be bound by its predecessors. There is one and only one limit to Parliament's legal power: it cannot detract from its own continuing sovereignty (Dicey, *Law of the Constitution* (10th ed, 1959)). A later Parliament can expressly repeal an earlier statute. A later Parliament can impliedly repeal an earlier statute – *Vauxhall Estates* v *Liverpool Corporation* [1932] 1 KB 733; *Ellen Street Estates Ltd* v *Minister of Health* [1934] 1 KB 590 – the only limitation on this rule is where the earlier statute is regarded as 'constitutional' (ie its subject matter relates to fundamental constitutional principles or human rights). In such cases the courts will only regard the later statute as repealing the earlier where the later statute expressly provides that this is to be the case: see *Thoburn* v *Sunderland City Council* (2002) The Times 22 February.

c) In theory once Parliament has legislated no court or other person can pass judgment upon the validity of the legislation. All the courts may do when faced with an Act of Parliament is apply it, subject to their limited powers of statutory interpretation. What the courts would do when confronted by a primary Act of Parliament that confounded all basic notions of fairness any civilised society remains a matter of academic speculation. It should not be assumed that the courts would not 'discover' a common law doctrine whereby they were not required to give effect to such an Act. At common law a Bill becomes an Act of Parliament when it has been approved by the House of Commons and the House of Lords (unless passed under the provisions of the Parliament Acts), and has received the royal assent. The enforcement of these procedural rules is entirely a matter for the House concerned and the courts refuse to consider the question as to whether there have been any procedural defects in the passage of a Bill through Parliament: *Pickin* v *British Railways Board* [1974] AC 765.

d) Only Parliament can limit its own sovereignty and such limitations must have been enacted in the form of a statute. However, no Parliament can bind its successors. Therefore, whatever limitations are imposed upon the sovereignty of Parliament by one statute may be repealed by a subsequent Act. However, in practice there are limitations upon the sovereignty of Parliament.

   i) Limitation as to the scope and subject matter of parliamentary legislation: Statute of Westminster 1931, s4.

   ii) Limitation as to the manner and form which legislation must take: *Attorney-General for New South Wales* v *Trethowan* [1932] AC 526 – but note that this applied to a colonial legislature.

   iii) Other practical limitations on the exercise of sovereignty:

   - the doctrine of the mandate;

   - public opinion;

   - political and economic constraints;

- judicial disobedience expressed through the power of interpretation of statutes.

3.3 Key cases and statutes

- *Attorney-General for New South Wales* v *Trethowan* [1932] AC 526 (PC)
  Sovereignty limited by 'higher' constitutional law where the constitution so provides

- *Bribery Commissioner* v *Ranasinghe* [1965] AC 172 (PC)
  Sovereignty limited by 'higher' constitutional law where the constitution so provides

- *Cheney* v *Conn* [1968] 1 WLR 242; [1968] 1 All ER 779
  Courts give precedence to domestic legislation

- *Edinburgh and Dalkeith Railway Co* v *Wauchope* (1842) 8 Cl & F 710 (HL)
  Courts will not adjudicate on procedural irregularity in statute

- *Ellen Street Estates Ltd* v *Minister of Health* [1934] 1 KB 590 (CA)
  Later statute takes effect over earlier inconsistent provisions

- *Harris* v *Minister of the Interior* (1952) (2) SA 428; [1952] 1 TLR 1245 (South African Supreme Court)
  Sovereignty limited by 'higher' constitutional law where the constitution so provides

- *Manuel* v *Attorney-General* [1983] Ch 77; [1982] 3 All ER 822 (CA)
  Statute prevails over convention

- *Pickin* v *British Railways Board* [1974] AC 765 (HL)
  Courts will not adjudicate on procedural irregularity in statute

- *R* v *Secretary of State for the Home Department, ex parte Simms; Same, ex parte O'Brien* [1999] 3 All ER 400
  Constitutional statutes not subject to implied repeal

- Act of Settlement 1700 – determines union of England and Scotland

- Bill of Rights 1689 – legal basis for parliamentary sovereignty

- European Communities Act 1972 – transfers sovereignty to the European Community institutions

- Statute of Westminster 1931 – limits sovereignty over dominions

3.4 Questions and suggested solutions

QUESTION ONE

'It is often said that it would be unconstitutional for the United Kingdom Parliament to do certain things, meaning that the moral, political and other reasons against doing them are so strong that most people would regard it as highly improper if Parliament did these things. But this does not mean that it is beyond the power of Parliament to do such things. If Parliament chose to do any of them the courts could not hold the Act of Parliament invalid.' (*Madzimbamuto* v *Lardner-Burke* (1969), per Lord Reid).

Discuss.

University of London LLB Examination
(for External Students) Constitutional Law June 1995 Q1

General Comment

This question is a general theoretical problem that requires some discussion of basic constitutional theory. The candidate must take care with this problem and not merely launch into it because it appears to be straightforward. Obtaining a strong mark in very generally based questions can be difficult unless the candidate is scrupulous to ensure that the answer is well structured. Beyond that, it is a question asking for a discussion of the interaction between Parliament and the courts, which might be useful to settle in the student, or as a general final question.

Skeleton Solution

Comparison with the USA – discussion of the scope of judicial review in English law to review executive action – discussion of the Criminal Justice and Public Order Act 1994 as an example of courts' ability to control Parliament – use of statutory interpretation to control legislation partially – overall sovereignty of Parliament explained.

Suggested Solution

There is a tension between the theoretical constitutional powers of Parliament and those acts that Parliament can perform without attracting political censure. The basic rule of constitutional law is that Parliament is the sovereign body and that any Act of Parliament passed by the Queen in Parliament supersedes any other rule or decree. Therefore, at least in theory, there is a possibility that Parliament can act in any way that it sees fit.

In the United States of America, the seminal decision of the Supreme Court in *Marbury* v *Madison* (1803) 1 Cranch 103 found that the Supreme Court has the power to review any legislative act of the executive or the legislature. Therefore, the principle of sovereignty under United States constitutional arrangements is that the Supreme Court has a residuary power to find that any particular Act is unconstitutional. There is no such power in the United Kingdom legal jurisdiction. The English law doctrine of judicial review has led to a power in the High Court to review certain acts of public bodies or the acts of ministers in the exercise of the prerogative powers of the Crown. There is, therefore, a development of the ability of the courts to look at the powers of the executive and their exercise. However, these powers derive from the common law, as recognised in the Supreme Court Act 1981. They cannot be seen as constitutional 'long-stop' functions. There are no judicial powers to directly curtail the exercise of parliamentary sovereignty. Judicial review cannot curtail the power of the legislature by overturning legislation, nor can it affect the power of the legislature, Parliament, to pass legislation. There is no ability to say that an Act of Parliament offends some principle of natural justice or that it is ultra vires in some way.

Under the Human Rights Act 1998 certain courts have the power to grant declarations of incompatibility where it proves impossible to interpret a primary Act so as to ensure compatibility with the European Convention on Human Rights. There is no constitutional guarantee, however, that Parliament will respond by amending the offending provision so as provide for compliance.

The question arises: to what extent does Parliament act against the interests of the constitutional order by doing things that are, per se, unconstitutional? The answer to that question is that Parliament does not tend to do things that are unconstitutional on such a regular basis that the constitutional order would be threatened. The system of democratic elections ensures that the House of Commons has a vested interest in not exercising powers which it would be unable to justify to the British electorate.

Therefore, legislation like the Criminal Justice and Public Order Act 1994 can be passed by Parliament, despite the fact that it seems to interfere with the rights of citizens to freedom of movement and action in prescribed circumstances. On the United States model, it would be possible for the Supreme Court to consider whether or not this exercise of power was unconstitutional. If it were found to be unconstitutional, then it would be possible to refer the legislation back to Parliament as constitutionally invalid.

The Westminster model, however, invests no such power in the courts. The Criminal Justice and Public Order Act 1994 cannot be declared invalid. The courts, however, are able to interpret it in such a way that the sense it appeared to have when passed through Parliament is tempered somewhat to ensure that it complies with a level of fairness on the facts of any case. Judges have developed the concept of 'constitutional' statutes that attract a different approach to statutory interpretation. Lord Hoffmann adverted to this in *R v Secretary of State for the Home Department, ex parte Simms; Same, ex parte O'Brien* [1999] 3 All ER 400, where he explained that parliamentary sovereignty means that Parliament can, if it chooses, legislate contrary to fundamental principles of human rights. The Human Rights Act 1998 does not detract from this power. He added, however, that fundamental rights could not be overridden by general or ambiguous words. The courts presume that even the most general words used in a statute are intended to be subject to the basic rights of the individual. The result is that the courts can now apply principles of constitutionality little different from those that exist in countries where the power of the legislature is expressly limited by a constitutional document. In practice it means that Parliament could pass an Act which was outrageous in its purported effect on individual rights, but the judges would interpret it very narrowly – to the point where no effect would be given to a statute that appeared to abrogate basic and inalienable rights. Examples of constitutional statutes attracting such protection include the Human Rights Act 1998, the European Communities Act 1972 and the Bill of Rights 1689.

The other key restraint on Parliament is clearly the democratic process. There is no obvious constituency of voters keen to support a major political party committed to the abrogation of basic human rights. Therefore, there is a gap between constitutional theory, which holds that Parliament is all-powerful, and the political realities of democratic power.

QUESTION TWO

'Constitutionalism, like an elephant, is hard to define but easy to recognise.'

Discuss.

University of London LLB Examination
(for External Students) Constitutional Law June 1997 Q4

General Comment

This is not a question about the constitution in any general sense, or indeed the sources of the constitution as such. Essentially it is concerned with an examination of government according to law. Hence, an examination of the rule of law is required, and the mechanisms that exist to ensure it operates properly.

Skeleton Solution

Explanation of constitutionalism – the nature of constitutional rules – the meaning of the rule of law – the extent to which the British constitution conforms to this – constitutionalism as a substantive concept – the role of the judiciary – the importance of non-legal constraints on political action.

Suggested Solution

Constitutionalism is hard to define in any precise sense. In general terms it could be described as government according to the rules of the constitution. This notion can perhaps be developed further by an examination of constitutionalism in terms of form and procedure on the one hand, and an examination of constitutionalism in terms of substantive content on the other.

In its narrow sense constitutionalism assumes that there are some constitutional rules within which the organs of government must operate. These rules might be found in a written document referred to as 'the constitution' (as is the case with most written constitutions), or by reference to the custom and practice of the organs of government, as is the case with a largely unwritten constitution.

Second, constitutionalism assumes that these rules, whether written or unwritten, will be obeyed as if they were binding, in other words as if they have the force of law. The essence of the rule of law is that even those who govern should be subject to some higher law and should govern in accordance with that higher law. In his *Law of the Constitution* (10th ed, 1959), Dicey identified three aspects of the rule of law that can be equated with the concept of constitutionalism. First, that individuals should not be subject to arbitrary decision-making – government should be according to known laws. Second, that the law should apply to all equally. Third, that the rights of the individual are determined by and are dependent upon the ordinary law of the land as developed by the ordinary courts adjudicating in particular cases.

To what extent does the British constitution adhere to this narrow concept of constitutionalism? As regards Parliament itself, it does not. Parliament is sovereign and can pass such laws as it thinks fit. It is effectively a law unto itself. An Act of Parliament could not be challenged in the courts on the basis that the correct procedure in Parliament had not been followed. Any discrepancies in the parliamentary process would be a matter for Parliament itself to deal with: see *Pickin v British Railways Board* [1974] AC 765. As regards administrative agencies such as ministers, tribunals and local authorities, the narrow concept of constitutionalism is much easier to enforce. If a procedural requirement laid down in a statute is not complied with the resulting administrative action can normally be challenged in the courts by way of an application for judicial review. Not all areas of ministerial activity are governed by statute, however. Whether or not a minister should resign in the event of some failure on his part, or that of his department, is governed by convention. The courts will pronounce on the existence of constitutional conventions, but will not enforce them as they do not form part of the law of the land: see *Re Amendment of the Constitution of Canada* (1982) 125 DLR (3d) 1.

Thus constitutionalism can, in the narrow sense, be taken to mean 'playing by the rules'. It is submitted, however, that constitutionalism also bears a wider meaning, in that it can relate to the substance of the decisions taken by those in power. Even if all the procedural rules relating to the enactment of legislation were followed there would still be some laws that would be regarded as unfair or invalid in the sense that they offended against natural justice, or violated certain basic rights regarded as inalienable. Examples might be legislation denying women the right to vote, or legislation permitting the persecution of a racial or religious minority. These would be valid laws in the procedural sense, but could nevertheless be described as 'unconstitutional' because they offend against the norms of fairness that pertain in most liberal, pluralistic, democracies. The examples given are necessarily extreme, in order to make the point. In reality it may be far more difficult to discern whether or not legislation is unconstitutional in the wider sense. A useful indicator may be public and press reaction. The legislation that introduced the Community Charge, or 'Poll Tax', was met with sustained criticism from many quarters, and resulted in riots, civil disobedience and non-observance. These are all clues that suggest that the government of the day may have gone too far. No matter how big a majority a government might have in the House of Commons, it must still be mindful of how the public at large is going to react to a change in the law.

Whilst judges cannot declare primary legislation to be invalid as such, they can strike down delegated legislation on the basis that it is ultra vires. Failure to conform to the standards of constitutionalism is not one of the grounds of judicial review as such, but judges will declare delegated legislation invalid on the grounds that, if put into effect, it will have unacceptable consequences. Hence, in *R v Secretary of State for Social Security, ex parte Joint Council for the Welfare of Immigrants* [1996] 4 All ER 385 the Court of Appeal held that regulations removing from asylum seekers any entitlement to income benefit were invalid because they meant that asylum seekers would effectively be unable to exercise their rights of appeal. Simon Brown LJ described the regulations as 'uncompromisingly draconian' and likely to result in a life for asylum seekers that was 'so destitute that no civilised nation could contemplate it'. The court will also quash an exercise of executive discretion if they feel that it causes a result which is unfair: see for example *Congreve* v *Home Office* [1976] QB 629 (minister using a regulatory power in order to raise revenue). The term constitutional is sometimes expressed as an issue of legality. As Lord Hoffmann explained in *R v Secretary of State for the Home Department, ex parte Simms; Same, ex parte O'Brien* [1999] 3 All ER 400, the principle of legality means that if Parliament seeks to introduce an Act that many would regard as 'unconstitutional' it must squarely confront what it is doing and accept the political cost. This means that only express words will persuade the courts that a statute means what it says as regards overriding basic human rights, or other fundamental constitutional principles.

In those areas not governed by statute, whether or not action is regarded as unconstitutional will depend on popular opinion and press comment. For example, failure to resign after losing a vote of 'no confidence' in the House of Commons; appointing individuals who are not Members of Parliament to key ministerial posts; lying to House of Commons; or forcing through significant constitutional changes, such as the introduction of proportional representation, or a single European currency, in the absence of any clear electoral mandate. Notwithstanding that a government, or individual ministers, may have the power to do all of these things (by which is meant there is no positive law against doing these things), many would still describe such actions as unconstitutional, in the sense that they lack political legitimacy. In this sense we do know unconstitutional action when we see it, even if a definition that would satisfy lawyers remains elusive.

QUESTION THREE

Critically assess the constitutional role of judicial review in upholding the sovereignty of Parliament and the rule of law. How effective are the courts in fulfilling this role?

University of London LLB Examination
(for External Students) Constitutional Law June 1997 Q8

General Comment

This question calls for an explanation of the constitutional basis for judicial review and the distribution of powers within the constitution. Candidates need to explain the dual role of the courts when exercising judicial review powers, namely giving effect to the intention of Parliament (the parliamentary sovereignty issue), and ensuring that the executive acts within the limits of its powers (the rule of law issue). Bear in mind that a critical assessment is called for, so candidates should not just describe what happens but should offer a view as to whether the courts are discharging these functions satisfactorily, supported by examples.

Skeleton Solution

The theoretical basis for judicial review – how the courts uphold the sovereignty of Parliament – possible exceptions – upholding the rule of law – the ultra vires doctrine – examples – critique of the role of the courts.

Suggested Solution

The High Court has a common law jurisdiction to review the legality of actions taken by inferior bodies, or bodies of limited jurisdiction. Arguably the only institutions which do not have limited jurisdiction are Parliament and the Crown, hence judicial review today extends to the whole range of executive and administrative agencies, from tribunals, local authorities and quangos to government ministers. Parliament frequently enacts enabling legislation creating administrative bodies, or enacts legislation that places duties on, and gives powers to, existing administrative agencies. In the event that an application for judicial review is made on the basis that an administrative agency has failed to comply with an enabling Act, it will be the task of the reviewing court to determine what Parliament intended when the legislation in question was enacted. In a sense the courts would describe themselves as enforcing the ultra vires principle (ie ensuring that administrative agencies act within the limits of their delegated powers and perform their statutory duties), but in reality they are making sure that the intention of Parliament is reflected in the way in which the administrative body exercises its powers.

Equally, when a court exercises its power of judicial review, it is seeking to ensure that the rule of law is upheld. The ultra vires principle holds that any action taken by an administrative agency that results in it exceeding its powers will be unlawful and invalid. In other words administrative bodies must act within the limits of the powers given to them, and in that sense are subject to the rule of law as imposed by means of judicial review. The courts can therefore ensure that there are known limits to the powers of administrative agencies, rather than them having arbitrary powers over individuals. The courts can also uphold the rule of law by ensuring that the law applies equally to all. Indeed, the significance of judicial review lies in the fact that it is a process by which the ordinary citizen can, in principle, challenge the legality of any action in the public law sphere, even that taken by a minister of the Crown. Ultimately, on the assumption that Parliament never intends any inferior body to exceed the limits of its powers, upholding the sovereignty of Parliament and the rule of law are the same thing. The courts will declare administrative action ultra vires because it is beyond what is permitted by an enabling Act. The court will have determined the limits of power by examining the statute in question. The court can justify its actions by claiming to be giving effect to the sovereign wishes of Parliament as expressed in the Act.

So much for the constitutional theory, how well does it work in practice? First, judicial review can only be effective if an application is made. There may be many ultra vires decisions that go unchallenged because those affected are ignorant, impecunious or simply accept the actions of administrators unquestioningly. Second, the courts may decline to intervene because what is being challenged is a policy issue, the legality of which the courts cannot comment upon. Hence in *R v Cambridge District Health Authority, ex parte B* [1995] 1 WLR 898 the court held that it would not review the budgeting decision taken by a health authority refusing to provide treatment due to lack of resources. The courts will also decline to intervene if they characterise an impugned decision as involving principally a question of fact. In *Puhlhofer v Hillingdon London Borough Council* [1986] 1 All ER 467 the House of Lords held that it was for a local housing authority to determine whether applicants had been provided with 'suitable accommodation'. A closer reading of the judgments will reveal, however, that the House of Lords was concerned that if it allowed the application for judicial review to proceed local authorities might face a huge increase in the number of judicial review cases. An application for judicial review may also be unsuccessful if the court determines that the decision in question falls into the 'non-justiciable' category. The speeches in *Council of Civil Service Unions v Minister for the Civil Service* [1984] 3 All ER 935 identify those matters traditionally considered to fall outside the scope of justiciability, including the conduct of foreign affairs, disposition of troops, appointment of ministers and so forth. Courts are particularly reluctant to intervene where a minister claims to have acted to protect national security. In *R v Secretary of State for the Home Department, ex parte Cheblak* [1991] 1 WLR 890 Lord Donaldson MR argued that where the courts declined to review a decision of a minister on the grounds of national security, the constitutional safeguard was supplied by ministerial responsibility to Parliament. The Scott Report (1996) perhaps casts doubt upon this view. Finally, decisions such as *R v Secretary of State for the Environment, ex parte Nottinghamshire County Council* [1986] AC 240 suggest that the courts will be reluctant to declare administrative action ultra vires if it has been expressly approved by the House of Commons, although this is not a bar to judicial review.

Hence, whilst in principle judicial review is a powerful weapon that the courts can use to uphold the rule of law, and therefore parliamentary sovereignty, it is of no use whatsoever if they decline to exercise it. In essence there will be no means of mounting any legal challenge to these decisions, thus placing them, in effect, above the law. Conversely, it can be argued that there are occasions where the courts actually subvert the notion of parliamentary sovereignty by way of judicial review.

In *Anisminic v Foreign Compensation Commission* [1969] 2 AC 147 (a case that would have been pursued by way of judicial review had it occurred now) the plaintiffs sought a declaration that the Commission had acted ultra vires in denying them the correct level of compensation. The statute in question provided that no determination of the Commission was to be called into question in any court of law. Despite the clear wording of the statute the House of Lords allowed a legal challenge to the Commission's decision, on the basis that the statute only prohibited challenges to intra vires (ie valid) determinations. As the House of Lords had decided that the determination was ultra vires it was not protected by the statute. The decision was quite contrary to the intention of Parliament. The aim of the Act was to prevent any legal challenges to the decisions of the Commission because it only had a finite amount of money to distribute. If it had distributed money and then had its decisions successfully challenged in the courts it could have found itself having to pay out more compensation, having already distributed the fund.

The case is perhaps an example of the courts upholding the rule of law (ie that no body should be above the law) in preference to the doctrine of parliamentary sovereignty. There are also many cases were the courts have struck down delegated legislation on the basis that Parliament cannot have intended ministers to have had the power to introduce such extreme measures, only for Parliament to quickly pass amending legislation making it clear that it did intend just that result: see for example *R v Secretary of State for Social Security, ex parte Joint Council for the Welfare of Immigrants* [1996] 4 All ER 385. In such cases the courts could argue that the legislation simply did not state Parliament's intentions clearly enough, but the reality is that the courts are not averse to throwing out a constitutional challenge to the legislature when it suits them to do so.

The concept of the rule of law can also be extended to encompass the notion that Parliament must accept the need for legality, in the sense of legitimacy, in the exercise of its legislative powers. As is well known, parliamentary sovereignty means that Parliament can enact any legislation it sees fit. Judges have no power to declare a statute invalid. Judges can, however, ensure that in interpreting an Act of Parliament the principle of legality is observed. Thus judges will presume that a statute will not impliedly remove basic human and civil rights – only express words can achieve this: see *R v Secretary of State for the Home Department, ex parte Simms; Same, ex parte O'Brien* [1999] 3 All ER 400.

In conclusion, it should be noted that, on the one hand, the courts deal with only a tiny fraction of the disputes between the citizen and the state. The majority is dealt with by tribunals and administrative appeal procedures. On the other hand, judicial review has developed over the last 50 years to become a powerful weapon against unlawful executive action. The effectiveness of judicial review depends on the willingness of the judiciary to be assertive and creative in their application of the ultra vires doctrine.

QUESTION FOUR

'Attempts to entrench legislation by legal means will inevitably be futile unless the basic rule of the United Kingdom's constitution is abandoned.'

Discuss.

University of London LLB Examination
(for External Students) Constitutional Law June 1991 Q1

General Comment

A question requiring an explanation of the terms used, particularly entrenchment, and the basic rule of the constitution. It is important to explain how parliamentary sovereignty manifests itself thus indicating the difficulties with entrenchment. Obviously the impact of European Union membership upon parliamentary sovereignty also needs to be considered.

Skeleton Solution

Explain nature of sovereignty – express and implied repeal – examples – nature of European Communities Act decisions thereunder – *Factortame* cases – conclusion.

Suggested Solution

Entrenchment of legislation involves the enactment of clauses that prevent the Act concerned from being repealed by simple majority vote by the legislative body. A typical example is provided by art V of the United States constitution under which two-thirds of the members of Congress have to approve an amendment to the constitution, which in turn has to receive the support of three-quarters of the state legislatures. The purpose of entrenchment is clearly to protect those constitutional measures that are seen as being particularly fundamental. A constitution that could not be altered at all would soon become obsolete and disregarded in practice. One that could be changed by a simple majority vote would be at the mercy of passing political trends, especially where a small party held power because an election had produced a 'hung' Parliament. The question under consideration refers to attempts at entrenchment within the British constitution being futile because of the constitution's basic rule. By this it is assumed that the question is referring to the doctrine of parliamentary sovereignty, under which Parliament has the ultimate power to pass or repeal any legislation it sees fit. In short it is being suggested that it will not avail Parliament to include entrenchment provisions in a piece of legislation in an effort to protect it, as a natural consequence of parliamentary sovereignty is that no parliament can bind its successor parliaments. To what extent does the operation of the British constitution support this view?

Traditionally constitutional lawyers have pointed to the operation of two doctrines as evidence of the inability of any parliament to bind its successors; express repeal and implied repeal. Under the former, any parliament could enact legislation expressly repealing existing legislation. The effect of the doctrine was that the courts would always apply the most recent legislation. Where two pieces of legislation appeared irreconcilable, but the later Act did not expressly state that its effect was to repeal the terms of the earlier Act, the latter doctrine of implied repeal would be brought into play by means of which the courts would assume that it was implicit in the passage of the later legislation that Parliament had intended to repeal the earlier legislation since they could not stand together. Attempts by Parliament to circumvent the doctrine of implied repeal in the earlier part of the twentieth century met with little success.

This is illustrated by the cases of *Vauxhall Estates* v *Liverpool Corporation* [1932] 1 KB 733 and *Ellen Street Estates Ltd* v *Minister of Health* [1934] 1 KB 590. In the first of these cases, the Corporation of Liverpool proposed a scheme for the improvement of a certain area of the city. The Minister of Health confirmed the scheme in an order that incorporated the provisions of the Acquisition of Land (Assessment of Compensation) Act 1919 and the Housing Act 1925. These two Acts each provided a different scheme of compensation for compulsorily acquired land. The 1919 Act provided in s7(1):

'The provisions of the ... order by which the land is authorised to be acquired, or of any Act incorporated therewith, shall in relation to the matters dealt with in this Act, have effect subject to this Act, and so far as inconsistent with this Act those provisions shall ... not have effect.'

The question arose as to whether the compensation due to the appellants should be calculated in accordance with the 1919 Act or in accordance with the 1925 Act. The appellants argued that, because of s7(1) of the 1919 Act, it must be calculated in accordance with that Act. It was held that the compensation should be assessed in accordance with the later Act. Parliament had exercised its power of overriding the provisions of s7(1) of the 1919 Act by enacting in the later Act of 1925 a set of provisions totally inconsistent with those of the 1919 Act. Similarly, in the *Ellen Street* case it was held that the provisions of an earlier Act could always be repealed, by implication, by provisions in a later Act which were inconsistent with those in the earlier Act. Maugham LJ stated the effect of the doctrine as follows:

'The legislature cannot, according to our constitution, bind itself as to the form of subsequent legislation, and it is impossible for Parliament to enact that in a subsequent statute dealing with the same subject matter there can be no implied repeal.'

It should be clear from the above that the doctrine of parliamentary sovereignty depends in large measure on the adherence by the judiciary to the practice of applying the later Act in preference to an earlier one.

The common law has recognised an exception to the doctrine of implied repeal where so-called 'constitutional' statutes are concerned. These are statutes dealing with fundamental constitutional principles such as the Bill of Rights 1689, or those dealing with key individual rights, such as the Human Rights Act 1998. Where a later statute is inconsistent with an earlier constitutional statute the courts will assume that Parliament did not intend to accidentally or impliedly repeal the constitutional statute. This does not mean that the constitutional statute is entrenched in the technical sense, merely that Parliament, if it seeks to repeal a constitutional statute or part thereof, must expressly say so – and accept the political consequences: see further Lord Hoffmann's speech in *R v Secretary of State for the Home Department, ex parte Simms; Same, ex parte O'Brien* [1999] 3 All ER 400.

The European Communities Act 1972 provides further evidence of this development. With the coming into force of the 1972 Act all EC law became part of United Kingdom law with effect from 1 January 1973. Section 2(4) further provides that:

> '... any such provision (of any such extent) as might be made by Act of Parliament, and any enactment passed or to be passed, other than one contained in this Part of this Act, shall be construed and have effect subject to the foregoing provisions of this section'.

In other words any subsequent Act passed by the United Kingdom Parliament was to take effect only to the extent that it did not conflict with the provisions of EC law. This was clearly another attempt to bypass the doctrine of implied repeal, but it was one that was necessary if the United Kingdom was going to be able to abide by its obligations under the terms of the Treaty of Rome, which requires each member state to give primacy to EC law: see *Costa v ENEL* [1964] ECR 585. The result has been that the domestic courts have modified the doctrine of implied repeal as regards domestic law and EC legislation, by holding that domestic law should always be interpreted in a manner that produces a result consistent with the United Kingdom's obligations under the Treaty: see *Macarthys Ltd v Smith* [1981] QB 180 and *Garland v British Rail Engineering Ltd* [1983] 2 AC 751, wherein Lord Diplock stated that, in a case of clear conflict, domestic courts would still have to produce an interpretation of domestic law that ensured conformity with EC law, no matter how wide a departure from the prima facie meaning may be need to achieve consistency.

Following *R v Secretary of State for Transport, ex parte Factortame (No 2)* [1990] 3 WLR 818, it is now clear that the domestic courts have to be prepared to go as far as effectively suspending the operation of an Act of Parliament if it is impugned on the ground that it conflicts with EC law whilst that issue is being considered by the European Court of Justice. It is submitted that short of the United Kingdom reneging upon its obligations under the Treaty of Rome, unilaterally withdrawing from the EC, and expressly repealing the European Communities Act 1972, the Act effectively entrenches EC law, by making it impossible for any later Act to be applied in preference to EC law by means of implied repeal.

In *Thoburn v Sunderland City Council* (2002) The Times 22 February Laws LJ observes that in the final analysis the 1972 Act is not to be regarded as entrenched, even though the institutions of the European Union might regard this as being the case. He is adamant that Parliament cannot bind its successors by stipulating against repeal, wholly or partly, of the 1972 Act. Neither can it stipulate as to the manner and form of any subsequent legislation. In his view it cannot stipulate against implied repeal any more than it can stipulate against express repeal. Being sovereign Parliament cannot abandon its sovereignty, making entrenchment a logical impossibility.

QUESTION FIVE

To what extent is it correct to assert that within the United Kingdom constitution the judiciary cannot invalidate Acts of the Westminster Parliament?

Written by the Editor

General Comment

This question requires an examination of parliamentary sovereignty and a review of the way in which the courts have dealt with challenges to the validity of legislation. Care should be taken to distinguish between challenges to validity on procedural grounds and challenges on substantive grounds. The answer also needs to address the extent to which judges use their powers of interpretation to limit the effect of primary Acts when they see fit to do so.

Skeleton Solution

Define sovereignty – provide examples – distinguish procedural and substantive invalidity – explain failure of the procedural cases – explain failure of substantive cases – explain growth of constitutional statutes – comment on new judicial attitude where human rights in play.

Suggested Solution

The concept of parliamentary sovereignty is often cited as one of the cornerstones of the United Kingdom constitution. It is assumed that Parliament is legally competent to legislate upon any subject matter and that no Parliament can bind its successors or be bound by its predecessors. As Laws LJ observed in *Thoburn* v *Sunderland City Council* (2002) The Times 22 February, Parliament cannot bind its successors by stipulating against repeal, wholly or partly, of any legislation – the common law does not recognise any such power. Being sovereign Parliament cannot abandon its sovereignty.

Examples of the major changes that can be brought about by the exercise of parliamentary sovereignty include the Act of Settlement 1700 and His Majesty's Declaration of Abdication Act 1936. In 1700 Parliament laid down in the Act of Settlement the law governing accession to the English throne. The House of Lords Act 1999 removed hereditary peers from the House of Lords, and the Human Rights Act 1998 incorporated the European Convention on Human Rights.

Over the years there have been a number of attempts to challenge the validity of primary Acts on the basis that the procedure leading up to the enactment was in some way defective. None of these actions has been successful. In *Edinburgh and Dalkeith Railway* v *Wauchope* (1842) 8 Cl & F 710 the respondent argued that an Act was invalid since it adversely affected his rights and according to the standing orders of the House of Commons should not have been introduced without his having been given notice. Rejecting the challenge Lord Campbell observed that all a court can do is look to the parliamentary roll. If from that it appears that a Bill has passed both Houses and received the royal assent, no court can inquire into the mode in which it was introduced into Parliament, nor into what was done previous to its introduction, or what passed in Parliament during its progress in its various stages through both Houses. The leading modern authority on this point is the House of Lords' decision in *Pickin* v *British Railways Board* [1974] AC 765. Again it was a challenge to the procedure leading up to the enactment of an Act – the plaintiff argued that the Board had obtained the unopposed passage of an Act by misleading Parliament by a false recital in the preamble to the Bill. Lord Reid regarded the idea that a court might be entitled to disregard a provision in an Act of Parliament on any ground as 'strange and startling to anyone with any knowledge of the history and law of our constitution'. He added that the function of the court was to construe and apply the enactments of Parliament. The court was not to be concerned with the manner in which Parliament or its officers might have carried out those standing orders or performed those functions.

Other challenges to validity have been substantive – ie that the Act touches upon matters that are contrary to some higher law, such as international law, or that the Act is incompatible with the United Kingdom's international obligations. Like the procedural challenges these have received short shrift from the courts. In *Cheney* v *Conn* [1968] 1 WLR 242 a taxpayer challenged his assessments of tax liability on the basis that the Finance Act 1964 contravened international law, in that it permitted spending of taxpayers' money on weapons of mass destruction despite the outlawing of genocide in the Geneva Conventions. Rejecting this challenge Ungoed-Thomas J observed that what a statute enacts cannot be unlawful, because what the statute says and provides is itself the law, and the highest form of law that is known to the constitution.

This begs the question of how the courts would deal with an Act that was widely regarded as having been enacted with complete disregard for basic human rights? Suppose an Act was passed removing votes from women, or one that stipulated that any person over the age of 80 was to be put to death. The traditional view, as espoused by Lord Scarman in *Duport Steels Ltd* v *Sirs* [1980] 1 WLR 142, suggests that the judiciary would be powerless. He saw it as the judge's duty to choose the construction which, in the judge's mind, best met the legislative purpose of the enactment. If the result proved to be unjust but inevitable, the judge may say so and invite Parliament to reconsider its provision. But he had no power to deny the statute.

Whilst Scarman's view is still technically correct, there is evidence that judges today would be prepared to provide more opposition. The growing recognition at common law that some statutes are so fundamental in their importance to the constitution that they fall into a special category known as 'constitutional' statutes has led the courts to the view that certain basic rights and constitutional principles cannot be altered or abrogated by primary legislation unless Parliament clearly states that this is to be the case: see for example Lord Hoffmann in *R v Secretary of State for the Home Department, ex parte Simms; Same, ex parte O'Brien* [1999] 3 All ER 400. This does not equate with judges declaring statutes to be invalid, but it does mean that a latter statute that appears to impliedly repeal an earlier 'constitutional' statute will not be allowed to have such an effect. As Lord Steyn observed in *R v Secretary of State for the Home Department, ex parte Pierson* [1997] 3 WLR 492 'unless there is the clearest provision to the contrary, Parliament must be presumed not to legislate contrary to the rule of law. And the rule of law enforces minimum standards of fairness, both substantive and procedural.' What he means is that the powers of statutory interpretation vested in the judiciary should be used to nullify, so far as is possible, legislative provisions that offend against basic principles of fairness.

If one extrapolates from this that the rule of law can be argued as taking priority over the doctrine of parliamentary sovereignty, it is conceivable that a judge might simply refuse to give effect to an Act on the basis that the measure lacks the hallmark of legality – ie compliance with the rule of law. Lord Woolf MR in his article 'Droit Public – English Style' [1995] PL 57 argues that if Parliament were to legislate to abolish the role of the courts in, for example reviewing the legality of executive action (ie judicial review), the courts would have to resist it because it would be seen as a measure designed to subvert the rule of law.

In conclusion, therefore, it would be true to say that there is no legal basis for asserting that judges can invalidate primary Acts of Parliament, but it would also be true to say that judges possess sufficient ingenuity and independence of mind to ensure that by use of their powers of statutory interpretation they can give primacy to the assumption that Parliament always legislates in the context of observing basic human rights – and will give effect to legislation accordingly.

Chapter 4

The Sovereignty of Parliament and EU Membership

4.1   Introduction

4.2   Key points

4.3   Key cases and statute

4.4   Questions ad suggested solutions

4.1 Introduction

The political integration of European countries has been a post-war objective within Europe. In 1957 Belgium, France, West Germany, Italy, Luxembourg and The Netherlands signed the Treaty of Rome establishing the European Economic Community. In 1973 Denmark, Ireland and the United Kingdom became members.

The United Kingdom became a member by virtue of the Treaty of Accession 1972. It was necessary for Parliament to pass legislation incorporating the provisions into domestic law. This was achieved by the European Communities Act 1972. Political and legal integration has proceeded since then. The political and legal issues are:

a) The extent to which the United Kingdom Parliament is obliged to pass legislation which is consistent with Community provisions – is this a negation of sovereignty?

b) The position of the United Kingdom courts where Community law and domestic law conflict.

4.2 Key points

As explained in Chapter 3, the phrase 'the sovereignty of Parliament' is generally used to mean the absence of any legal restraint on the legislative powers of the United Kingdom Parliament. Accession to the European Union in 1973, and the enactment of the European Communities Act 1972, have had profound practical effects on the concept of sovereignty, however. Subject to Parliament exercising its undoubted power to repeal the 1972 Act, the courts will give precedence to EU law, notwithstanding any conflict with domestic legislation, even where the domestic legislation has been enacted post-1972. Hence membership of the European Community has lead to a reassessment of the doctrine of parliamentary sovereignty, given that the Community acquires its sovereignty as a result of member states each giving up sovereignty to some extent in order to be bound by Community law. The Community organs have law-making, executive and judicial powers.

The institutions of the EU

a) The Council of Ministers – the final policy and law-making body of the Community. It has representatives from each member state with a president holding office for six months. Note the decision-making process of the council.

b) The European Commission – members are chosen by national governments. The Commission can propose law, make law itself and enforce Community law against member states.

c) The European Parliament – members of the European Parliament are directly elected by member states. They are independent of national party policies. The Parliament has no law-making powers but is consulted by the council. Both the Council and the Commission are accountable to the Parliament.

d) The European Court of Justice – the European Court of Justice consists of 15 judges appointed by member states. Its function is to enforce Community law and treaty provisions. The role of the Court is crucial to Community law being applied uniformly through all member states.

The sources of Community law

The treaties

Proceedings can be brought in the European Court if a member state fails to fulfil its obligations.

Acts of the Community institutions

a) Regulations – made by Council of Ministers or the Commission, these are directly applicable in member states.

b) Directives – these establish Community objectives but leave the responsibility of implementation to member states: see *Van Duyn* v *Home Office* [1974] 3 All ER 178.

Decisions of the Court of Justice

a) Actions against member states.

b) Rulings on the interpretation of Community law referred by national courts: art 234 EC; see *Bulmer (HP)* v *J Bollinger SA* [1974] Ch 401 and *Finnegan* v *Clowney YTP* [1990] 2 AC 407.

Note s3(1) European Communities Act 1972:

'For the purpose of all legal proceedings any question as to the meaning or effect of any of the Treaties, or as to the validity, meaning or effect of any Community instrument, shall be ... for determination as such in accordance with the principles laid down by ... the European Court.'

Direct applicability

Section 2(1) of the European Communities Act 1972 provides:

'All such rights, powers, liabilities, obligations and restrictions from time to time created or arising by or under the Treaties, and all such remedies and procedures from time to time provided for by or under the Treaties, as in accordance with the Treaties are without further enactment to be given legal effect or used in the United Kingdom shall be recognised and available in law, and be enforced, allowed and followed accordingly; and the expression "enforceable Community right" and similar expressions shall be read as referring to one to which this subsection applies.'

The effect of this subsection is that all the provisions of Community law which are, in accordance with Community law, intended to take direct effect in the United Kingdom are given the force of law. This applies to Community law made both before and after the coming into force of the Act.

Direct effect

The term 'direct effect' refers to the enforceability of Community law. 'Vertical' direct effect is the term applied to those measures that can be invoked by a private individual against a member state. 'Horizontal' direct effect applies to those provisions that can be invoked by an individual against another private party. Essentially, the criteria to be satisfied before a provision can be regarded as having direct effect are that it is sufficiently precise in its terms to be said to be creating individual rights, and does not require any further implementation in order to become effective in law. Treaty provisions and regulations are normally regarded as having both vertical and horizontal direct effect provided the above criteria are met: see *Van Gend en Loos* v *Nederlandse Administratie der Belastingen* [1963] ECR 1; *Politi* v *Ministry of Finance* [1971] ECR 1039; *Walrave and Koch* v *Union Cycliste Internationale* [1974] ECR 1405; and *Defrenne* v *SABENA* [1976] ECR 455. Directives can also have vertical direct effect (see *Van Duyn* v *Home Office* Case 41/74 [1974] ECR 1337), but not horizontal direct effect: see *Marleasing SA* v *La Comercial Internacional de Alimentacion SA* Case C–106/89 [1992] 1 CMLR 305 and *Faccini Dori* v *Recreb Srl* Case C–91/92 [1994] ECR 1–3325. In *Marleasing SA*, however, the European Court of Justice ruled that, whilst directives were not of themselves capable of having direct effect between individuals, the national courts of member states were obliged to interpret domestic law so as to ensure conformity with EC directives, whether the domestic law originated before or after the incorporation of the directive.

The supremacy of Community law over national rules

Section 2(4) of the European Communities Act provides:

'The provision that may be made under subsection (2) above includes, subject to Schedule 2 of this Act, any such provision (of any such extent) as may be made by Act of Parliament, and any enactment passed or to be passed, other than one contained in this part of this Act, shall be construed and have effect subject to the foregoing provisions of this section.'

The 'foregoing provisions' include s2(1), which states that directly applicable Community law shall have effect in the United Kingdom. Therefore s2(4) seems to amount to a statement that United Kingdom Acts of Parliament 'shall be construed and have effect subject to' directly applicable Community law. The primacy of Community law over national law can be seen in decisions of the European Court of Justice: *Costa v ENEL* [1964] ECR 585; *Amminstrazione delle Finanze dello Stato* v *Simmenthal SpA* Case C–106/77 [1978] 3 CMLR 263; [1978] ECR 629.

Community law and the United Kingdom

European law will be followed in preference to inconsistent pre-1972 statutes: *Conegate v HM Customs and Excise* [1987] 2 WLR 39. The doctrine of implied repeal would, in theory, mean that any post 1972 domestic Act found to at odds with EC law introduced under the 1972 Act would have to take precedence over EC law. To avoid this conclusion, which would make EC membership unworkable, the courts have developed a new canon of statutory interpretation so that relevant provisions of United Kingdom law can bear a meaning that is consistent with Community law: *Garland* v *British Rail Engineering Ltd* [1983] 2 AC 751; *Macarthys Ltd* v *Smith* [1979] 3 All ER 325; *Pickstone* v *Freemans plc* [1988] 2 All ER 803. In effect, as Laws LJ explained in *Thoburn v Sunderland City Council* (2002) The Times 22 February, the doctrine of implied repeal has no operation in respect of statutes, such as the European Communities Act 1972, that deal with constitutional fundamentals. The 1972 Act, or parts of it, can be repealed by Parliament, but only where this is expressly stated to be the purpose of the later legislation. In effect a type of 'manner and form' restriction has been developed by the judiciary.

As the litigation in *R* v *Secretary of State for Transport, ex parte Factortame Ltd (No 2)* [1990] 3 WLR 818 makes clear, the courts will grant such remedies as are required to nullify the effects of domestic legislation found to be inconsistent with EC law.

Conclusion

The doctrine of direct applicability and the supremacy of Community law over national rules has led to a surrender or transfer of sovereignty on the part of the Westminster Parliament. But while there can be no implied repeal of Community law by national legislation, the position regarding the express repeal of Community law by Act of Parliament is a matter of controversy. While the European Court of Justice maintains that a national court should give effect to Community law even when subsequent national legislation is inconsistent with it, some lawyers argue that the express wish of Parliament must prevail.

4.3 Key cases and statute

- *Costa* v *ENEL* [1964] ECR 585; [1964] CMLR 425 (ECJ)
  EC law takes precedence over domestic law

- *Garland* v *British Rail Engineering Ltd* [1983] 2 AC 751; [1982] 2 All ER 402 (HL)
  Implied repeal inoperative regarding EC law

- *Macarthys Ltd* v *Smith* [1981] QB 180; [1979] 3 All ER 325 (CA)
  Implied repeal inoperative regarding EC law

- *R* v *Secretary of State for Transport, ex parte Factortame (No 1)* [1990] 2 AC 85 (HL);
  (No 2) [1991] 1 AC 603 (HL) and *(No 4)* [1996] All ER (EC) 301 (ECJ)
  Remedies to prevent domestic law prevailing over EC law

- *Thoburn* v *Sunderland City Council* (2002) The Times 22 February
  No implied repeal of European Communities Act 1972

- *Van Gend en Loos* v *Nederlandse Administratie der Belastingen* [1963] CMLR 105
  EC law takes precedence over domestic law

- European Communities Act 1972 – provides for the primacy of EC law

4.4 Questions and suggested solutions

QUESTION ONE

Parliament wishes to promote affirmative action and decides to allow women to be paid more than men for the same work. It passes the Turning the Tables Act 1995, s1 of which states:

'This Act is to be given effect notwithstanding any decision of the European Court of Justice or any provisions of Community law or any provisions of the European Communities Act 1972.'

Would a British judge still give primacy to Community law if this new Act came into conflict with it?

Adapted from University of London LLB Examination
(for External Students) Constitutional Law June 1987 Q3

General Comment

A relatively simple question concerning the effect of membership of the European Communities on the sovereignty of the Westminster Parliament.

Skeleton Solution

Introduction: the European Communities Act 1972 – the principles of direct applicability and the supremacy of Community law over national rules: s2(1) and (4) of the European Communities Act 1972 – the sovereignty of Parliament, express repeal and the doctrine of implied repeal, effect of Community law – effect of parliamentary legislation expressly contrary to Community law: *Macarthys Ltd* v *Smith* (1979); *R* v *Secretary of State for Transport, ex parte Factortame (No 2)* (1990) – *Thoburn* v *Sunderland City Council* (2002): express and implied repeal – the position with regard to the Turning the Tables Act 1995.

Suggested Solution

The United Kingdom became a member of the European Communities with effect from 1 January 1973, by virtue of the Treaty of Accession 1972. For the Treaty of Accession and the Community treaties and law to have legal effect in the United Kingdom it was necessary for Parliament to pass legislation incorporating them into domestic law. This was achieved by the European Communities Act 1972.

The legal regime of the European Community is founded upon the principle of direct applicability. Certain rules of Community law contained both in the treaties and in regulations made by the Council or the Commission are directly applicable in that, of their own force, they create legal rights and duties enforceable in municipal courts. Community law also forms part of the national law of every member state. The European Court of Justice has held that Community law prevails over national law to the extent that they are inconsistent with one another. These two principles are given effect in the law of the United Kingdom by virtue of s2(1) and (4) of the European Communities Act 1972.

By virtue of s2(4) of the European Communities Act 1972 therefore all United Kingdom legislation shall only take effect to the extent that it is consistent with Community law however clearly it may appear from the United Kingdom legislation that it is intended to have effect notwithstanding any Community law to the contrary: *Costa* v *ENEL* [1964] ECR 585; *Amministrazione delle Finanze dello Stato* v *Simmenthal SpA* [1978] ECR 629. It is clear both from the Treaty and from statements made by the European Court of Justice that community law should prevail over national law in all circumstances. Any United Kingdom constitutional law doctrine of the legislative sovereignty of Parliament is irrelevant. This approach taken by the European Court of Justice runs completely contrary to the traditional doctrine of the sovereignty of Parliament as enunciated in *Vauxhall Estates* v *Liverpool Corporation* [1932] 1 KB 733 and *Ellen Street Estates Ltd* v *Minister of Health* [1934] 1 KB 590. Certainly the doctrine of implied repeal as set out in *Ellen Street Estates* v *Minister of Health*, that later United Kingdom legislation always, by implication, repeals earlier legislative provisions with which it is inconsistent, would not survive.

But what about the situation such as that under the Turning the Tables Act 1995, where Parliament legislates expressly contrary to Community law? In such a case it may be possible to treat s2(4) as amounting to a rule of interpretation that there shall be a presumption that the United Kingdom Parliament, in passing legislation, intends to legislate consistently with Community law. This approach allows that if the United

Kingdom Parliament were to make it clear in a piece of legislation that it intended to legislate contrary to Community law or that it intended the legislation to take effect notwithstanding any provision of Community law to the contrary, then the United Kingdom legislation would prevail over the inconsistent Community law. This is the approach that was favoured by the Court of Appeal in *Macarthys Ltd* v *Smith* [1979] 3 All ER 325. A man had been employed as a stockroom keeper at £60 per week. Subsequently a woman was employed in this position at £50 per week. She took the matter to an industrial tribunal on the grounds that this was contrary to law. Two questions arose. First, was this contrary to art 119 of the Treaty of Rome (now art 141 EC) which provides that each member state shall ensure and maintain the application of the principle that men and women should receive equal pay for equal work? Second, in the event of a conflict between the United Kingdom legislation and art 119 of the Treaty, which should prevail in English courts?

In the Court of Appeal Lord Denning MR felt that if there were a conflict between the United Kingdom legislation and art 119 of the Treaty (now art 141 EC), art 119 should prevail since this is required by s2(1) and (4) of the European Communities Act 1972. Lord Denning here assumed that Parliament, when it passes legislation, intends to fulfil its obligations under the Treaty. But he felt that if the time should come when Parliament deliberately passes an Act with the intention of repudiating the Treaty or any provision in it or intentionally of acting inconsistently with it and says so in express terms, then it would be the duty of the United Kingdom courts to follow the Act of Parliament. But unless there is such an intentional and express repudiation of the Treaty, it is the duty of the United Kingdom courts to give priority to the Treaty.

Thus Lord Denning put forward the view that if Parliament in an Act stated an express intention to legislate contrary to Community law or notwithstanding Community law, then in that one situation the United Kingdom court would give preference to the United Kingdom legislation over the Community law. This interpretation was also favoured by Lord Diplock in *Garland* v *British Rail Engineering Ltd* [1983] 2 AC 751 when he too stated that statutes must be construed in a way consistent with Treaty obligations if they are capable of bearing such a meaning.

This amounts to a retention of the doctrine of express repeal of earlier law by later legislation, but involves the abandonment of the doctrine of implied repeal as far as Community law is concerned.

In the case of *R* v *Secretary of State for Transport, ex parte Factortame (No 2)* [1990] 3 WLR 818 the court granted temporary injunctive relief suspending those parts of the Merchant Shipping Act 1988 which were in conflict with Community law. A reference to the European Court of Justice ruled that domestic courts were required to give effect to directly enforceable provisions of Community law. The approach is not consistent with the traditional United Kingdom doctrine of the sovereignty of Parliament. However, it is yet to be seen how the United Kingdom courts would act if faced with a United Kingdom Act of Parliament expressing a clear intention of Parliament to legislate contrary to Community law. The more recent case of *Thoburn* v *Sunderland City*

Council (2002) The Times 22 February also confirms the abandonment of implied repeal as regards the 1972 Act, but leaves open the possibility of a later Act taking effect even though incompatible with Community law where Parliament expressly provides that such is its intention.

Regarding the Turning the Tables Act 1995 therefore the position is far from clear. The court may be inclined to uphold the express wish of Parliament and give effect to the Act notwithstanding art 141 EC. However, the European Court of Justice would almost certainly declare this to be invalid and hold that s1 of the 1995 Act amounts to a blatant repudiation by the United Kingdom of its international obligations under the European Community Treaties.

QUESTION TWO

Discuss, by reference to decided cases, the legal status of European Community law within the United Kingdom and its priority in relation to provisions in domestic Acts of Parliament.

University of London LLB Examination
(for External Students) Constitutional Law June 1996 Q4

General Comment

This is a relatively straightforward question involving the case law relating to the United Kingdom's membership of the European Community. The candidate should highlight the leading cases in this area and avoid getting enmeshed in a descriptive analysis of the plethora of cases in this area. A detailed knowledge, inter alia, of the course and implications of the Factortame litigation is required.

Skeleton Solution

United Kingdom's membership of the EC and the method by which treaties are signed – implications for domestic law of the signing of treaties – ss2(1), 2(4) and 3 European Communities Act 1972 – question of express and implied repeal – *Macarthys* v *Smith* – *Factortame* cases – art 234 EC – how the EC sees itself and conclusion.

Suggested Solution

The United Kingdom as an international legal personality joined the European Economic Community (as it then was) by the act of signing and ratifying the Treaty of Rome under the power vested in the royal prerogative. This was not as such a departure from previous practice dealing with treaties. The power so to do cannot be impugned or questioned in the courts: *Blackburn* v *Attorney-General* [1971] 2 All ER 1380. The royal prerogative is not, however, capable of enacting new laws and, as the *Case of Proclamations* (1611) 12 Co Rep 74 established, the Crown is unable to make new prerogative powers or laws imposing rights or obligations upon the Crown's subjects.

Therefore, in order to give domestic effect to the Treaty of Rome it was necessary to incorporate the Treaty into United Kingdom municipal law. This was done by the enactment of the European Communities Act 1972. The terms of the statute are far-reaching. By s2(1) both primary – the Treaty – and secondary Community law is to be given legal effect in the United Kingdom.

This applies to Community law past, present and future. Moreover, under s3 of the 1972 Act the interpretation of Community treaties and legislation is regarded as a question of law to be interpreted either by the European Court of Justice at Luxembourg or, if it is decided by the courts of the United Kingdom, the matter is to be decided in accordance with European Court of Justice decisions. The wording of s2(4) presents the United Kingdom courts with the dilemma of how to interpret Community law and subsequent Acts of Parliament, stating that: 'any existing or future enactments are to be construed and have effect subject to the foregoing provisions of this section'.

This would appear to be constitutional nonsense. According to the traditional doctrine of parliamentary sovereignty one Parliament cannot bind future Parliaments. Sovereignty is continuing and one Parliament cannot see itself up as being superior to any future Parliament or Parliaments. A subsequent Act of Parliament may expressly or impliedly repeal any previous legislation. English case law contains a plethora of decisions substantiating the above proposition. In the case of *Ellen Street Estates Ltd* v *Minister of Health* [1934] 1 KB 590 Maugham LJ held, inter alia:

'If in a subsequent Act, Parliament chooses to make it plain that the earlier statute is being to some extent repealed, effect must be given to that intention just because it is the will of the legislature.'

Such is, or was, the theory. In the case of *Blackburn* v *Attorney-General* Lord Denning chose to cast doubt on the orthodox theory and its relation to reality. Speaking obiter he said:

'We have all been brought up to believe that in legal theory one Parliament cannot bind another and that no Act is irreversible. But legal theory does not always march alongside political reality.'

He then went on to discuss the unlikely instance of Parliament reversing an Act of independence to a former colony, arguing 'Freedom once given cannot be taken away. Legal theory must give way to practical politics.'

What then is the position with relation to European Union law and any conflicting Acts of Parliament? In the case of *Macarthys Ltd* v *Smith* [1979] 3 All ER 325 Lord Denning again turned his attention to this problem. Speaking obiter he hypothesised:

'Thus far I have assumed that our Parliament whenever it passes legislation intends to fulfil its obligations under the Treaty. If the time should come when our Parliament deliberately passes an Act – with the intention of repudiating the Treaty or any provision in it – or intentionally acting inconsistently with it – and says so in express terms – then I should have thought that it would be the duty of our courts to follow the statute of our Parliament. I do not, however, envisage any such situation.'

Thus Lord Denning is acknowledging that if Parliament intends to repudiate Community law (as it then was), then the United Kingdom courts will give effect to it. However, one should be aware and pay attention to the phrase used: 'express terms'. It is submitted that this is less than express repeal and an implied repeal may be in express terms. In his judgment Lord Denning also provides for an escape clause from any possible conflict by talking about 'some oversight of our draftsmen' when a conflict with Community law is apparent. So what is 'express terms' or what is 'an oversight of our draftsmen' is conveniently left to the United Kingdom courts to interpret.

Another aspect of the potential conflict between the two jurisdictions, which the courts have had to tackle, arises when there is a perceived conflict between the United Kingdom law and EC law. This is discussed in the series of *Factortame* cases. The Common Market Fishing Policy devised a system to conserve fish by fixing quotas for national fishing fleets. The British government established a licensing system in 1985, which was expanded upon in the Merchant Shipping Act 1988 and which empowered the Secretary for Transport to make regulations and introduce a new register of British fishing vessels designed to prevent so-called 'quota hopping', whereby non-British Community nationals, Spanish fishermen, established companies in the United Kingdom in order to avail themselves of the British fishing quota. The question that arose before the United Kingdom courts was if a United Kingdom Act of Parliament supposedly infringed a party's Community rights – in this case as a result of discrimination based on the grounds of nationality – could that Act could be suspended pending a final outcome? The House of Lords (*R v Secretary of State for Transport, ex parte Factortame* [1989] 2 WLR 997) initially answered 'no' but referred the case to the European Court of Justice, under art 177 (now art 234 EC), for a preliminary ruling. The United Kingdom courts will avail themselves of art 234 EC when, inter alia, a question of interpretation of Community law needs to be answered: *Bulmer Ltd v Bollinger* [1974] Ch 401; see also *Customs and Exercise Commissioners v APS Samex* [1983] 1 All ER 1042.

The European Court of Justice in its preliminary ruling argued that the full effectiveness of Community law would be impaired if the United Kingdom argument that they could not suspend an Act of Parliament in such circumstances were to prevail. The European Court of Justice (*R v Secretary of State for Transport, ex parte Factortame* [1990] 3 CMLR 807) argued that, pending a final outcome, interim relief should be granted and the House of Lords (*R v Secretary of State for Transport, ex parte Factortame (No 2)* [1991] 1 AC 603) granted the said relief. A temporary injunction was issued against the Secretary of State preventing him from enforcing the offending provisions of the statute. Injunctive relief was therefore granted against the Crown and an Act of Parliament was suspended. In *Factortame (No 3)* [1991] 3 All ER 769 the ruling of the European Court of Justice upheld the complaints of the Spanish fishermen. Therefore, for the first time in United Kingdom constitutional history an Act of Parliament was suspended upon the basis of a violation of alleged rights, never mind established rights, and injunctive relief was given against the Crown.

The legal revolution as a result of joining the European Community has also been commented upon in other areas of litigation. Hoffmann J (as he then was) put it succinctly:

'The EC Treaty is the supreme law of this country, taking precedent over Acts of Parliament. Our entry into the EC meant that Parliament surrendered its sovereign right to legislate contrary to the provisions of the Treaty on matters of social and economic policy which it regulated': *Stoke-on-Trent City Council* v *B & Q plc* [1991] 2 WLR 242.

Whether or not the courts of the United Kingdom would disallow an Act of Parliament if it were to say 'notwithstanding EC law to the contrary' such and such is to apply is an open question. As it is the United Kingdom courts have clearly absorbed the philosophy of the European Court of Justice in *Costa* v *ENEL* [1964] ECR 585, when it argued in effect that a new legal order had been created. The United Kingdom courts will now not only suspend the workings of a statute but will also entertain an application for judicial review from, for example, the Equal Opportunities Commission (*R* v *Secretary of State for Employment, ex parte Equal Opportunities Commission* [1994] 2 WLR 409) for a declaration that United Kingdom law is incompatible with Community law. It is indeed true to say, as Lord Denning stated in *Bulmer* v *Bollinger*, that 'the Treaty [ie the Treaty of Rome] is like an incoming tide. It flows into the estuaries and up the rivers. It cannot be held back.'

QUESTION THREE

'Membership of the European Community requires a fundamental reassessment of the traditional theory of parliamentary sovereignty.'

Do you agree? To what extent does the case law support such a view?

University of London LLB Examination
(for External Students) Constitutional Law June 1997 Q1

General Comment

The question requires an explanation of the traditional theory of parliamentary sovereignty and an assessment of whether or not that doctrine has undergone any significant changes since 1972. It is important to put the issue in perspective and examine the view of the ECJ on this matter. Candidates should explain how judges have tried to accommodate the changes, and note that the European Communities Act 1972 is itself a manifestation of parliamentary sovereignty.

Skeleton Solution

What the European Community believes the impact of Community law to be – why this is a problem for the UK – the wording of s2(4) of the Europan Communities Act 1972 – the approach of the courts – whether this amounts to a fundamental change.

Suggested Solution

Membership of the European Community has profound implications for the doctrine of parliamentary sovereignty as it operates within the British constitution. In simple terms the doctrine provides that the Parliament at Westminster has unlimited power and is free to make or repeal laws as it sees fit – it is not a body of limited jurisdiction.

In practice this means that a later statute passed by Parliament at Westminster can expressly repeal an earlier one, no matter how significant the earlier Act. On those occasions where a later Act is found to be inconsistent with an earlier one, the courts invoke the doctrine of implied repeal. This is illustrated by *Vauxhall Estates Ltd* v *Liverpool Corporation* [1932] 1 KB 733. The Corporation of Liverpool proposed a scheme for the improvement of a certain area of the city. The Minister of Health confirmed the scheme in an order which incorporated the provisions of the Acquisition of Land (Assessment of Compensation) Act 1919 and the Housing Act 1925. These two Acts each provided a different scheme of compensation for compulsorily acquired land. Notwithstanding the clear terms of the 1919 Act, the court applied the less favourable terms of the 1925 Act, on the basis that Parliament had exercised its power of overriding the provisions of the 1919 Act (albeit unwittingly) by enacting in the later Act of 1925 a set of provisions totally inconsistent with those of the 1919 Act. *Ellen Street Estates Ltd* v *Minister of Health* [1934] 1 KB 590 provides a further illustration.

The view of the European Court of Justice as regards the sovereignty of member states is equally clear, ie membership of the European Community involves a pooling of sovereignty by member states. In *Costa* v *ENEL* [1964] ECR 585 it explained that the European Community derived its power and identity from 'a limitation of sovereignty or a transfer of powers from the States to the Community' and concluded that member states had limited their sovereign rights, within certain fields, to create a body of law binding on their nationals and themselves. The Court stressed in particular the point that if the European Community was to work properly it would have to ensure that European Community law applied equally and to the same extent within each member state. This necessarily limits the scope of each member's legislature to enact laws inconsistent with European Community law – hence the conflict with the traditional theory of parliamentary sovereignty. Similar statements can be found in the decision of the ECJ in *Re Export Tax on Art Treasures (No 2)* [1972] CMLR 699, where it was held that the grant to the European Community by member states of the rights and powers envisaged by the provisions of the Treaty of Rome implied a 'definitive limitation of their sovereign powers' over which no appeal to provisions of international law of any kind whatever could prevail. In effect, as far as the European Court of Justice is concerned, the United Kingdom doctrine of the legislative sovereignty of Parliament is irrelevant where the primacy of European Community law is in issue.

The United Kingdom became a member of the European Community with effect from 1 January 1973, the incorporation of the Treaty of Rome being achieved by the enactment of the European Communities Act 1972. The significance of the 1972 Act is that, from the date it came into force, all existing European Community law became part of domestic law. Following the doctrine of implied repeal this meant that any pre-1972 domestic law could now only have effect to the extent that it was consistent with European Community law – ie the doctrine of implied repeal applied. The real problems, however, arose as to the status of domestic law enacted post-1972 that was found to be in conflict with European Community law. The 1972 Act does not expressly deal with the issue of sovereignty, but provision is made in s2(4) for the resolution of such conflicts, where it is stated that any domestic legislation enacted after 1972 will be 'construed and have effect subject to' European Community law. In other words this provision suggests that the traditional doctrine of implied repeal cannot apply where domestic legislation passed after 1972 is found to be in conflict with existing European Community law.

The courts have responded to this problem by developing a rule of interpretation whereby it is presumed that Parliament, in passing legislation, intends to legislate consistently with Community law. On the basis of *Macarthys Ltd* v *Wendy Smith* [1979] 3 All ER 325 and *Garland* v *British Rail Engineering Ltd* [1983] 2 AC 751, this approach still allows the United Kingdom Parliament to make it clear in an Act that it intends to legislate contrary to Community law, or that legislation will take effect notwithstanding any provision of Community law to the contrary. It would appear that, to the extent that it was in conflict with European Community law, the United Kingdom legislation would prevail. This 'rule of construction' approach is neither consistent with the traditional United Kingdom doctrine of the sovereignty of Parliament, nor with the Community doctrine of the supremacy of Community law over national law. Although the courts have not had to deal with the problem of a United Kingdom Act of Parliament expressing an intention to legislate contrary to Community law, in the *Factortame* litigation *(R* v *Secretary of State for Transport, ex parte Factortame (No 2)* [1990] 3 WLR 818) the courts had to consider the validity of domestic legislation that was wholly inconsistent with European Community law, and the House of Lords held that domestic courts had no power to grant interim relief to prevent the operation of a statute passed by Parliament, unless it could be shown that there was some overriding principle of Community law which provided that member states must provide such relief. On a reference under art 177 (now art 234 EC) however, the ECJ ruled to the contrary. Following this ruling, the House of Lords held that a litigant could be given interim interlocutory relief to suspend the operation of the offending domestic legislation.

On the one hand, therefore, it could be said that there has been a fundamental change to the doctrine of parliamentary sovereignty simply on the basis there is now a legislative body that can create law to which the judges will, normally, give precedence over domestic law. On the other hand, it can be argued that this state of affairs is simply a manifestation of parliamentary sovereignty. The United Kingdom is only a member of the European Community because Parliament passed the European Communities Act 1972. When judges give precedence to European Community law they are simply carrying out Parliament's instructions as contained in s2(4) of that Act. When the *Factortame* case returned to the House of Lords for implementation of the ECJ ruling

Lord Bridge expressed the view that Parliament has always loyally accepted the obligation to make appropriate and prompt amendments where the ECJ has found domestic law to be in breach of European Community law, and that there was nothing novel in according supremacy to rules of Community law in those areas to which they applied.

The forfeiture of sovereignty is best described as limited and partial. The European Communities Act 1972 is not entrenched and Parliament can in theory repeal the Act at any time and thus regain its full supremacy as a sovereign legislature. The longer the United Kingdom remains a member , however, the more difficult it will be to extricate itself in political and economic terms. Joining a single currency will accelerate this process. Ultimately the situation may be reached where legislation to withdraw from the European Community may regarded in the same way as, for example, legislation to make Hong Kong a Crown colony again – theoretically possible, but unlikely.

QUESTION FOUR

By what means does the Court of Justice of the European Communities ensure the supremacy of Community law over national law?

> University of London LLB Examination
> (for External Students) Constitutional Law June 1998 Q7

General Comment

There are a variety of ways in which this question can be approached. One is to look at it entirely from the perspective of the domestic courts of the United Kingdom and the way in which they have tried to cope with the impact of ECJ rulings. It is probably preferable, however, to look at it from outside the confines of the United Kingdom constitution. Examine what the court does, the jurisprudence it has developed and the way in which doctrines such as direct applicability, direct effect and indirect effect have ensured the primacy of European Community law. An explanation of sanctions is also necessary.

Skeleton Solution

Outline the role of the ECJ – explain the approach taken to treaties – look at the methods adopted to ensure primacy of other sources of law – direct applicability – empowerment of citizens – direct effect – vertical and horizontal – indirect direct effect – the accommodation of the UK courts – evidence of supremacy of European Community law in the United Kingdom – sanctions for non-compliance.

Suggested Solution

The primary function of the European Court of Justice is to ensure that the provisions of the various treaties that underpin the European Union are observed by the various member states and applied properly by the courts of those member states. The Court therefore interprets and applies the whole corpus of European Community law from the basic treaties to the various implementing regulations, directives and decisions issued by the Council and the European Commission.

All member states agree to relinquish a degree of sovereignty when joining the European Union but the Court is there to ensure that this theory becomes reality. Since its inception the court has developed a body of jurisprudence that confirms the supremacy of European Community law over the domestic law of the member states. In *Costa* v *ENEL* [1964] ECR 585 the Court ruled that the executive force of European Community law could not be allowed to vary from one state to another in deference to subsequent domestic laws, without jeopardising the attainment of the objectives of the EC Treaty. Hence the EC Treaty and its provision would always prevail over any inconsistent domestic law. The provisions contained in the treaties and in EC regulations enacted by the Council have therefore been held by the Court to be of 'direct applicability', by which is meant that they become part of the law of a member state without further intervention by the member state: see further *Van Duyn* v *Home Office* Case 41/74 [1974] ECR 1337.

The extent to which the primacy of European Community law is made effective depends largely upon the degree to which compliance is policed. Clearly, large-scale failure by a member state to comply with the requirements of European Community law would be raised by the European Commission, or other member states. It is through the empowerment of individual European Union citizens, however, that the monitoring process is made most effective, and this has been achieved by the European Court's development of the concept of 'vertical direct effect', whereby a given provision of European Community law can be invoked by a individual against a member state in the courts of the relevant member state. The concept of member state here encompasses public bodies that can be regarded as emanations of the state. For a provision to have direct effect it must be sufficiently precise in its terms, it must be creating individual rights and it must not require any further implementation in order to become effective in law.

Treaty provisions and regulations can have this type of direct effect: see *Van Gend en Loos* v *Nederlandse Administratie der Belastingen* [1963] ECR 1. Subject to certain conditions, the court has ruled that directives can also have direct effect: see *Van Duyn* v *Home Office* (above). *Becker* v *Finanzamt Munster-Innenstadt* [1982] ECR 53 makes clear that the conditions for direct effect of directives are that the member state against whom the action is brought must have failed to transpose the directive into domestic law, or failed to do so correctly, and the directive must be sufficiently unconditional and precise in its terms.

Although the European Court of Justice has been unwilling to accept that directives can have horizontal direct effect (ie between private parties of member states), it has developed a doctrine of indirect effect whereby member states become obliged to ensure that its domestic courts interpret domestic law in such a way as to secure compliance with the objectives of a given directive: see *Marleasing SA* v *La Commercial Internacional de Alimentacion SA* [1992] 1 CMLR 305, where the doctrine of indirect effect was developed further to cover the situation where a directive had not been implemented.

The United Kingdom became a member of the European Community with effect from 1 January 1973, the incorporation of the Treaty of Rome being achieved by the enactment of the European Communities Act 1972. The approach of the European Court of Justice has posed particular problems for the United Kingdom's courts because of the doctrine of parliamentary sovereignty, particularly in relation to domestic law enacted post-1972 found to be in conflict with European Community law. The 1972 Act does not expressly deal with the issue of sovereignty, but provision is made in s2(4) for the resolution of such conflicts, where it is stated that any domestic legislation enacted after 1972 will be 'construed and have effect subject to' European Community law. The solution developed by the United Kingdom courts is, in a sense, a testament to the achievement of the European Court of Justice in securing the supremacy of European Community law within the legal systems of member states. The United Kingdom courts have developed a rule of interpretation whereby it is presumed that Parliament, in passing legislation, intends to legislate consistently with European Community law. On the basis of *Macarthys Ltd* v *Wendy Smith* [1979] 3 All ER 325 and *Garland* v *British Rail Engineering Ltd* [1983] 2 AC 751 this approach still allows the United Kingdom Parliament to make it clear in an Act that it intends to legislate contrary to Community law, or that legislation will take effect notwithstanding any provision of Community law to the contrary, but this is a largely theoretical possibility. To the extent that real conflict has arisen the domestic courts have followed the European's court's line: see *R* v *Secretary of State for Transport, ex parte Factortame (No 2)* [1990] 3 WLR 818.

Ultimately the European Court of Justice can have resort to a range of punishments in order to cajole member states into compliance with European Community law and rulings of the court. The Treaty on European Union 1992 provided a framework for the introduction of a system of fines imposed upon member states for non-compliance with European Community obligations: see art 68 EC (formerly art 73p). The European Commission has agreed that fines are to be imposed on a sliding scale related to the 'wealth' of member states.

The failure of a member state to ensure compliance with the provisions of the EC Treaty or other Community legislation, or indeed to implement directives accurately and within given time limits, may also give rise to a right in damages on the part of an individual adversely affected by the failure: see *Francovich* v *Italian Republic* [1992] IRLR 84. The Court based its reasoning on the ground that the full effectiveness of European Community law might be called into question, and the protection of the rights which they conferred would be weakened, if individuals could not obtain compensation where their rights were infringed by a breach of European Community law for which a member state was responsible. In other words, a member state should not be able to hide behind its own failure to implement a directive when defending such proceedings. The European Court of Justice has since gone on to extend this right to damages to other instances of non-compliance by Member States, notably in *Brasserie du Pêcheur SA* v *Federal Republic of Germany* Case C–46/93; *R* v *Secretary of State for Transport, ex parte Factortame Ltd and Others (No 4)* Case C–48/93 [1996] 2 WLR 506.

QUESTION FIVE

To what extent is it correct to view the European Court of Justice as a dynamic force for achieving the supremacy of Community law over domestic law? By what means does the Court ensure the supremacy of Community law?

University of London LLB Examination
(for External Students) Constitutional Law June 1999 Q8

General Comment

This question is virtually identical to Question 7 on the June 1998 paper. What is required is an explanation of the sources of European Community law and the various doctrines that the European Court of Justice has developed since its inception to ensure the primacy of European Community law. Candidates should explain the doctrine of direct applicability, direct effect and indirect effect, illustrating each with appropriate case law. Some reference of the impact this has had on the United Kingdom constitution will illustrate how influential the European Court of Justice has been.

Skeleton Solution

Explain the role of the Court – outline sources of European Community law – explain direct applicability regarding treaties and regulations – outline the development of direct effect and the thinking behind it – mention indirect effect and the role of damages – consider the impact on the United Kingdom constitution – illustrate with *Factortame* – conclusion.

Suggested Solution

Since its inception the European Court of Justice has been startlingly dynamic in its interpretation of its role as guardian of the European Community treaties, in the sense that it has boldly developed its jurisprudence to introduce doctrines that have successfully ensured not only the primacy of European Community law, but have also ensured that member states have not been able to undermine European Community law by failing to meet their obligations to implement it.

There are essentially five sources of European Community law: treaty articles; regulations; directives; decisions; and rulings of the European Court of Justice. The provisions of the EC Treaty are the primary source of European Community law. A regulation can be issued by the European Council of Ministers or the European Commission. Under art 249 EC (formerly art 189) a regulation will be of general application to all member states and will normally be directly applicable. A directive will normally be of general application to all member states, but will not be directly applicable. The EC Treaty leaves it to each member state to take the appropriate steps to adjust its domestic law so as to ensure conformity with the aims and objects of the directive.

How has the European Court of Justice ensured that these sources of European Community law have supremacy over the laws of the member states? The view of the Court as regards the sovereignty of member states is that membership of the European Community involves a pooling of sovereignty. In *Costa v ENEL* [1964] ECR 585 it explained that the European Community derived its power and identity from 'a limitation of sovereignty or a transfer of powers from the States to the Community', and concluded that member states had limited their sovereign rights, within certain fields, to create a body of law binding on their nationals and themselves. The Court stressed in particular the point that, if the European Community was to work properly, it would have to ensure that European Community law applied equally and to the same extent within each member state. This necessarily limits the scope of each member's legislature to enact laws inconsistent with European Community law – hence the conflict with the traditional theory of parliamentary sovereignty. Similar statements can be found in the decision of the European Court of Justice in *Re Export Tax on Art Treasures (No 2)* [1972] CMLR 699, where it was held that the grant to the European Community by member states of the rights and powers envisaged by the provisions of the Treaty of Rome implied a 'definitive limitation of their sovereign powers' over which no appeal to provisions of international law of any kind whatever could prevail.

The European Court of Justice has further developed the concept of direct applicability as regards treaties and regulations enacted by the Council, by which is meant that they become part of the law of a member state without further intervention by the member state: see further *Van Duyn v Home Office* Case 41/74 [1974] ECR 1337 and *Re Export Tax on Art Treasures* (above).

Provided they are sufficiently precise and unconditional, the European Court of Justice has held that both treaty provisions and regulations can give rise to direct effect. Normally, when a member state violates a treaty provision, or regulation, the response would be for the Commission or another member state to commence proceedings against the alleged defaulting state before the European Court of Justice. An important aspect of European Community law, however, is the extent to which the European Court of Justice has sought to empower individual EU citizens to invoke European Community law before both the domestic courts of a member state and the European Court of Justice. Where a provision of European Community law is described as giving rise to direct effect, therefore, it means that it can be invoked by an EU citizen against an EU member state in the domestic courts of that state: see *Van Gend en Loos v Nederlandse Administratie der Belastingen* [1963] ECR 1.

The European Court of Justice has also developed the concept of directives having direct effect, but the circumstances in which this will be the case are limited. In *Von Colson* v *Land Nordrhein-Westfalen* [1984] ECR 1891 the European Court of Justice broke new ground by recognising that even if a directive did not have direct effect, the courts of a member state would still be obliged to give effect to domestic law so as to achieve compliance with European Community law. Hence courts should indirectly give effect to directives by using them as guides to interpretation. This concept applied whether the litigation was between an individual and the state, or between private parties.

It should be borne in mind that directives are not directly applicable in that they require further enactment by a member state before they can take effect within its domestic law. Member states have no discretion as regards the object to be achieved by the implementation of the directive, but do have discretion as to how that objective is to be achieved. To ensure compliance, however, the European Court of Justice ruled in *Marleasing SA* v *La Commercial Internacional de Alimentacion SA* [1992] 1 CMLR 305 that this doctrine could apply even if a member state had not taken steps to implement a directive in its domestic law.

The European Court of Justice has also developed the doctrine of damages being payable by member states to individuals for failure to implement directive correctly. In *Francovich* v *Italian Republic* [1992] IRLR 84 the European Court of Justice held that the provision of such a remedy was necessary in order to prevent a member state relying on its own failure to implement a directive as the basis for denying rights accruing under European Community law to its citizens. Damages will also be available in cases of inadequate or incomplete implementation: see *Brasserie du Pêcheur SA* v *Federal Republic of Germany* Case C–46/93; *R* v *Secretary of State for Transport, ex parte Factortame Ltd and Others (No 4)* Case C–48/93 [1996] 2 WLR 506 where the European Court of Justice held that the principle established in *Francovich* applied provided three conditions were met: (i) the rule of law infringed must be intended to confer rights on individuals; (ii) the breach must be sufficiently serious; and (iii) there must be a direct causal link between the breach of the obligation resting on the state and the damage sustained by the injured party.

The extent to which the supremacy of European Community law has been made plain can be illustrated by looking at the case of *R* v *Secretary of State for Transport, ex parte Factortame (No 2)* [1990] 3 WLR 818. The United Kingdom constitution has, since the seventeenth century been based upon a doctrine of parliamentary sovereignty, a concept that does not sit well with the jurisprudence of the European Court of Justice. A conflict was inevitable. The House of Lords ultimately gave effect to the ruling of the European Court of Justice that domestic law, in the form of the Merchant Shipping Act 1988, had to be disapplied to the extent that it conflicted with European Community law. A litigant can now obtain interim interlocutory relief in the United Kingdom courts to suspend the operation of offending domestic legislation. Damages may also be available in respect of any loss suffered.

In conclusion, therefore, it can be seen that through the development of concepts such as direct applicability, direct effect, indirect effect and damages for non-compliance, the European Court of Justice has truly fulfilled a dynamic role in ensuring that the courts of all members states are obliged to give primacy to European Community law.

Chapter 5

The Electoral System

5.1   Introduction

5.2   Key points

5.3   Key cases and statutes

5.4   Questions and suggested solutions

5.1 Introduction

The membership of the House of Commons is elected on the basis of adult suffrage. A general election must be held at least every five years: Parliament Act 1911.

5.2 Key points

The Electoral Commission

a) The Electoral Commission was created by the Political Parties, Elections and Referendums Act 2000 to oversee the conduct of the electoral process and the Act introduces controls over donations to political parties and expenditure by political parties during campaigns. By virtue of s5 the Commission is placed under a duty, following each election or referendum to which the Act applies, to publish a report on the administration of the election or referendum. A Speaker's Committee oversees the operation of the Commission, both in terms of its use of resources and in terms of approving the Commission's 'five year plan'.

b) Under ss16–20 of the Political Parties, Elections and Referendums Act 2000 the functions of the various Boundary Commissions are transferred to the Commission, which is required, by s14, to establish four Boundary Committees, one for each of England, Scotland, Wales and Northern Ireland. Each Committee comprises between two and four members – only an Electoral Commissioner or a deputy Electoral Commissioner may be appointed a member of a Boundary Committee.

The registration of political parties

Part II of the Political Parties, Elections and Referendums Act 2000 replaces the provisions of the Registration of Political Parties Act 1998. Political parties have to register in order to field candidates under a party name. Registration is also a gateway to receipt of funding and participation in party political broadcasts.

The person registered as a party's treasurer is responsible for compliance with the accounting and reporting regime laid down in the Political Parties, Elections and Referendums Act 2000. The Electoral Commission can refuse to register offensive or inappropriate party names.

Controls on party funding and election expenditure

a) Part III of the Political Parties, Elections and Referendums Act 2000 provides for limits on the size of donations to political parties, requirements for donors to be identified, and provides for accounting procedures to be followed. The Act relaxes the rules on campaign expenditure to some extent – although candidates contesting a constituency are still subject to certain limitations. The restrictions apply to general election campaigns and those for the European and regional parliaments. Expenditure on local government election campaigns is not included for these purposes.

b) Under s75 of the 2000 Act it is a criminal offence to incur, without reasonable excuse, campaign expenditure by, or on behalf of, a registered party without the authority of the treasurer of the party. Section 79 and Sch 9 impose limits on campaign expenditure incurred by or on behalf of registered parties. It is an offence for the treasurer of a registered party to authorised expenditure to be incurred by or on behalf of the party where he knows or ought reasonably to have known that the expenditure would be incurred in excess of the statutory limit. In general terms the limit imposed by the Act is £30,000 multiplied by the number of constituencies contested by a party. Sections 80–84 provide for the auditing of party treasurer returns in respect of campaign expenditure and the delivery of returns to the Commission.

c) Expenditure by third parties during a national election campaign, aimed at securing the election of a particular party, is dealt with by Ch I of Pt VI of the Act. A third party for these purposes is any individual or organisation intending to incur controlled expenditure in excess of £10,000 during a regulated period, effectively the period of the election campaign. Any such third party must comply with the registration, notification and accounting requirements of the Act. Controlled expenditure is defined by s85 as including expenditure incurred by or on behalf of the third party in connection with the production or publication of election material that is made available to the public at large or any section of the public. Limits on campaign expenditure in respect of referendums are introduced by Pt VII of the Act.

d) The funding of, and expenditure by, individual candidates is addressed by ss130–135 of the Act. The regime introduced by the Act to regulate donations to registered political parties and third parties is extended to cover donations to individual candidates with appropriate modifications. In any event a candidate will only be able to spend money so donated for election purposes within the limits outlined below. In response to the ruling of the European Court of Human Rights in *Bowman* v *United Kingdom* (1998) The Times February 23, s131 amends s75 of the

Representation of the People Act 1983 by increasing the expenditure that may be incurred in meeting election expenses by persons other than the candidate or his agent from £5 to £500 for a parliamentary election. For local government elections the maximum figure is £50 plus 0.5p for every entry in the register of local government electors for the electoral area in question. The 2000 Act does alter the rules relating to the limits on expenditure by individual candidates in constituencies. That figure is calculated on the basis of £4,965 plus 5.6p per elector in county constituencies, and 4.2p per elector in borough constituencies. Under s132(6), however, the maximum expenditure that may be incurred by a candidate contesting a constituency at a parliamentary by-election is increased to a flat rate £100,000, reflecting the fact that many by-elections are keenly fought contests attracting national interest.

The franchise

In order to vote in a parliamentary election a person must be included on the electoral register for a parliamentary constituency: Representation of the People Act 1983, as amended by the Representation of the People Act 2000. To qualify for inclusion a person must:

a) be 18 years of age (or be due to attain his eighteenth birthday within 12 months of the publication of the register);

b) be a British subject or a citizen of the Republic of Ireland;

c) not be subject to any legal incapacity;

d) be registered as a voter in accordance with the procedures by the 2000 Act.

Disqualification

The following persons are not entitled to vote, even if their names appear on the register.

a) Aliens (excluding citizens of the Republic of Ireland).

b) Minors (persons under 18 years of age).

c) Convicted persons serving sentences of imprisonment, as upheld in *R (Pearson and Another)* v *Secretary of State for the Home Department* (2001) The Times 17 April. Remand prisoners retain the right to vote under the 2000 Act.

d) Persons convicted of corrupt practices at elections are disqualified from voting for five years. Persons convicted of illegal practices at elections are disqualified from voting for five years in the constituency in question.

e) Those who for reasons such as mental illness, subnormality or other infirmity lack the capacity at the moment of voting of understanding what they are about to do. Note however that the 2000 Act does provide that a person who is detained in a mental hospital as a voluntary patient may be registered as a voter provided his stay is sufficient in length for him to be regarded as resident.

The electoral system

At present Members of Parliament are elected under the simple majority voting system. Each parliamentary constituency returns a single member. Each elector can vote for one candidate only and the candidate who polls the most votes within a given constituency wins the seat.

Disadvantages of the simple majority voting systems

a) There are many wasted votes.

b) It is a very crude system.

c) There is no relationship between the number of votes cast nationally for a particular party and the number of seats allocated to that party in the House of Commons.

d) The system produces exaggerated majorities for the two major parties and discriminates against the minority parties.

Advantages of the simple majority voting system

a) The voting procedure is simple and the results may be quickly calculated.

b) There is a link between the member and his constituency.

c) One party usually obtains an absolute majority of seats in the House of Commons thus leading to strong government.

Electoral reform

The three main alternatives to our present system are:

a) The alternative vote. Voters list the candidates in order of preference. If no candidate gains an absolute majority of first preference votes then the lowest candidate is eliminated and his second preference votes are distributed among the other candidates. The process may be repeated until a candidate emerges who has an absolute majority.

b) The party list system. This system operates on the basis of large multi-member constituencies. The parties present lists of candidates and electors vote not for individual candidates but for the whole party list. Seats are then allocated to the parties in proportion to the votes received by each party list. The system is now used for elections to the European Parliament and is proposed for the election of members to the House of Lords, whenever this is introduced. Party list systems are also used to select the 'additional members' to the Scottish Parliament and the Welsh Assembly.

c) The single transferable vote. This requires multi-member constituencies of between five and seven members. Voters list the candidates in order of preference. The candidate needs a quota of votes to be elected. Any votes he receives beyond this figure are surplus and so they are redistributed among the other candidates according to second preference. The quota is usually established by the following formula:

$$\frac{\text{number of votes cast} + 1}{\text{number of seats} + 1}$$

5.3 Key cases and statutes

- *Bowman* v *United Kingdom* (1998) The Times 23 February (ECHR)
  United Kingdom electoral expenditure restrictions – whether a violation of art 10 of the European Convention on Human Rights

- *Matthews* v *United Kingdom* (1999) The Times 30 March (ECHR)
  Right to vote – whether a breach of Protocol 1, art 3

- *R (Pearson and Another)* v *Secretary of State for the Home Department* (2001) The Times 17 April
  Prisoner – loss of the right to vote – whether incompatible with rights protected by the European Convention on Human Rights

- *R (Quintavalle)* v *BBC* (2002) The Times 19 March
  Ban on party political broadcast a violation of the right to free speech

- *R (Robertson)* v *Wakefield MDC* (2001) The Times 27 November
  Electoral register – refusal to register if electoral register sold to commercial interests – whether legal duty to register compatible with European Convention on Human Rights

- European Parliamentary Elections Act 1999 – introduced party list system for United Kingdom elections to EU Parliament

- Political Parties, Elections and Referendums Act 2000 – establishes Electoral Commission, new election rules on expenditure and replaces the Boundary Commission

- Representation of the People Act 1983 – provides basic rules on electoral process, as amended by later Acts

- Representation of the People Act 2000 – introduces rolling registration and clarifies issues of disqualification

5.4 Questions and suggested solutions

QUESTION ONE

'In a really equal democracy, every or any section would be represented, not disproportionately, but proportionately.' (J S Mill)

Discuss this statement with respect to the British system of general elections.

University of London LLB Examination
(for External Students) Constitutional Law June 1995 Q3

General Comment

This is a beguilingly straightforward question about differing forms of electoral systems. The statement is brief and therefore gives a lot of scope to the candidate to use all the knowledge that can be amassed. The statement itself focuses on 'sections' of society rather than the individual voter. This aspect should be discussed to focus on the right aim for an electoral system, before considering the variety of possible electoral systems.

Skeleton Solution

Discuss the detail of the statement in the question – discuss the pros and cons of the first-past-the-post system – discuss the pros and cons of the party-list system – discuss the pros and cons of the single transferable vote – discuss the pros and cons of the alternative member system – conclusion.

Suggested Solution

The question of the desirability of equality in systems of democracy is one that is easy to answer in rhetorical terms, but difficult to deal with in systemic terms. In general, it is possible to say that an ideal system of elections would aim to provide each citizen of majority age with one vote that would be of equal value to the vote of every other citizen. However, Mill's formulation of this proposition looks at society not in terms of individual citizens but rather in terms of 'sections'.

The difficulty with this formulation is that it requires it to be possible for every section to be identified in a two-dimensional format. To identify the opinions of the electorate as sectional interests casting their votes in the same manner is to ignore the broad range of issues which are active in the minds of the voters, and which may cause people of ostensibly similar backgrounds and with seemingly similar views to vote or act in very different ways. One may choose not to vote, whereas the other might decide that one should vote for the least worst option. Both are valid choices, but it is difficult to identify exactly which 'section' best represents each voter. Therefore, the individual citizen model, it is suggested, offers the better model for assessing whether or not a given democratic system is 'equal' or not.

Mill's conception of the issue is more useful when looking at the issue of proportional representation. While it is still focused on the notion of 'sections', it does identify the need to create a Parliament that does, to some extent, reflect the political composition and views of society. The result of an election is the creation of a Parliament that enacts the political programme of the majority party or a coalition of parties.

The first-past-the-post system fails to admit the views of the minority interests in society. Where there is insufficient support for a particular interest or shade of opinion in a given geographic region, there will not be enough support to elect a Member of Parliament in any constituency. Therefore, special interest groups are unrepresented. The growing cynicism of the population with the political system can potentially be traced to the failure of the current electoral system to reflect adequately the opinions of the population in more than a two-party, two-dimensional format. The weight of a vote for Party A will be weaker in a constituency where Party A either stands no prospect of victory or where Party A is sure to win. A vote for Party A will be more important in a constituency where Party A might win or lose by a very few votes.

The advantages of this system appear in ways other than straightforward 'equality' or parity of votes. The constituency system does provide representation for a particular region through a given individual politician. Therefore, there is a mechanism for ensuring responsiveness from the political system to the local needs of a particular constituency. The conduct of representational and democratic politics can therefore be made more accountable to specific units of the population. Voting patterns mirror more closely the views of general geographic areas measured in trends large enough to affect those overall local majorities. The simple majority system also aids ease of comprehension, which makes it easier for politicians to analyse the views of the population and also, more importantly, for the population to understand the outcomes of elections.

The proportional representation models are many and varied. The simplest system is that used in Israel where people vote on a party-list, non-constituency basis. The proportion of the total national vote obtained by each party is then attributed to that party. The percentage of the total that represents is then allotted to each party as a corresponding percentage of seats in the parliamentary assembly. The advantage of this system is that every vote has exactly the same weight. Similarly, each section in society is represented precisely. The disadvantages with this system are, first, that there is no link between local people and any individual politician: therefore local democratic ties are very weak. Second, the system places enormous powers in the hands of the parties to select who the politicians are. Party list systems are used as the basis for the election of 'additional members' to the Scottish Parliament and the Welsh Assembly. The Scottish Parliament comprises 73 constituency members (elected on the first-past-the-post basis) and 56 party list members; the Welsh Assembly has 40 constituency members and 20 party list members. Following the May 1999 elections no single party gained an overall majority in the Scottish Parliament or the Welsh Assembly – immediately calling into question the merits of this form of proportional representation, not least because those parties seeking to form coalition governments are forced to renege on manifesto commitments as the price for entering into a deal with other minority parties.

A form of the party list system is also used for the election of MEPs under the European Parliamentary Elections Act 1999, with England divided into nine electoral regions returning a total of 71 MEPs. Scotland, Wales and Northern Ireland are each classified as a single region returning eight, five and three MEPs respectively. A major criticism is that under this scheme voters do not have a choice between candidates selected by the parties. Voters can, of course, vote for independent candidates, but the chances of any such candidates succeeding are slim. It is the 'closed list' aspect of these proposals that has attracted so much criticism, from both left and right. Critics argue that power is being transferred from the electorate to a 'selectorate' of party managers.

The single transferable vote method is a more complicated system of proportional representation. This system retains the use of large constituencies from which a number of candidates are elected at the same time. Voters mark their ballot papers with their candidates placed in order of preference. A threshold level of votes is calculated above which a candidate is elected. This threshold is itself calculated by reference to the mean number of votes required for the prescribed number of candidates to be selected out of the votes cast. This enables a broader range of preferences to be tested because, once a candidate crosses the threshold, the remaining votes for that candidate as first choice are reallocated to the second choice on the ballot paper. The drawbacks are the complication of the system and the loose ties that are established on a local democratic basis. There is also an element of mathematical chance involved with the reallocation of votes.

The alternative member system is practised in a variety of countries, and it enables the voter to vote for a constituency MP and then to have that vote counted a second time as a vote for a party-list candidate selected by the party. Therefore, there are two cadres of MP, one who represents the constituency and another who is selected by the political party. There is a drawback to having two streams of politicians in that it raises questions as to which of the two has a better mandate from the electorate. The electoral process is also slightly complicated by the use of this system.

It is clear that there are a number of means of carrying out elections. However, it is difficult to measure which is the best electoral system to use. Mill's conception points towards a simple party list system that may, in fact, diminish the service and representation that many constituents are able to obtain from the first-past-the-post system.

It is interesting in this regard to note that the Jenkins Commission, which published its report on alternatives to the first-past-the-post system in October 1998, proposed that it should be replaced by an enhanced alternative vote system. There is no sign, however, of a more representative system being introduced for general elections. Governments tend to be loyal to the electoral process that put them in power in the first place.

QUESTION TWO

Consider the view that 'our method of election to the House of Commons is in the highest degree unjust, unsatisfactory and dangerous'.

University of London LLB Examination
(for External Students) Constitutional Law June 1996 Q3

General Comment

This question invites a discussion of the workings of the present electoral system. Candidates should discuss not only the present electoral system but also its consequences in the representation of the parties in Parliament. The advantages and disadvantages of the system should be set out and the student must be willing to agree or disagree with the polemical statement. A brief summary of some of the alternative electoral systems needs to be included to complete the essay.

Skeleton Solution

Introduction? the franchise in the United Kingdom.– constituency basis of the MP – first past the post – the reflection of first past the post in the Commons – advantages of the present system – disadvantages of the present system – alternative electoral systems – conclusion.

Suggested Solution

The membership of the House of Commons is elected on the basis of universal adult suffrage. In order to vote in a parliamentary election the individual must be listed in the electoral register for a parliamentary constituency. To be placed on the register the individual must be a British subject, a Commonwealth citizen or a citizen of the Irish Republic (such citizens are not classified as aliens for electoral purposes), be 18 years of age or be due to attain his/her eighteenth birthday within 12 months of the publication of the register, not suffer any legal incapacity and be resident in the constituency as required under the rolling registration system introduced under the Representation of the People Act 2000.

The above is without controversy and has raised little or no political discussion. It is the electoral system rather than those eligible to vote that is the cause of political disquiet. It is perhaps worth noting that the Labour Party, whilst still in opposition in 1996, suggested that it would initiate a referendum on reforming the electoral system if it were to gain power.

How then is the electoral system to the House of Commons based? The United Kingdom is divided into 659 parliamentary constituencies, each of which is represented by one member in the House of Commons. Under ss16–20 of the Political Parties, Elections and Referendums Act 2000 functions previously exercised by the various Boundary Commissions are transferred to the Electoral Commission, which is required, by s14, to establish four Boundary Committees, one for each of England, Scotland, Wales and Northern Ireland. Each Committee comprises between two and four members – only an Electoral Commissioner or a deputy Electoral Commissioner may be appointed a member of a Boundary Committee.

The premise is that each constituency should have the same number of voters within it to ensure that all votes in the country are of equal value. This is summed up by the maxim: 'one man, one vote, one value'. There are periodic reviews of the electoral population of the parliamentary constituencies and changes may be recommend, ie that extra constituencies be formed in an area under-represented owing to an increase in population, or an abolition of constituencies owing to a decrease in population. Changes have tended to reflect the change in the balance of the population away from urban areas and into the shires.

This division of the United Kingdom by the Electoral Commission is normally accepted by the political parties. Challenges have, historically, not fared well; see *R v Boundary Commission for England, ex parte Foot* [1983] QB 600.

Of much more controversy though is the United Kingdom's adherence to the first-past-the-post system in general elections. Each elector is eligible to vote for one candidate only and the candidate who obtains the most votes within a constituency wins. It is possible, therefore, for a candidate to win even though the majority of the electorate in a constituency vote against him. If, for instance, J Bloggs obtains 10,000 votes, J Smith obtains 7,000 votes and J Jones obtains 6,000 votes, J Bloggs wins despite the fact the majority of the electorate voted against him. All the votes given to J Bloggs over 7,001 are 'wasted'. The number of wasted votes may be significant in a safe Labour seat, for example in South Wales, or in a safe Conservative seat, for instance in Surrey. There is no way in the existing system that the votes, or more accurately the surplus votes, may be distributed elsewhere in the country.

This system is reflected in the final outcome of the votes as there is little relationship between the number of votes cast nationally for a party and the number of seats that party may obtain in the House of Commons. Thus, in the 1992 general election the Conservatives obtained 41.9 per cent of the votes but achieved 51.6 per cent of the seats. Minority parties do particularly badly in this system, as illustrated by the Liberal Democrats who obtained 17.8 per cent of the votes in 1992 but only 3.1 per cent of the seats. The figures for the general election of June 2001 were as follows:

Party	Seats won	As a % of seats	% of the total vote
Conservative	166	25	32
Labour	412	63	41
Liberal Democrats	52	8	18
Others	29	4	10

Again the disparity between votes cast and seats won is obvious. As with racing, or even more so, there is little merit in coming second. Parties that come second in a significant number of constituencies may as well have come third or fourth. The only minority parties likely to survive in such a system are those with a strong regional base, such as the Scottish Nationalists. They are able to target particular constituencies rather than have their votes spread out throughout the country.

It should be pointed out, however, that the first-past-the-post system has a number of advantages. It is simple and the electorate has a clear understanding of how it works. The results are easily arrived at and it avoids delays in establishing the winner on both a national and local level. It also establishes a link between the MP and his/her constituency; the other systems (see below) often fail to achieve this. The link between an MP and his/her constituency enables other institutions such as the Parliamentary Commissioner for Administration (PCA) to function effectively as the MP puts forward the complaints and grievances of the constituent. An MP may also pursue a particular matter that is of concern to his or her constituents. For example, MPs who have a large proportion of immigrants amongst their constituents are more likely to be involved in immigration issues. In taking up an issue raised by a constituent the MP is obliged to help the constituent to his or her best ability no matter whether the constituent is likely to vote for the MP or not.

A further advantage of the present system is that it usually creates an absolute (overall) majority of seats in the House of Commons. At the end of the day the electorate can understand the result of the election, while in other electoral systems (see below) this is not necessarily the case. The majority of British elections do not result in inter- and intra-party manoeuvres as a government is trying to be formed. A proportional representation system, with its possible result of a 'hung' Parliament, would also have the effect of politicising the role of the monarch as she would have to exercise her discretion as to which candidate would be the most suitable Prime Minister.

While it may be seen as unjust in the manner in which it penalises minority parties, the present electoral system does have the beneficial effect of preventing extremist minority parties obtaining a presence in the House of Commons. In the 1930s the British Fascist Party led by Oswald Mosley failed to obtain a seat in the House of Commons because its followers were spread throughout the country and the party failed to gain enough following to achieve a majority in a single constituency. Indeed, countries with a system of proportional representation, such as Germany, have a threshold requirement of about 5 per cent before a party can enter Parliament, the purpose being to prevent extremist minority parties gaining a platform.

What then are the alternatives to the British electoral system? The main options are these systems: alternative vote; party list; and single transferable vote.

The alternative vote system operates by the voter listing the candidates in their constituency in order of preference. If no candidate gains an absolute majority of the first preference then the lowest candidate is eliminated and his/her second preference votes are distributed amongst the other candidates. This process can be repeated until one candidate emerges with an absolute majority. The principal inadequacy of the system is that the overall result does not reflect the actual proportions of the votes. The voter has the potential to be confused with the procedure and the winner might not have a clear mandate from the voters.

The party list system is perhaps the method which best reflects the real proportion of the votes. The country is classified as one constituency and the parties present lists of candidates and the electors vote for the whole party list. Seats in Parliament are allocated to the parties in proportion to the votes received by each party list. Such a system strengthens the party bureaucracy as potential candidates compete to be placed as near the top of the list as possible. The link between the MP and the constituency is destroyed and minority parties will be given greater potential power as they offer their conditional support to any putative government. This effect is increased, as an outright winner in such a system is unusual. This is the alternative system that seems to appeal to the present Labour government as it has used it for elections to the Scottish Parliament, the Welsh Assembly and for the election of United Kingdom MEPs. It is also in favour of using the system to elect members of the House of Lords, should such a change be introduced. It is significant that it is not so enamoured of the system that it is willing to embrace it for elections to Parliament at Westminster. A major defect of the party list system is that it marks a shift away from election towards selection. Party managers can determine who gets into power by reference to how near the top a candidate is listed.

The single transferable vote (STV) is the system that is looked upon with most approval by the advocates of electoral reform. This system would see a diminution in the number of constituencies in Parliament as it requires multi-member constituencies with between five and seven members. Voters list the candidates in order of preference. The candidate needs a quota of votes to be elected. The 'surplus' votes of the winning candidate are then redistributed among the other candidates in accordance with the voter's second preference. While this system would weaken the link between the MP and his constituents it is not unknown in the United Kingdom. In the nineteenth century multi-member constituencies (usually two MPs) were present in the United Kingdom Parliament.

The call for reform of the electoral system in the United Kingdom is heard especially from those parties such as the Liberals who are penalised by being minority parties. There is no manner in which their votes may be distributed. The Labour Party has flirted with reform but shows no appetite for it as regards General Elections. The advocates of electoral reform point to the German voting system while the detractors point to Israel or Ireland. The message elsewhere is unclear; while New Zealand has introduced a system of proportional representation, Italy has moved away from it. One might conclude that our method of election is unjust and unsatisfactory, but so are all the others.

QUESTION THREE

What, if any, has been the impact of the European Convention on Human Rights on the electoral processes in the United Kingdom?

Written by the Editor

General Comment

This question requires a knowledge of what the European Convention on Human Rights provides in respect of voting rights and a good knowledge of recent case law developments relating to the electoral process. The question is not limited, however, to the right to vote. Note how it brings in other rights issues, such as privacy and freedom of expression.

Skeleton Solution

Explain what the European Convention on Human Rights provides – example of the way it requires enfranchisement – look at specific examples – election expenditure – legislative response – right to vote – freedom of expression – conclusion.

Suggested Solution

It is often overlooked that the European Convention on Human Rights extends beyond the obvious individual rights, such as those relating freedom of the person, privacy and the right to a fair trial. Article 3 of the First Protocol provides for signatory states to ensure free elections at reasonable intervals by secret ballot, under conditions that will ensure the free expression of the opinion of the people in the choice of the legislature.

The significance of the European Convention on Human Rights provisions regarding domestic law in these matters was underlined in *Matthews* v *United Kingdom* (1999) The Times 30 March, where the applicant successfully brought proceedings against the United Kingdom in respect of the fact that, as a British citizen living in Gibraltar, she was not entitled to be registered as a voter for the elections to the European Parliament on the basis that Gibraltar was not included in the franchise for those elections. The European Court of Human Rights held that the European Parliament was a 'legislature' for the purposes of the First Protocol as the term did not relate solely to the national legislature of a signatory state. The term could apply to a supranational body such as the European Parliament, especially given the extent to which EC law could be directly applicable in, and take precedence over, the domestic law of, member states. The Court also felt that the role of the European Parliament was sufficiently 'legislative' given its involvement in the law making processes of the EC.

Although, by and large, there has been no challenge to the United Kingdom electoral process as a whole there have been a number of challenges that have highlighted defects in the system and some of these have led to reforms. Not all of these challenges relate to the right to vote in the narrow sense as disputes have thrown up issues relating to other Convention rights, such as the right to free speech and the right to privacy.

Bowman v *United Kingdom* (1998) The Times 23 February arose out of events leading up to the 1992 general election when the applicant, an anti-abortion campaigner, distributed 25,000 leaflets, at a cost of £10,000, in the Halifax parliamentary constituency outlining the views of the various parliamentary candidates on abortion. She was, in due course, charged with incurring unauthorised expenditure with the view of promoting or procuring the election of a candidate contrary to s75 of the Representation of the People Act 1983 (since amended, see below). The 1983 Act imposed a limit of £5 on such unauthorised expenditure. As a result of the summons being issued out of time the applicant was in fact acquitted of the s75 charges, but nevertheless took her case to the European Court of Human Rights alleging that s75 amounted to a violation of her right to freedom of expression, contrary to art 10 of the European Convention on Human Rights. The Court agreed that the operation of s75 of the 1983 Act amounted to a violation of the applicant's rights under art 10 of the Convention. Although s75 restricted freedom of expression in a manner that was prescribed by law, and was introduced to secure a legitimate aim, namely equality between candidates seeking election, it was important to ensure that views could be freely expressed in the period leading up to elections, in order to ensure the proper functioning of the democratic process. Similarly, it was important to ensure the free expression of the opinion of the people in the choice of legislature, and this might mean restricting the right to freedom of expression. In striking the balance between these two considerations a margin of appreciation would be allowed to contracting states. In the circumstances, however, the Court concluded that s75 effectively imposed a complete ban on the applicant disseminating her views effectively in the pre-election period, as the spending limit was so low and she had no access to other forms of broadcasting. As a consequence of this ruling Parliament amended the relevant law in the Political Parties, Elections and Referendums Act 2000, s131 of which amends s75 of the Representation of the People Act 1983 by increasing the expenditure that may be incurred in meeting election expenses by persons other than the candidate or his agent from £5 to £500 for a parliamentary election.

The disqualification of prisoners as voters at elections was challenged by the applicant in *R (Pearson and Another)* v *Secretary of State for the Home Department* (2001) The Times 17 April. The relevant provisions of the Representation of the People Act 1983 then in force provided that a convicted person who was detained in a penal institution in pursuance of his sentence was legally incapable of voting at parliamentary or local government elections. The applicant argued that this disqualification was in breach of the European Convention on Human Rights, especially as he had completed the 'punitive' element of his sentences. Dismissing the application the House of Lords observed that, notwithstanding the ruling in *Raymond* v *Honey* [1983] AC 1, to the effect that a convicted prisoner still retained his civil rights, the European Court of Human Rights recognised in *Mathieu-Mohinand Clerfayt* v *Belgium* Application No 9267/81 (1987) 10 EHRR 1 that the implied right to vote enshrined in art 3 of the First Protocol was not absolute and there was room for implied limitations. The 1983 Act satisfied the requirements under the European Convention that any restrictions on the right to vote should not be such as to impair the essence or remove the effectiveness of that right, should be imposed in pursuit of a legitimate aim, and the means employed should not be disproportionate or thwart the free expression of the opinion of the people in the choice of the legislature. In assessing whether restrictions imposed met these criteria the court would bear in mind that contracting states had a wide margin of appreciation in subjecting the right to conditions. The Court noted that Parliament, following careful consideration of the issues, had determined by means of primary legislation that prisoners being detained for preventative purposes should still be denied the right to vote. Deference would be given to the will of the legislature on this point.

The practice of imposing criminal liability on those failing to register to vote, but then selling on the details provided to commercial organisations for marketing purposes, was declared unlawful in *R (Robertson)* v *Wakefield MDC* (2001) The Times 27 November. The applicant was a registered voter whose name was entered on the relevant electoral register. Under regulations made pursuant to the Representation of the People Act 1983 electoral registration officers were required to supply copies of the register to those wishing to purchase copies. Commercial organisations wishing to purchase copies of the register for direct marketing purposes could thus obtain names and addresses of all those registered to vote. The applicant objected to this practice, contending that whilst he was under a legal duty to register to vote he did not want his details released to commercial organisations without his consent. Although his argument also succeeded on grounds related to the Data Protection Act 1998, the court held that given modern marketing techniques, the selling of personal details to direct marketing organisations did raise a potential threat to privacy under art 8 of the European Convention on Human Rights, and that there had been a breach of the First Protocol. As things stood under domestic law a voter could only register to exercise his democratic rights by accepting that his registration details would be sold for commercial purposes – this amounted to an unjustified and disproportionate fetter on the right to vote contrary to art 3 of the First Protocol.

Finally, the developing law relating to freedom of expression was clearly instrumental in the court's ruling in *R (Quintavalle)* v *BBC* (2002) The Times 19 March, where it was held that the BBC and the ITC had been in breach of their public law obligations by refusing to broadcast a party political broadcast by an anti-abortion group on the basis that the content of the film to be broadcast was shocking and offensive. The film in question contained footage of abortions being performed and showed the effect on aborted foetuses. Laws LJ observed that in political debate the right to freedom of expression was of paramount importance. The decision of the broadcasters to refuse to televise the film was subject not only to tests of reasonableness but also test of proportionality. The interference with the fundamental right to free expression in the run up to a general election resulting from the refusal to broadcast the film was a disproportionate response to the desire not to shock and offend viewers.

Hence it can be seen that the European Convention on Human Rights is having an increasing influence on the electoral process and this trend is likely to continue as the courts become more accustomed to apply the jurisprudence of the European Convention on Human Rights.

QUESTION FOUR

'Recent reforms have ensured that the electoral processes operating in the United Kingdom are essentially sound. The problem remains, however, as regards the extent to which the system is capable of accurately reflecting voters' preferences.'

Consider the accuracy of this statement.

Written by the Editor

General Comment

This question is really in two parts. The first requires a good working knowledge of recent changes – principally those relating to the Electoral Commission and the reform of party funding. The second part requires a critique of the first-past-the-post system.

Skeleton Solution

Outline changes in the Political Parties, Elections and Referendums Act 2000 – Electoral Commission – party funding – new rules on donations – cleaning up sleaze – more modest changes on registration and voting rights – Representation of the People Act 2000 – critique of first-past-the-post system – analysis of recent figures – mention alternatives used – conclusion.

Suggested Solution

The past few years have seen a flurry of legislative activity directed at improving the electoral processes operating within the United Kingdom. Some of these changes have been at the level of detail. Some have been fundamental.

The most significant development by far has been the enactment of the Political Parties, Elections and Referendums Act 2000. The Act establishes an Electoral Commission to oversee the conduct of the electoral process, introduces controls over donations to political parties and expenditure by political parties during campaigns and reforms the law relating to third-party expenditure. By virtue of s5 of the Act the Commission is placed under a duty, following each election or referendum to which the Act applies, to publish a report on the administration of the election or referendum, and to keep under review, and from time to time submit reports to the Secretary of State on, matters relating to local, regional and national elections, referendums, the redistribution of seats at parliamentary elections, the registration of political parties, the regulation of their income and expenditure, and political advertising in the broadcast and other electronic media. The Commission may be required to conduct reviews into specific aspects of the electoral process as determined by the Secretary of State.

For the first time, therefore, there is an established body to keep all aspects of the electoral process under review. This must be seen as a positive step.

The Political Parties, Elections and Referendums Act 2000 also consolidates an earlier development in that it deals with the registration of political parties (largely replacing the provisions of the Registration of Political Parties Act 1998). In order to submit a valid nomination at a relevant election a candidate must be standing for election in the name of a qualifying registered party, be a candidate who does not purport to represent any party (ie an independent candidate or one not indicating any party name), or be a qualifying registered party, where the election is one for which registered parties may be nominated (ie where the 'party list' system is in operation). Again the avoidance of rogue candidates and the prevention of confusion on the part of voters must be seen as a step forward.

Although it introduces measures dealing with constituency expenses and the conduct of referendums, perhaps the biggest change brought about by the 2000 Act is in relation to party funding. The criticism levelled at the electoral system prior to the Act coming into force was that parties could win elections by spending more money than their opponents on campaigning, and that individual donors could gain influence and favour with prospective governments through their generosity in donating to the party funds. These factors lead to allegations of 'sleaze' and undue influence in the electoral process.

The Political Parties, Elections and Referendums Act 2000 addresses these issues by introducing a regime that ensures greater accountability and transparency as regards such donations. A donation for these purposes includes (inter alia): any gift to a party of money or other property; any sponsorship; any subscription or other fee paid for affiliation to, or membership of, the party; any money spent (otherwise than by or on behalf of the party) in paying any expenses incurred directly or indirectly by the party; any money lent to the party otherwise than on commercial terms; and the provision otherwise than on commercial terms of any property, services or facilities for the use or benefit of the party (including the services of any person). Single donations of less than £200 in any financial year fall outside the scope of these restrictions. A registered political party may only accept donations from individuals who are registered as voters in the United Kingdom (donations cannot be accepted if they are anonymous), or from companies registered in the United Kingdom. The Commission may order the forfeiture of donations received in circumstances where the requirements of the Act are not met. Sections 62–69 of the Act provide for a reporting regime as regards donations received by registered parties. Quarterly reports have to be provided detailing donations in excess of £5,000, along with information about the donor. During the run-up to a general election more regular (ie weekly) reports may be required. Under ss139–140 directors proposing that their companies should make donations to political parties or organisations for political purposes in excess of £200 are required to seek the approval of the company in general meeting. Any such payments must be disclosed in the relevant directors' annual report.

The Political Parties, Elections and Referendums Act 2000 also addresses the issue of campaign expenditure, reflecting to some extent concern that the party with access to the most funds might be able to 'buy' success at an election. The Act also reflects the fact that whilst, during the nineteenth century, concern was correctly directed at corrupt and illegal electoral practices at a the constituency level, such as the bribing and treating of voters, in more recent years, particularly with the advent of mass telecommunications, the emphasis has shifted to the national campaign during general elections. The Act imposes limits on campaign expenditure which, for these purposes, is defined, in s72, as expenses incurred by or on behalf of the party for election purposes, falling within those matters listed in Pt I of Sch 8 to the Act (eg party political broadcasts, manifestos, rallies, transport and advertising). The restrictions apply to general election campaigns and those for the European and regional parliaments.

Section 79 and Sch 9 impose limits on campaign expenditure incurred by or on behalf of registered parties. It is an offence for the treasurer of a registered party to authorised expenditure to be incurred by or on behalf of the party where he knows or ought reasonably to have known that the expenditure would be incurred in excess of the statutory limit. In general terms the limit imposed by the Act is £30,000 multiplied by the number of constituencies contested by a party. Sections 80–84 provide for the auditing of party treasurer returns in respect of campaign expenditure and the delivery of returns to the Commission. In practical terms this means that the Labour and Conservative parties would not be permitted to spend more that £20 million each at any forthcoming general election. This compares with expenditure of £26 million and £28 million respectively in the run up to the May 1997 election.

It is perhaps too early to come to any considered conclusion as to the extent to which the changes to the rules on donations to parties have been successful. Loopholes have emerged in respect of matters such as loans to political parties. The government has not ruled out the possibility of providing significant public funding for each party based on electoral support, as is the case in many other countries.

At a more detailed level useful changes have been introduced by the Representation of the People Act 2000 to ensure that it becomes easier for people to register to vote. The Act also narrows the former rules on disqualification – the aim being to enable traditionally excluded groups, such as the homeless, remand prisoners and mental patients, to register as voters. Section 5 of the 2000 Act now permits such a prisoner to register as a voter if the length of time spent on remand in prison is sufficient for him to be regarded as a 'resident'. The registration rules were simplified by removing the concept of residency on a 'qualifying date' as a crucial factor in being able to register as a voter. In determining whether a person is resident at a particular address the officer must have regard to the purpose and other circumstances, as well as to the fact, of his presence at, or absence from, the address on the 'relevant date'.

In contrast to the many changes that have been made to the mechanics of the electoral system, there has been no move away from the first-past-the-post system for general elections and the psephological distortions that it produces. If one takes the figures for the 1997 general election, the unfairness speaks for itself. The results were:

Party	Actual seats	% Seats	% Popular vote
Conservative	165	25	31
Labour	419	64	45
Liberal Democrats	46	7	17
Others	29	4	7

By dividing the number of votes cast for each party by the number of seats won it can be seen that in the 1997 general election it took: 58,124 votes to elect each Conservative MP; 32,342 votes to elect each Labour MP; 113,985 votes to elect each Liberal Democrat MP; and 108,049 votes to elect each 'minor party' MP.

The result of the 1997 general election is commonly referred to as a landslide victory for the Labour Party, but the statistics reveal that it polled only 1.9 million votes more than it had in 1992. The problem for the Conservative Party appeared to be defections to the Liberal Democrats and abstentions by those who would normally have supported the party. The curious variable geometry of the electoral system ensures that any party thus squeezed suffers disproportionately.

The government has dabbled with alternative, arguably more representative systems – for example, party list systems are used as the basis for the election of 'additional members' to the Scottish Parliament and the Welsh Assembly – but it shows no enthusiasm for embracing such systems for general elections. Could this be because it knows that the price to be paid for a more accurate representation of voters' preferences is the prospect of sharing power with a minority party?

In conclusion it can be said that recent reforms deal with many issues peripheral to the fairness of the electoral process, but fail to address the lack of representativeness that lies at its heart.

QUESTION FIVE

What difference, if any, would reforming the electoral system make to the British constitution?

Written by the Editor

General Comment

This is a very straightforward question involving discussion of the present electoral system and the effect reform would have on the British constitution.

Skeleton Solution

Introduction – the operation of the relative majority system (the first-past-the-post system) – the problems with the present system – parliamentary seats not allocated on a proportional basis; discrimination against small parties; wastage of votes; problems with constituency size – the advantages of the present system – simplicity; results in strong government; constituency link with MP – effect of reform – loss of the advantages of the present system; election of a Parliament but not a government.

Suggested Solution

Under the present parliamentary electoral system the United Kingdom is divided into 659 parliamentary constituencies, each of which returns a single member to the House of Commons. Each elector may vote for one candidate only and the successful candidate is the one who receives the highest number of valid votes in the constituency. This system of 'first past the post' is known as the relative majority system as wherever there are more than two candidates in a constituency, the successful candidate need not have received an absolute majority of votes, but simply a majority over the runner-up. This system has the advantage of being very simple, but as a means of providing representation of the electorate in Parliament it is very crude. It is a system which, according to its critics, is not truly democratic and one which has several inherent disadvantages which, it is argued, can only be overcome by reform.

Certainly any reform of the present electoral system will seek to remedy the major problem that at present the system does not ensure that the distribution of seats in the House of Commons is in any way proportionate to the national distribution of votes. There is no consistent relationship between the number of votes cast nationally for a political party and the seats that they obtain. This is illustrated by the May 1997 general election result. The Labour Party polled 45 per cent of the votes cast and won 419 seats. The Conservative Party polled 31 per cent of the votes cast and won 165 seats. The Liberal Democrats polled 17 per cent of the votes cast and won only 46 seats. The Liberal Democrats were therefore was under-represented in relation to their national vote. By dividing the number of votes cast for each party by the number of seats won it can be seen that, in the 1997 general election, it took: 58,124 votes to elect each Conservative MP; 32,342 votes to elect each Labour MP; 113,985 votes to elect each Liberal Democrat MP; 108,049 votes to elect each 'minor party' MP.

The result of the 1997 general election is commonly referred to as a landslide victory for the Labour Party, but the statistics reveal that it polled only 1.9 million votes more than it had in 1992. The problem for the Conservative Party appeared to be defections to the Liberal Democrats and abstentions by those who would normally have supported the party. The curious variable geometry of the electoral system ensures that any party thus squeezed suffers disproportionately. The figures for the 2001 election tell a similar story:

Party	Seats won	As a % of seats	% of the total vote
Conservative	166	25	32
Labour	412	63	41
Liberal Democrats	52	8	18
Others	29	4	10

This tendency of the system to exaggerate the representation of the large parties and reduce that of the smaller parties leads to the allegation that the present electoral system makes no provision for the representation of minority interests. It discriminates against the smaller parties whose support is evenly spread throughout the country rather than being concentrated in particular constituencies. Votes for the smaller parties are, in effect, wasted votes. It matters not whether the person elected has one single vote, or twenty thousand votes, more than his nearest rival does. So where there are more than two candidates a person may be elected by less than 50 per cent of the total votes cast in that constituency. The votes for the losing candidate have no parliamentary importance, they are in a sense wasted. This system, it is argued, perpetuates the two party system and helps destroy any possibility of consensus politics in the United Kingdom.

A further problem arises from the constituency basis of the present system. If votes are to carry equal weight throughout the country each constituency must be of equal size. The size of every constituency is determined by the Boundary Committees who keep the situation under constant review and try to ensure that each constituency has the same number of voters in it. However, disparity does exist between constituency populations and, as a result, the weight of your vote may vary according to where you live.

Reforming the electoral system would therefore help remove these problems and help achieve fairer representation for all political parties in the House of Commons. But it must always be remembered that the present electoral system has considerable advantages and that these advantages may be lost as a result of any reform. For example the voting procedure itself is very simple and easy to understand, ensuring quick results. The outcome of the election is known within a matter of hours of the close of poll. The system also ensures a close link between the Member of Parliament and his constituency. The constituents know who their parliamentary representative is and can approach him with their problems. He in turn will serve their interests, in the knowledge that their continued support is necessary if he is to be re-elected.

But the major advantage claimed for the present system is its tendency to produce an absolute majority of seats in the House of Commons for one party. The function of a general election is to elect a government as well as a parliament and the present system does precisely that, producing strong government. The United Kingdom system avoids the problems, often found in European countries, which use different electoral systems, of coalition or minority governments, which can find it difficult to govern effectively because of their unstable electoral position.

Despite these advantages there is a case for reforming the electoral system so as to secure better representation of minority parties and a distribution of seats which bears some relation to the votes cast. The most favoured alternative systems are the alternative vote system, the party list system and the single transferable vote system. The adoption of any one of these systems would bring about changes to the British constitution which, while welcomed by some, would be abhorrent to others.

The Jenkins Commission's key proposal is that the current first-past-the-post system should be replaced by an enhanced alternative vote system. Approximately 80 per cent of MPs would be elected on a constituency basis – the number of constituencies being reduced to around 525. The remaining MPs would be drawn from party lists and would represent other geographical areas such as cities and counties. Electors would cast two votes in order to elect a constituency MP, numbering the candidates in their order of preference. If a candidate secured a 50 per cent share of the votes on the first count he or she would be elected as the MP for that constituency. If no candidate secured 50 per cent of the votes on the first count, the candidate with the lowest number of first preference votes would be eliminated and his or her second preference votes redistributed amongst the remaining candidates. The process of eliminating lowest scoring candidates would continue until a candidate achieved 50 per cent of the first preference and redistributed second preference votes. Voters would also cast a party list, or 'top-up' vote for MPs who would represent cities or counties. The proposal is that this vote could simply be for a party, or for a specific candidate appearing on the party list. If the 1992 and 1997 general elections had been conducted using the enhanced alternative vote system proposed by the Jenkins Commission the allocation of seats would have been as follows:

1997: Conservatives – 167 seats; Labour – 367 seats; Lib Dem – 92 seats; Nationalists – 14 seats.

1992: Conservative – 316 seats; Labour – 240 seats; Lib Dem – 74 seats; Nationalists – 11 seats.

The major result of adopting these systems is that they will help achieve legislative representation that accords with the relative electoral strengths of the political parties. Minority parties and independent candidates will therefore stand a better chance of election and the number of wasted votes will be reduced. But while these systems may to an extent maintain a local basis for representation, they may weaken the link between Members of Parliament and constituents. These systems of election are also complex. Most important, however, is the likely result that the traditional two party system may be destroyed. To some of course this may be no bad thing but, if the European experience is repeated and one party is less likely to secure an absolute majority of seats in the House of Commons, this will lead to minority or coalition governments giving smaller parties political importance out of all proportion to their popular support. Such a system of government is totally alien to the British tradition.

Chapter 6

The Legislature: The House of Commons and the House of Lords

6.1   Introduction

6.2   Key points

6.3   Key statutes

6.4   Questions and suggested solutions

6.1 Introduction

The monarch is one of the three constituent parts of the legislature but the role of the monarchy is now largely ceremonial and formal. The United Kingdom has a bicameral legislature – there are two Houses of Parliament – the House of Commons and the House of Lords. The House of Commons dominates.

One of the central issues relating to the legislature is the accountability of government to Parliament. The House of Commons is dominated by the government particularly if following a general election the government has a large majority. The House of Lords challenges the government at a political level on unpopular policies. However, ultimately the Commons can successfully achieve its political will in the unlikely event of a confrontation.

The House of Lords is currently a non-elected chamber. It plays a part in the legislative process but ultimately its powers are very limited. Nevertheless many argue that the quality of debate in the House of Lords is high and the House can sometimes effectively challenge the Commons.

The reform/abolition of the House of Lords has been on the political agenda for many years. The Life Peerages Act 1958 was very successful in creating a re-vitalised House, but the most significant recent change has been the House of Lords Act 1999 which removed the right of hereditary peers to sit and vote in the second chamber. Despite a Royal Commission and a White Paper addressing further reforms, it is not clear at present what further changes might be made, or indeed when they will occur.

6.2 Key points

The main functions of Parliament include the passing of legislation and the scrutiny of the administration through debate, the committee system and the control of national finance.

The legislative process

A distinction must be drawn between Public and Private Bills:

a) Public Bills seek to alter the general law and affect the whole community.

b) Private Bills affect only a section of the community and relate to matters of individual, corporate or local interest.

c) Hybrid Bills are Public Bills that are classified by the Speaker as having a particular effect on one section of the community.

Public Bill procedure

Most Public Bills are government Bills, but some may be Private Members Bills introduced by backbench Members of Parliament. Bills may be introduced into either House, but legislation that is politically controversial, or legislation concerned with financial or electoral matters begins in the House of Commons.

a) First reading. The Bill is presented to Parliament.

b) Second reading. The House considers the principles and merits of the Bill.

c) Committee stage. The Bill is normally referred to a standing committee for detailed clause by clause consideration.

d) Report stage. The Bill as amended is reported to the whole House.

e) Third reading. The Bill is debated in general terms with only oral amendments allowed.

f) House of Lords stages and amendments. After its third reading, the Bill is sent to the House of Lords where it goes through stages similar to those in the Commons. But note the effects of the Parliament Acts 1911–1949.

g) Royal assent. Now a formality. After the royal assent has been given the Bill becomes an Act.

Private member's Bill procedure

There are a number of procedures under which private members may initiate Bills.

a) The Ballot. The Ballot establishes an order of priority enabling those members successful in it to use the limited private members' time for debate of their Bills which, given the governments' control of the parliamentary timetable, might otherwise not make progress.

b) The Ten Minute Rule. Not, in general, serious attempts at legislation. The member may speak briefly in support of the Bill and an opponent may reply. The House may then decide on whether the Bill should be introduced.

c) Standing Order No 39. Allows every member the right to introduce a Bill of his choosing after due notice.

Private Bill procedure

Private Bills are initiated by petition from persons or bodies outside Parliament. Full notice must be given to those whose legal rights may be affected by the proposed legislation so that they may oppose it. In the House of Commons the Bill is introduced by being presented at the Table by the Clerk of the Private Bill Office. It is then deemed to have been read for the first time. At the Second Reading Debate, the House determines whether the Bill is unobjectionable from the point of view of national policy. If read a second time, the Bill is committed to a committee of four members in the Commons (or five members in the Lords). The committee stage has some of the features of a quasi-judicial proceeding.

Hybrid Bill procedure

The Standing Orders for private business apply to a Hybrid Bill so that if opposed after its second reading it goes before a select committee, where those whose legal rights are affected by the Bill may raise their objections and petition against it. After the petitioners have been heard by the select committee, the Bill then passes through its committee stage and later stages as if it were an ordinary Bill.

Opportunities for debate in the House of Commons

Apart from the opportunities for debate during the legislative process, there are various other opportunities for debate in the House of Commons.

Adjournment debates

At the end of every day's business, when the adjournment of the House is formally moved, half an hour is made available for a private Member to raise a topic in debate and for a ministerial reply to be given.

Standing Order No 10 – Motion to Adjourn

This allows members to suggest that a specific and important matter should have urgent consideration and that an emergency debate be held upon it.

Other opportunities

The final day before each of the four parliamentary recesses is also devoted to a series of private members' debates and ten Fridays per session are also set aside for private members' Motions. Other opportunities for debate occur in the debate on the address in reply to the Queen's Speech, the debate on the Budget, debates on motions of censure, the twenty Opposition Days, the three Estimate Days and on the second reading of Consolidated Fund Bills.

Devices for curtailing debate

Delay of Bills in the House of Commons is a threat to the government's legislative programme. To overcome this threat, various methods of curtailing debate have been adopted by the House.

a) Standing Order 22. The Speaker or Chairman may require a member to discontinue his speech if he persists in irrelevance or tedious repetition.

b) The Closure. Any member may move 'that the question now be put'. If not less than 100 members vote for the motion the debate ceases and the motion under discussion must be voted upon.

c) The Kangaroo. This is the power of the Speaker at the Report Stage to select from amongst the various proposed amendments those that are to be discussed.

d) The Guillotine Motion. Such a motion provides that one or more stages of a Bill be disposed of either by a fixed date, or by a fixed number of sittings.

Parliamentary questions

There are three categories of question:

a) Question for oral answer, which is intended to be given an oral answer in the House during Question Time.

b) Private notice question, which can be asked if the Speaker judges its subject matter to be urgent and important. These are taken orally in the House at the end of Question Time.

c) Question for written answer, which is not taken orally in the House but is printed in the official report (Hansard).

Parliamentary committees

The committees of the House of Commons fall into two main categories:

Standing committees

These are responsible for the committee stage in the passing of a Bill.

Select committees

a) Ad-hoc select committees. These are set up for a specific purpose when the need arises.

b) Sessional select committees. These are set up at the beginning of the session and remain throughout the session.

c) Departmental select committees. These are appointed to examine the expenditure, administration and policy of the principal government departments and associated public bodies.

Parliamentary control of national finance

Parliamentary control of national finance has two aspects:

Parliamentary control of government expenditure

a) Estimate Days. There are now three annual days devoted to consideration of the main and Supplementary Estimates.

b) The Public Accounts Committee. This is a select committee concerned with public money already spent, to see that it has been spent economically, and not wastefully.

c) National Audit Act 1983. This Act provides for the appointment of the Comptroller and Auditor General, establishing a Public Accounts Commission and a National Audit Office and making new provisions for promoting economy, efficiency and effectiveness in the use of public money by government departments and other authorities and bodies.

Control over taxation

Budget Resolutions and the Finance Bill. These provide an opportunity for members to debate government proposals for taxation and duties etc.

The composition of the House of Lords

a) The Lords Spiritual. Archbishops of Canterbury and York, the Bishops of London, Durham and Winchester, and the next 21 diocesan bishops of the Church of England in seniority of appointment.

b) The Lords Temporal:

i) life peers created under the Life Peerages Act 1958 (hereditary peers were removed by virtue of the House of Lords Act 1999);

ii) Lords of Appeal in Ordinary.

The functions and work of the House of Lords

The 1968 Government White Paper, *House of Lords Reform*, referred to seven functions of the House of Lords:

a) its appellate role as the supreme court of appeal;

b) the provision of a forum for free debate and matters of public interest;

c) the revision of Public Bills brought from the House of Commons;

d) the initiation of Public Bills;

e) the consideration of subordinate legislation;

f) the scrutiny of the activities of the executive;

g) the scrutiny of private legislation.

The White Paper on House of Lords reform, *Completing the Reform* (Cmd 5291), published in 2001 summarised these functions more succinctly as:

a) serving as a revising and deliberative assembly;

b) serving as a powerful deliberative Assembly, both in its debates and in the work of its committees, particularly its Select Committees on Delegated Powers and Regulatory Reform and the European Union;

c) holding the government to account – the second chamber can question and criticise individual ministers appointed to the Lords.

House of Lords' reform

The Parliament Act 1911

a) A Bill certified by the Speaker as a Money Bill should receive the royal assent and become an Act of Parliament without the consent of the House of Lords if, having been sent up from the House of Commons at least one month before the end of the session, it had not been passed by the Lords without amendment within one month of its being sent up.

b) Any other Public Bill, except one for extending the life of Parliament, could become an Act of Parliament without the consent of the House of Lords if it had been passed by the House of Commons in three successive sessions, two years having elapsed between its second reading and its final passing in the House of Commons, and if it had been sent up to the House of Lords at least one month before the end of each of the three sessions.

c) The maximum duration of a Parliament was reduced from seven years to five.

The Parliament Act 1949

Amends the Parliament Act 1911 by reducing the number of sessions in which a Bill must be passed by the House of Commons from three to two, and reducing the period between the second reading and final passing in the House of Commons from two years to one.

Life Peerages Act 1958

This Act empowers the Crown to create life peers who vote in the House of Lords. The on-going result of the Act is that the House of Lords has become rejuvenated and appointments are made from people with wide ranging experience in different walks of life. The role of the House of Lords as a debating chamber is consequently significant.

House of Lords Act 1999

The House of Lords Act 1999 removed the rights of hereditary peers to sit and vote in the House of Lords. Section 1 of the Act provides that 'No-one shall be a member of the House of Lords by virtue of a hereditary peerage.' Section 2 of the Act goes on to provide for 92 hereditary peers to remain as members of the House of Lords, but only as life peers. Under Standing Orders of the House 15 peers were selected by the whole House to serve as deputy speakers or in any other office required by the House. The remaining 75 (42 Conservative, 28 crossbenchers, three Liberal Democrat and two Labour) were selected by a ballot conducted amongst the hereditary peers.

The Royal Commission

Further to the enactment of the House of Lords Act 1999 the government set up a Royal Commission on the House of Lords chaired by Lord Wakeham. The ensuing report – *A House for the Future* – came out in favour of a revised second chamber comprising some 550 members. It envisaged that the majority of these members would be appointed by an independent Appointments Commission, with a minority being elected (65 under model A; 87 under model B; 195 under model C). The 92 hereditary peers spared under the House of Lords Act 1999 would be removed over a period of time. Elected members would be drawn from regional lists, such as those now used for the election of MEPs, with one-third being elected every five years. Once elected a term of office would be for 15 years. The Law Lords and Lords Spiritual would continue to enjoy membership of the second chamber by virtue of office.

The proposals placed considerable power in the hands of the Appointments Commission, which was charged with ensuring that those appointed were representative of the nation as a whole, in terms of gender, ethnicity, background and representation of the regions. It recommended that existing life peers should remain in office until death, envisaging that the change over to an appointed and/or elected chamber would take between 20 and 30 years. The Appointments Commission began the task of soliciting applications in the summer of 2000. In the interim between the abolition of hereditary peers' voting rights and the more radical stage two reforms, the Prime Minister began the process of appointing Labour life peers with a view to equalising party support in the House of Lords.

White Paper – Completing the Reform (Cmd 5291)

This was the government's response to the Royal Commission Report. It proposed that the House of Lords should lose its power to veto subordinate legislation, the power of veto being replaced with a power to delay such legislation for up to three months. Under the White Paper proposals the membership of the reformed second chamber would eventually (over a ten-year period of transitional change) be capped at 600. Those appointed to the second chamber would not be made peers, but would be given the title 'Member of the Lords' designated 'ML'. Whereas the Royal Commission envisaged an elected element in a reformed second chamber of 87 members (model B figures), the White Paper favours an elected membership of 120. A further 120 members would be appointed by the Appointments Commission. The remaining 332 members would be political appointees nominated by the major political parties. At least 12 Law Lords would continue to sit as members of the second chamber, but the representation of Church of England bishops would be reduced from 26 to 16.

6.3 Key statutes

- House of Commons Disqualification Act 1975 – limits the number of ministers in the Commons

- House of Lords Act 1999 – abolished the right of hereditary peers to sit and vote in the House of Lords

- Life Peerages Act 1958 – allowed for appointed peers to sit in the House of Lords without an hereditary title

- Parliament Acts 1911–1949 – limited the power of the House of Lords to veto or delay legislation passed by the Commons

6.4 Questions and suggested solutions

QUESTION ONE

Discuss the ways in which the British Parliament seeks to scrutinise the administrative and legislative acts of the European Community.

University of London LLB Examination
(for External Students) Constitutional Law June 1995 Q4

General Comment

This question requires an explanation of the sources of Community law and the various ways in which they are transmuted into domestic law. An account of the processes in Parliament should be given, with appropriate distinctions being made between the various sources of Community law.

Skeleton Solution

Sources of Community law – status within the UK – European Communities Act 1972, s2 – treaties and use of delegated legislation – scrutiny committees – functions – effectiveness – conclusion – realities of Community law.

Suggested Solution

There are three main sources of EC law: the Community treaties; the Acts of the Community institutions; and the decisions of the Court of Justice of the European Communities. Essential to the effective operation of the EC is the principle that its primary law, the treaties, applies to the same extent in the legal system of each member state, and that it takes precedence over the domestic law of any member state. As regards the secondary legislation of the European Union, namely regulations, directives and decisions, art 249 EC provides that a regulation shall have general application and will be binding in its entirety and directly applicable in all member states.

Provisions contained in the treaties and regulations enacted by the Council of Ministers are of 'direct applicability', by which is meant that they become part of the law of a member state without further intervention by the member state: see further *Van Duyn* v *Home Office* Case 41/74 [1974] ECR 1337 and *Re Export Tax on Art Treasures (No 2)* [1972] CMLR 699. Directives, by contrast, are not directly applicable in that they require further enactment by a member state before they can take effect within its domestic law. Member states have no discretion as regards the object to be achieved by the implementation of the directive, but do have discretion as to how that objective is to be achieved. In the United Kingdom, for example, the implementation of a directive may take the form of primary or delegated legislation as appropriate.

Under s2 of the European Communities Act 1972 Community law becomes part of domestic law and takes precedence over domestic law to the extent that there is any conflict between the two. As Lord Denning observed in *Bulmer* v *Bollinger* [1974] Ch 401, Community law 'is like an incoming tide. It flows into the estuaries and up the rivers. It cannot be held back'.

Given the importance of the subject matter dealt with by Community law, and scope for major changes being made by way of treaties, regulations and directives, the question arises as to the extent to which Parliament is being bypassed in this process.

As regards treaties Parliament arguably retains its full powers of scrutiny because treaties cannot become part of domestic law unless incorporated into domestic law – that is the process of ratification required in a 'dualist' legal system. Hence Parliament can debate and examine the enabling legislation of the incorporation of a treaty in the same way that it can examine any other piece of legislation. The 1972 Act is itself an example of this process, which has been repeated each time the EC treaties have been amended or added to. For example in December 1991, the Treaty on European Union (TEU) 1992 (the Maastricht Treaty) was signed by all member states. The Treaty accelerated the move towards a federal, unified, Europe and laid down a timetable for monetary union. As with previous EC treaties, and in accordance with constitutional requirements, the TEU 1992 had to be incorporated into United Kingdom law by means of domestic legislation, hence the enactment of the European Communities (Amendment) Act 1993. The only limitation on the effectiveness of this scrutiny is that fact that the relevant Bill will be sponsored by the government and there will be reliance on the 'payroll' vote to ensure it successfully passes through Parliament. Failure to incorporate such a treaty would have major political ramifications for the government in its dealing with other EU member states.

Where Community law is directly applicable, such as is the case with regulations, Parliament can debate the likely effect of such measures when they are being considered as proposals by the institutions of the European Union. The relevant minister will make announcements to both Houses, time will be set aside for debate, and time will be earmarked during Question Time sessions to permit further discussion. Both Houses have a select committee charged with the task of examining and reporting on Community legislation and legislative proposals. These committees will also consider statutory instruments issued in order to give effect to directives. Under Standing Orders 102 and 127 (as amended) the House of Commons has established two Standing Committees charged with the task of considering developments in Community law. The Standing Committees report to the House of Commons on the matters referred to them. It is the custom and practice observed by successive governments that no major changes to domestic law (consequent on legislative acts of the EU institutions) will be introduced without the Standing and Select Committees being given the opportunity to investigate and report back.

Of the various committees it is widely agreed that the House of Lords' Select Committee on the European Community, established in 1974, has played a particularly effective watchdog role. Its terms of reference are to consider Community law proposals and to obtain all necessary information about them; to report on such matters and to bring to the attention of the House matters of importance. The Committee operates with seven sub-committees and produces approximately 20 reports a year, each of which is debated in the House of Lords. The White Paper on House of Lords reform, *Completing the Reform* (Cmd 5291), went so far as to observe that the House of Lords was a powerful deliberative assembly, both in its debates and in the work of its committees, particularly its Select Committee on the European Community. The White Paper highlighted the fact that the Committee was especially strengthened by the role of independent experts sitting as crossbenchers, and that reform of the second chamber should be geared to strengthening this capacity, without duplicating the work of the House of Commons.

Despite this activity, it has to be concluded that in all but the most significant matters Parliament at Westminster has been reduced to the role of interested onlooker in respect of Community law. The various committees can report and act as watchdogs but cannot stop the juggernaut of Community law from rolling on. Indeed Parliament itself can do little when more and more matters fall to be decided by the EU Council of Ministers under the system of qualified majority voting. The House of Commons can opt to refuse to ratify an EU treaty, or to refuse to enact the primary or delegated legislation required to give effect to a directive, but that is a measure of the last resort that sets the United Kingdom on a collision course with the European Court of Justice.

In reality the only room to manoeuvre that the United Kingdom Parliament has is in relation to the way in which effect is given to directives.

QUESTION TWO

In the British Parliament today, are a government's backbenchers its most effective opposition?

University of London LLB Examination
(for External Students) Constitutional and Administrative Law June 1992 Q4

General Comment

This is not the usual question on the power of backbenchers, therefore it is not a general essay on the methods open to the backbencher to check the executive. It requires a discussion of the role of the government's own backbenchers, who will often exercise their influence in less overt ways. As a result it is quite a difficult question to answer fully.

Skeleton Solution

Introduction – the whips – backbench groups – procedural opportunities – debates – restrictions on the backbencher – conclusion.

Suggested Solution

A party that wins an election with an outright majority of seats in the House of Commons is virtually unassailable. Even if the opposition gathers together all the minority parties, the government cannot be defeated. In such a position, only a backbench revolt will threaten the government. Where the majority is smaller, the need for party discipline increases. Whatever the case, it is true that the government's backbenchers can be a most effective check on the government.

Immediately following the general election in 1992 John Major's government had an outright majority of 21 seats – 81 seats fewer than that of the previous Conservative government. In due course he lost his overall Commons majority, and faced the prospect of backbench revolts over monetary union, the ban on handguns, and the culling of livestock affected by BSE. It is during such times that a small number of dissident backbenchers can exercise an inordinate amount of power, effectively blackmailing the front bench with treats to defeat the government on key votes. The only weapon the Prime Minister has is to threaten an election at a time when the same backbenchers might lose their seats because of the government's unpopularity. By contrast, following the elections of 1997 and 2001, Tony Blair has enjoyed large Commons majorities and has had the luxury of being able to ignore backbench feeling when it has suited him to do so.

What can the backbencher do? He is under the control of the party whips, to the extent that they will try to ensure that MPs will turn up and vote when needed and will perform such parliamentary duties as are required. Most of the time, most MPs obey the whips. Ambitions of joining the front benches will soon be thwarted if an MP takes too independent a line, but, that apart, most of the time MPs willingly follow the party line.

The whips also convey to the party leaders the feeling amongst the backbenchers. These feelings are more directly conveyed by backbench groups. For example, the Conservative 1922 Committee is quite capable of taking ministers, even the Prime Minister, to task over their policies. Any Conservative Prime Minister faced with contentious legislation must first ensure he has the 1922 on his side – faced as he will be with unanimous opposition from the other parties, he needs to rely on his own members and these unofficial channels will tell him whether this support will be provided.

There are, of course, plenty of opportunities within House of Commons' proceedings, short of voting against the government, by which a backbencher can make his voice heard. Parliamentary questions – both oral and written – are one such opportunity. Another would be through participation in parliamentary committees. To some extent, the selection process will ensure that maverick MPs are kept away. However, the select committees have shown themselves quite capable of confronting government policies and criticism may well come from the government's backbench members as, for example, in the Select Committee on Defence during the 'Westland Affair' (1986). In other words, their loyalty to the government does not prevent them from taking a critical stance. The government is not directly threatened by that stance and yet its source probably makes the criticism more effective.

A further opportunity for the backbencher will be during debates. During Mrs Thatcher's premiership the most significant backbench speeches came from those she had just removed from the front bench. Sir Geoffrey Howe's speech shortly after his departure is a good example. If such a speech voices opposition and if others share that view then it is obviously of greater significance than the inevitable opposition from the other side of the House.

In conclusion it should be said that most politicians are ambitious; none would want to see their own government defeated. These two factors limit the extent of backbench opposition. Further, MPs are answerable to their constituents who might take a dim view of opposition. A government may not wish to call the backbencher's bluff, but the backbencher certainly does not hold all the cards.

QUESTION THREE

Critically evaluate the current practices and procedures by which the House of Commons scrutinises and approves government Bills.

University of London LLB Examination
(for External Students) Constitutional Law June 1998 Q3

General Comment

Whilst answering this question obviously requires an examination of the processes of the House of Commons, it is vital to adopt a critical stance. A straight recital of procedural detail will not suffice. It must also be borne in mind that the question specifically relates to government Bills – hence it does not require an account of all types of legislative process.

Skeleton Solution

First reading – Bill published – second reading – debate – role of minister – party loyalties – Human Rights Act 1998 – committee stage – party divisions – lack of expertise – limitation on time for consideration – report stage – consideration of reform proposals – conclusions.

Suggested Solution

The procedure by which the House of Commons scrutinises government Bills essentially comprises five stages: the first reading; the second reading; the committee stage; the report stage; and the third reading.

The first reading is largely ceremonial. A 'dummy' copy of the Bill is placed 'on the table' in the House of Commons on the day of presentation. When the moment of presentation is reached, after Questions, the Speaker calls the sponsoring minister and the Clerk reads the short title of the Bill and the minister, or a whip acting on his behalf, names a (notional) day for the Bill's second reading. No debate takes place at this stage. Once the first reading procedure is complete the Bill is printed and published. To encourage more informed debate at an earlier stage most government Bills are now published with accompanying guidance notes. These are designed to assist the lay person (which for these purposes may include a good many backbench MPs) in understanding the purpose and effect of the Bill.

Wherever possible the government aims to leave two weekends between the printing and second reading of a Bill. The second reading is the stage at which significant parliamentary scrutiny of legislative proposals becomes possible. The House considers the principle and merits of the Bill, and a vote is taken on whether to give the Bill a second reading. Although the opposition will seek to score parliamentary points in the course of debates, the outcome of the second reading will hardly ever be in doubt. It is rare however for a government Bill to be denied a second reading. The government, after all, by definition has the majority of seats in the House of Commons. Its MPs will be subject to the party whip in order to get the legislation through. Defiance of the party whip can mean a long wait for any hope of political advancement. It may even result in a backbench MP being cast out into the political wilderness. Real scrutiny of the legislation at this stage is, therefore, unlikely to occur. It should be noted, however, that under s19 of the Human Rights Act 1998 the minister in charge of a Bill is under a duty to make a statement, prior to the second reading, to the effect that in his view the provisions of the Bill are compatible with the Convention rights as protected by the 1998 Act. Alternatively, he must make a statement explaining that, although he is unable to make a statement of compatibility, the government nevertheless wishes the House to proceed with the Bill. This at least draws the attention of the House to a specific matter of importance.

Following its second reading, a Bill is normally referred to a standing committee consisting of between 16 and 50 members nominated by a committee of selection and reflecting party strength in the House. Standing committees are constituted to deal with Bills as and when necessary. The committee stage involves detailed clause-by-clause consideration of the Bill, and the committee may generally amend the Bill as it thinks fit, provided that the amendments made are relevant to the subject matter of the Bill. Amendments and new clauses may be moved by the minister, the opposition spokesmen, or by any member of the committee. Provision also exists for non-party political Bills to be referred to special standing committees, where a more informed discussion can take place and evidence can be taken, but this procedure has only rarely been used, not least because of the delay that would ensue in the passage of the legislation.

Bills of first-class constitutional importance, those requiring a very rapid passage, and certain financial measures, including at least part of each year's Finance Bill, are often referred to a committee of the whole House enabling all MPs to engage in more detailed scrutiny. When a Bill has completed its committee stage it is reported as amended to the whole House. Further amendments, alteration of amendments made by the committee, and new clauses, may be made at this stage. All members may speak and vote at this stage, unlike in a standing committee. The final Commons stage of the Bill is the third reading. The Bill is debated once more in general terms with only verbal amendments allowed. Except for Bills of major political or constitutional importance the third reading is usually brief and formal.

One of the major problems with the whole process of scrutiny is the control exerted by the executive over the House of Commons. As indicated above the government will enforce the party line through the whips' office to ensure legislation is carried, regardless of what contributions are made in the course of the debate. The bigger the government's majority the more this is the case. Whereas select committees are powerful because they involve MPs from all parties working together to scrutinise the performance of government departments, standing committees are weakened because membership divides along party lines. A further problem is that of expertise and resources. The second reading looks at the 'big picture' – scrutiny at that stage is not going to persuade the government to abandon a piece of legislation. The committee stage is designed for examination of close detail. The government might take on board amendments at this stage – but this assumes MPs have the requisite experience and knowledge to move amendments on very technical points. Given the preponderance of academics and lawyers in the House of Commons this is highly questionable.

The government can also use its voting power in the House of Commons to introduce measures that limit the time for debate and consideration of amendments. The term 'guillotine motion' is a colloquial expression for an allocation of time motion. The purpose of such a motion is to provide that one or more stages of a Bill be disposed of either by a fixed date, or by a fixed number of sittings of the House, or a committee, or both. Each guillotine motion is specific and devised by the government for the particular Bill or Bills to which it applies. If a Bill before a standing committee is the subject of an 'allocation of time order', a detailed timetable is recommended to the standing committee. The effect of the order is that at the end of each allotted period the part of the Bill in question is voted upon forthwith, although substantial parts of the Bill may not yet have been discussed at all.

On the whole, these devices are unpopular with parliamentarians because they can restrict valuable criticism and amendment of legislation. If used extensively – and they are being used increasingly – it can be argued that they deny the legislative role of Parliament. The problem lies in striking the balance between ensuring adequate opportunity for debate, and ensuring the opposition does not use the debate simply to try and 'talk out' Bill.

The House of Commons Modernisation Committee, in its report published in July 1997, confirmed that the proceedings of standing committees were often devoted to political partisan debate rather than constructive and systematic scrutiny. It observed that the role of government backbenchers on standing committees was to remain silent and to vote as directed. The result of these tactics is that important sections of Public Bills sometimes receive little or no scrutiny at the committee stage because of the imposition of time allocation orders (ie 'the guillotine') which bring deliberations to an end at a specified point in time.

The report suggested a number of reforms, including proposals that all members of standing committees should be provided with notes on clauses produced at the time of presentation of a Bill; that clauses should be considered as a whole, before amendments, so as to isolate common points of agreement and criticism; and that more time should be made available for deliberation by permitting standing committees to meet during the parliamentary recess.

The committee further suggested that scrutiny of government Bills in the House of Commons could be improved if there was more systematic consideration of draft Bills prior to the first reading, rather than government ministers presenting draft legislation to the House of Commons as a fait accompli, resisting any proposals for significant change for fear that this might be taken as evidence of political weakness.

The report concluded in favour of pre-legislative scrutiny by a committee of the House of Commons but was not specific as to what form the committee should take.

Overall the quality of the scrutiny of government Bills by the House of Commons is inevitably limited by a number of factors, including the control exerted by the executive and the time available for debate. The paradox is that the greater the government's majority the greater the need for scrutiny. Governments with large majorities are perhaps more tempted to push through radical measures. A government with a small majority is likely to tailor the contents of its Bills before they are even published so as to take account of likely opposition and improve the chances of enactment.

QUESTION FOUR

Upon what legal and constitutional principles should the composition of the House of Lords be determined?

University of London LLB Examination
(for External Students) Constitutional and Administrative Law June 1998 Q4

General Comment

This is not an altogether easy question. The danger is that candidates will fall into the trap of thinking that it simply requires a description of House of Lords membership, and an account of the attempts at reform. What the question is trying to bring out are the constitutional values that underpin the debates about reform. Hence the need to examine issues such as legitimacy, representativeness and accountability.

Skeleton Solution

Examine what the House of Lords does – relate this to the issue of membership – explain the abolition of hereditary peers' rights – House of Lords Act 1999 – set out the various values underpinning the debate – the pros and cons of election and appointment – the Royal Commission – the desire of the government to retain control – conclude by contrasting two possible solutions.

Suggested Solution

It is pointless to debate the legal and constitutional principles that should determine the composition of the House of Lords, or indeed that of any second chamber in a bicameralist system, without first giving thought to what that second chamber is meant to do.

The House of Lords at present serves an essential role as a delaying and revising chamber. Where legislation is rushed through the House of Commons, sometimes with the use of a time-allocation order, it can receive more detailed scrutiny in the Lords. At the beginning of a parliamentary session, when there would otherwise be little for the second chamber to do, non-controversial Bills can be introduced into the House of Lords, so that they need not be reconsidered again by that chamber when they have completed the legislative process in the House of Commons. By virtue of the Parliament Acts 1911 and 1949, the House of Lords also acts as an essential brake on the otherwise sovereign power of the House of Commons to enact any law it wishes. Where controversial legislation is put forward, this delaying power provides further time for consideration, lobbying and reform. In particular, the House of Lords can veto any Bill to extend the life of a Parliament beyond five years, and thus prevent an unpopular government from postponing a general election. In constitutional terms these are all significant functions. Hence it is vital that those who serve as members of the second chamber should be able to discharge these functions with appropriate expertise and legitimacy.

How then is such a composition to be achieved? Prior to the enactment of the House of Lords Act 1999, the House of Lords comprised both life peers and hereditary peers. The hereditary peers outnumbered the life peers, although it was the life peers who tended to attend more regularly and take an active part in the proceedings of the House. This arrangement ensured that there was always a built-in Conservative majority in the House of Lords. If there was a particularly contentious vote, many of the hereditary peers who seldom otherwise attended (so-called 'backwoodsmen') would turn up to vote for the Conservative Party and disappear again. Not surprisingly it was the Labour Party that campaigned most fervently to change this state of affairs, the change eventually being brought about by the 1999 Act.

As indicated above, the House of Lords Act 1999 has the effect of removing the rights of hereditary peers to sit and vote in the House of Lords. Section 2 of the Act provides for 92 hereditary peers to remain as members of the House of Lords, but only as life peers. The Act swiftly achieved one of the long-term aims of the Labour Party by redressing, to some extent, the political balance in the House of Lords. At the commencement of the 1999/2000 session there were 230 Conservative peers, 185 Labour, 55 Liberal Democrats, 160 crossbenchers, plus bishops and law lords.

It is submitted that few would seriously seek to defend the hereditary principle as the basis of the right to sit and vote in a modern legislature. Most would also accept that it is not fair that one political party should have a perpetual majority in the second chamber, notwithstanding the fact that its powers are much reduced when compared with the House of Commons. The House of Lords Act 1999 has, however, left the Labour government with the difficult question of how membership should be determined in the future.

What key constitutional values can be detected in this debate? The first is the issue of democratic legitimacy. Some have called for an elected second chamber. This would undoubtedly increase its status. The composition would reflect the democratic will. The problem is that it would immediately start to rival the House of Commons. If it was as powerful as the House of Commons a constitutional stalemate could develop. If it was less powerful, would people bother to turn out to vote in elections for membership? If it was given more power than the House of Commons, elections for the first chamber would become less significant.

The second key value is accountability. Elected members of a second chamber would be answerable to the electorate – whether at large, or on a specific constituency basis. Appointed members would be unaccountable. This has the attraction of ensuring that they are more likely to be freethinkers, and thus counterbalance the 'lobby fodder' mentality of many backbench MPs in the House of Commons. It places an enormous power of patronage in those making the appointments, however. There is a danger, as has been the case with life peerages, that appointment to the second chamber is used as a political reward.

The third key value is fairness. As indicated above it is unfair for one party always to be in the majority. The composition of the second chamber should be determined by a mechanism that seeks to prevent this. But again there are problems. If the membership of the second chamber, in terms of party political allegiance, mirrors that of the first chamber, it is unlikely to act as an effective brake on the first chamber. If the government of the day does not have a majority in an appointed second chamber, and that second chamber obstructs the passage of government Bills, it is open to criticism on the basis that it is thwarting the will of the democratically elected first chamber.

The question of how to achieve an acceptable mechanism for determining membership of the second chamber has, therefore, proved to be one of the great current constitutional conundrums. It was not surprising that the Labour government opted to refer the question to a Royal Commission chaired by Lord Wakeham. In its report, published in January 2000, the Commission envisaged a second chamber of about 550 members, the majority of the members being appointed by an Independent Commission. A minority, somewhere between 65 and 195 members, would be elected from 12 UK regions. Elected members would serve a single 15-year term, with elections every five years. Measures would be put in place to ensure the representativeness of the second chamber, both in terms of current voting patterns, race, gender and socio-economic groupings.

The report, it is submitted, represents an unworkable compromise – seeking to ensure that the second chamber becomes more representative, but still a poor relation of the House of Commons. Notwithstanding proposals announced in September 2000 to invite 'ordinary members of the public' to apply for membership of the House of Lords, the way remains open for the 'good and the great' to be appointed, but it is inconceivable that this process could really be free from political influence.

The government's response, in the form of its White Paper *Completing the Reform* (Cmd 5291), does little to clarify or advance matters. It envisages a second chamber with 600 members – the elected membership amounting to 120 representing constituencies based on those used for the election of members of the European Parliament, successful candidates being selected on the basis of a party list system. A further 120 members would be appointed by the Appointments Commission, the Commission being under a duty to ensure a balanced and representative selection of members, reflecting the demographic and ethnic mix of the population as a whole. The remaining members would be political appointees nominated by the major political parties. The Appointments Commission would have a supervisory role in respect of such nominations in that it would be required to vet nominees for propriety, and would be required to ensure an appropriate political balance across the political parties. The right of each party to nominate members would be based on its electoral support at the most recent general election, subject to a proviso that no one political party should have an overall majority. The White Paper is a political fudge –having elected members is either desirable or it is not. And having a 20 per cent elected element sends mixed messages as to the value of democratic representation. There may also be issues regarding the relative legitimacy of elected and appointed members of the second chamber. Given current levels of voter apathy questions might also be asked as to the extent to which voters might be bothered to register their preferences in elections for members of the Lords. The White Paper, perhaps wisely, envisages elections for the Lords being held on the same day as general elections, thus masking what may be a high level of voter indifference regarding who their representative might be in the second chamber.

The White Paper reflects the conflict in which any government advocating Lords' reform inevitably finds itself. It seeks to attack the iniquities of hereditary membership and the historic pro-Conservative bias, but at the same time it is fearful of creating an institution that could be said to rival the Commons in terms of power and legitimacy. Nothing short of a complete constitutional resettlement will solve this conundrum, hence the uneasy and not altogether coherent compromise offered in the White Paper.

Ultimately the problem is one of power and control. Under the United Kingdom constitution the Prime Minister controls the executive which in turn controls the majority in the House of Commons. A second chamber made up of those who are not accountable to the government of the day is at best a nuisance to the government of the day, and at worst can wreck its legislative programme. It is not surprising, therefore, that the Labour government, for all its rhetoric about reforming the House of Lords, has not been radical enough to embrace the idea of a truly empowered second chamber.

If the second chamber is to be effectively toothless, and simply make gently reproving noises in respect of government Bills in the hope that some amendments might be accepted, it might as well remain an appointed body – the power of patronage resting in the hands of the prime Minister, subject to the convention that new appointments should be made from across the political spectrum. If the second chamber is to have real power it must, to have any legitimacy, be elected – thus throwing into sharp relief its relationship with the House of Commons.

QUESTION FIVE

Critically assess the adequacy of the Parliament Acts 1911–49 as the legal basis for relations between the two Houses of Parliament. What functions and powers should a reformed House of Lords possess?

University of London LLB Examination
(for External Students) Constitutional Law 1999 Q3

General Comment

This is a question that might deceive many candidates. The temptation is for candidates to simply write an account of what the House of Lords does. What is required is an explanation of the mechanics of the Parliament Acts and a critical comment on the effectiveness of the legislation. The question then asks for consideration of the functions of the second chamber, but note it refers to a reformed second chamber. It does not tell the candidates what reforms these might be. Candidates therefore need to link changes in membership rights in the second chamber to the appropriateness of functions.

Skeleton Solution

Explain why the 1911 Act was introduced – what it achieved – 1949 reforms – new balance of power – how have the Acts been used – problems remaining – delaying powers – the 'Salisbury Convention' – consider how the second chamber might be reformed – House of Lords Act 1999 – Wakeham Commission report – how would this impact on functions? – what should an appointed body be able to do? – future of the Law Lords.

Suggested Solution

The United Kingdom legislature is bicameralist, by which is meant it consist of two houses – the Commons and the Lords. In the absence of a written constitution relations between the two chambers have come to be regulated by a mixture of statute and convention. The distinguishing feature of the relationship over the last 100 years is the increasing power of the House of Commons, derived from its legitimacy as the directly elected chamber. This increase in the power of the House of Commons is as a direct result of the spread of universal adult suffrage. Given this increase in the power of the House of Commons, and the increasing ideological polarisation between the membership of the two chambers (the House of Lords having historically maintained a perpetual Conservative majority through its hereditary members), clashes were inevitable. In 1909 the Lords rejected the Budget that Lloyd George had presented to the Commons. The Liberal government, once re-elected, introduced a Parliament Bill to restrict the powers of the House of Lords. This Bill (which became the Parliament Act 1911) was passed by the House of Lords in August 1911, under the threat that sufficient Liberal peers would be created to ensure its passage should the Bill be rejected. The Parliament Act 1911 made a number of significant changes: a money Bill (certified as such by the Speaker) could become an Act of Parliament without the consent of the House of Lords if, having been sent up from the House of Commons at least one month before the end of the session, it had not been passed by the Lords without amendment within one month of its being sent up; any other Public Bill, except one for extending the life of a Parliament, could become an Act of Parliament without the consent of the House of Lords if it had been passed by the House of Commons in three successive sessions, two years having elapsed between its first second reading and its final passing in the House of Commons, and if it had been sent up to the House of Lords at least one month before the end of each of the three sessions.

The Labour government elected immediately after the Second World War was committed to a radical programme of popular socialist reform. Many of its measures were opposed by the Conservative peers. The result was the introduction of a Bill designed to amend the 1911 Act by means of further reducing the delaying power of the House of Lords to 12 months. The House of Lords refused to pass the Bill, with the result that it was presented for the royal assent without having been passed by the House of Lords, and became the Parliament Act 1949.

In summary, the effect of the Parliament Acts 1911 and 1949 is that the House of Lords can significantly delay the progress of a Public Bill brought from the House of Commons. A Commons Bill lost because it is not accepted by the Lords can be passed in the following session, without the Lords' consent, if the provisions of the Parliament Act 1911, as amended by the Parliament Act 1949, apply. The Parliament Acts' procedure does not apply to Bills introduced in the House of Lords. The three Acts passed under the Parliament Act 1911 are the Welsh Church Act 1914 (disestablishing the Church of Wales), the Government of Ireland Act 1914 (providing for Irish home rule) and the Parliament Act 1949. The 1949 Act was invoked to ensure the passage of the War Crimes Act 1991 and the European Parliamentary Elections Act 1999.

The Parliament Acts provide a clear demarcation of functions between the two chambers in respect of financial matters, but they leave scope for uncertainty where non-money Bills are concerned. The Acts clearly indicate that the House of Commons can legislate without the consent of the House of Lords, but the Lords' delaying power can put pressure on the government to accept amendments to its legislation rather than risk losing it before the end of the parliamentary session. Much will depend on the time left between the introduction of a Bill and the next general election. Where, for example, a government has a large majority and has recently come to power it can afford to be defeated in the House of Lords and simply reintroduce the Bill again in the House of Commons in the following session. This is illustrated by the current Labour government's Bill to reform the right of the defendant's to elect the mode of trial in criminal cases. Where a government is reaching the end of its term of office the House of Lords becomes more powerful. The government may be very keen to ensure that a Bill is enacted despite opposition from the Lords. The Bill may be rejected by the Lords, but the government has no guarantee that, come the next parliamentary session after the general election, it will still be in power. The House of Lords can exploit this situation by insisting on significant changes to a Bill to guarantee its passage. It has been suggested from time to time that the delaying power should be reduced to six months, to give the House of Commons greater leverage. The rules on introducing the same Bill twice in one parliamentary session could also be abolished.

The Parliament Acts also fail to address the point of principle concerning the extent to which an unelected second chamber should be able to prevent the enactment of legislation passed by the elected lower chamber. Under the 'Salisbury Convention' the House of Lords should not use its power to veto or amend legislation in order to bar the progress of any Bill that the government of the day claims embodies a manifesto commitment upon which it was elected. The debate inevitably surrounds the extent to which the government does have a clear mandate for its legislative proposals. Again, the proposals to limit the defendant's right to opt for trial by jury in criminal cases has provided scope for debate on this point. The government has claimed a manifesto commitment to reform and speed up criminal justice. Opponents say this is not a mandate to remove centuries old civil liberties. One solution might be to extend the Speaker's certification power under the Parliament Acts to include a ruling as to whether a Bill was a 'manifesto measure ' or not – thus clarifying the legitimate role of the House of Lords.

The functions and powers of a reformed House of Lords were discussed in the government's White Paper, *Completing the Reform* (Cmd 5291), published in response to the report of the Royal Commission on the future of the House of Lords chaired by Lord Wakeham. The White Paper sees the principle function of the second chamber as being the consideration and revision of legislation, scrutiny of the executive, and the provision of a forum for the debating of, and reporting on, public issues. In recommending that there be no significant changes in the functions of the second chamber, the White Paper observed that the House of Lords' most important function should continue to be as a revising chamber for legislation, providing further scrutiny of legislation, obliging the government to justify further its legislative proposals and examining them in a less partisan spirit than the Commons.

At the beginning of each parliamentary session the House of Lords has less work to do as it is waiting for measures to come up from the House of Commons. Using this time to initiate non-controversial measures is an efficient use of resources. Given the pressure created by the government's legislative programme in the House of Commons there is often insufficient time for consideration of Bills in the Lower House. Debates in the House of Lords cannot be terminated by 'guillotine' motions, and the nature of the debate is less partisan, hence it can provide an effective focus for continued scrutiny and wider public debate. It is submitted that, absent a written constitution, the second chamber should have the power to veto any measure introduced with a view to postponing or abolishing general elections, thus preventing a government from remaining in power in perpetuity.

The House of Lords was seen to play an important role in holding the government to account, and that for this purpose it was important that ministers should continue to be appointed from the Lords in broadly the number that obtains at present. The feeling was that a measure of parliamentary scrutiny would be lost if ministers were directly accountable only to the House of Commons. The White Paper saw no case for giving specific new functions to the House of Lords, however. But the White Paper does propose that the House of Lords should lose its power to veto subordinate legislation, the power of veto being replaced with a power to delay such legislation for up to three months. The justification for this being that although the second chamber would lose the nominal power to reject Statutory Instruments absolutely, it would become more effective in assuring the quality of secondary legislation, as it would be able to point out flaws and urge some recasting of the terms of a Statutory Instrument, without rejecting it outright.

The White Paper, as the Royal Commission had done, rejected any further reform of the delaying powers of the House of Lords as regards primary legislation on the basis that any changes would be 'far from simple to enact, and the practical effect insufficient to justify the parliamentary time and effort required.'

In general terms, the greater the elected element of its membership, the greater the justification for giving the House of Lords more power. The problem, however, is that the more powerful it becomes, the greater the scope for conflict with the House of Commons. The more 'legitimate'' the second chamber, the stronger the case for reviewing the balance of power as laid down in the Parliament Acts. Indeed, it could be argued that the whole rationale for the Parliament Acts is called into question if the second chamber becomes more representative.

The one function that might be removed from a reformed second chamber is that of providing the highest appeal court. It is largely a matter of historical happenstance that the House of Lords is also the final domestic court of appeal, and a reform of the second chamber could reflect this by providing for the establishment of a demonstrably independent 'Supreme Court'. This would very much reflect the spirit of the age and would be timely with the coming into force of the Human Rights Act 1998.

Chapter 7

Parliamentary Privilege

7.1   Introduction

7.2   Key points

7.3   Key cases and statutes

7.4   Questions and suggested solutions

7.1 Introduction

For a Member of Parliament to carry out his duties to his constituents properly he must be free to raise matters without the fear of being sued for slander or libel. Parliamentary privilege allows him to do so within the confines of Parliament itself. There is, of course, the risk of abuse and, in any event, the counter argument that those attacked may not have a chance to defend themselves.

It is sometimes said that the rules of parliamentary privilege constitute a clear case of 'power without responsibility', but it has to be accepted that over the years parliamentary privilege has been essential to the exposure of injustices and malpractices which the restrictive English libel laws might otherwise have allowed to continue unchecked.

As with most of constitutional law it is a matter of striking the right balance; in this area the need for freedom of speech in Parliament has to be respected and, perhaps, all that needs to be changed to achieve the balance is for Parliament itself to be much more willing to impose heavy penalties on those members who are deemed to have abused this privilege.

7.2 Key points

It is important that students understand the following issues regarding parliamentary privilege:

Definition

Parliamentary privilege is defined by Erskine May in *Parliamentary Practice*, 21st edn, as:

'... the sum of the peculiar rights enjoyed by each House collectively as a constitutional part of the High Court of Parliament and by members of each House individually, without which they could not discharge their functions, and which exceed those possessed by other bodies or individuals.'

Privileges of the House of Commons

'Ancient and undoubted rights and privileges'

At the opening of each Parliament, the Speaker formally claims from the Crown for the Commons 'their ancient and undoubted rights and privileges'. These are:

a) Freedom of speech in debate

The right is guaranteed in art 9 of the Bill of Rights 1689 which provides:

'... the freedom of speech and debates or proceedings in Parliament ought not to be impeached or questioned in any court or place out of Parliament.'

Thus the basic rule is that no MP may be made liable in the courts for words spoken in the course of parliamentary proceedings – what is said in Parliament cannot be used to support a cause of action in defamation: *Church of Scientology of California* v *Johnson-Smith* [1972] 1 QB 522. Whilst this protects MPs as defendants it also has the effect of preventing them from putting in evidence things said in Parliament in order to bring defamation actions as plaintiffs. This aspect of the law has now been amended with the enactment of s13(1) of the Defamation Act 1996 which provides:

'Where the conduct of a person in or in relation to proceedings in Parliament is in issue in defamation proceedings, he may waive for the purposes of those proceedings, so far as concerns him, the protection of any enactment or rule of law which prevents proceedings in Parliament being impeached or questioned in any court or place out of Parliament.'

Note also that in *Pepper* v *Hart* [1993] 1 All ER 42 the court held that account could be taken of extracts from Hansard to assist in statutory interpretation. Emphasis was, however, made of the need to give effect to Parliament's intentions, rather than to undermine the independence of MPs.

A likely point for consideration in the examination question is what constitutes 'proceedings in Parliament'. Remarks made in debate, discussions in committee, parliamentary questions and answers, and votes are clearly within the definition. Other words spoken within the precincts of Parliament unconnected with parliamentary proceedings are not protected: *Rivlin* v *Bilainkin* [1953] 1 QB 485. Students should note the following statement from Viscount Radcliffe in *Attorney-General for Ceylon* v *De Livera* [1963] AC 103 in which he was considering what was meant by a proceeding in Parliament:

'... the answer given to that somewhat more limited question depends upon the following consideration, in what circumstances and in what situations is a member of the House exercising his "real" or "essential" function as a member? The most that can be said is that, despite reluctance to treat a member's privileges as going beyond anything that is essential, it is generally recognised that it is impossible to regard his only proper functions as a member as being confined to what he does on the floor of the House.'

Particular problems have frequently arisen regarding the status of communications between MPs and ministers: *Case of GWR Strauss MP* (1957–58) HC 227. Such communications may only enjoy qualified privilege under the law of defamation: *Beach v Freeson* [1972] QB 14. Letters from members of the public to MPs enjoy only qualified privilege under the law of defamation: *R v Rule* [1937] 2 KB 375. Communications between MPs and the Parliamentary Commissioner for Administration are accorded absolute privilege in the law of defamation: s10(5) Parliamentary Commissioner Act 1967. It is instructive to note that s13(5) of the Defamation Act 1996 envisages parliamentary proceedings as encompassing:

i)   the giving of evidence before either House or a committee;

ii) the presentation or submission of a document to either House or a committee;

iii) the preparation of a document for the purposes of or incidental to the transacting of any such business;

iv) the formulation, making or publication of a document, including a report, by or pursuant to an order of either House or a committee; and

v)   any communication with the Parliamentary Commissioner for Standards or any person having functions in connection with the registration of members' interests.

At common law the fair and accurate reporting of parliamentary proceedings is protected by qualified privilege at common law: *Wason v Walter* (1869) LR 4 QB 73; *Cook v Alexander* [1974] QB 279. The defence now has a statutory basis: see s15 Defamation Act 1996. Fair and accurate extracts from, or abstracts of, papers published under the authority of Parliament enjoy qualified privilege in the law of defamation: Parliamentary Papers Act 1840.

b) Freedom from arrest

The immunity only applies to civil arrest and extends while Parliament sits and for 40 days before and 40 days after: *Stourton v Stourton* [1963] P 302.

The immunity does not protect members from arrest on criminal charges.

c) Freedom of access to Her Majesty whenever occasion shall require; and that the most favourable construction should be placed upon all their proceedings.

Other privileges

The other privileges of the House of Commons, not expressly claimed by the Speaker include:

a) The right of the House to regulate its own composition

The House retains the exclusive right to determine by resolution when a writ for the holding of a by-election shall be issued.

The House maintains the right to determine whether a member is qualified to sit in the House and can declare a member's seat vacant on grounds of legal disqualification or for any other reason it thinks fit.

The House may expel a member whom it considers unfit to sit: the *Case of Gary Allighan MP* (1947) HC 138.

b) The right to take exclusive cognisance of matters arising within the precincts of the House

The House maintains the right to control its own proceedings and regulate its internal affairs without interference from the courts: *Bradlaugh* v Gossett (1884) 12 QBD 271.

If a statute is to bind the House it must do so clearly: R v *Graham-Campbell, ex parte Herbert* [1935] 1 KB 594.

The right to punish both members and non-members for breach of privilege and contempt

The House has the power to maintain its privileges and to punish those who break or commit contempt of the House.

Contempt of the House is a very wide concept. Erskine May describes it as:

> ' ... any act or omission which obstructs or impedes either House or Parliament in the performance of its functions, or which obstructs or impedes any member or officer of such House in the discharge of his duty, or which has a tendency, directly or indirectly, to produce such results may be treated as a contempt even though there is no precedent of the offence.'

Thus while the House cannot create new privileges, except by statute, there is no complete list of behaviour which constitutes contempt.

Complaints of breach of privilege may be raised by a member or in the House by the Speaker. If the Speaker rules that a prima facie case has been made out a motion is proposed that the matter be referred to the Committee on Standards and Privileges.

The Committee comprises 15 senior members of the House. It is the master of its own proceedings. It can compel the attendance of witnesses and the production of documents; failure to comply being a contempt. There is no requirement of legal representation.

The Select Committee on Parliamentary Privilege in 1967 recommended that persons directly concerned in the Committee's investigations should have the right to attend its hearings, make submissions, call, examine and cross-examine witnesses, and be legally represented and apply for legal aid.

Offenders may be reprimanded or admonished or committed to prison. Members may be suspended or expelled from the House.

The right of impeachment (now obsolete).

The courts and parliamentary privilege

The House of Commons claims to be the absolute and sole judge of its own privileges and maintains that its judgment cannot be called into question by any other court. The courts do not agree. They maintain the right to determine the nature and extent of parliamentary privilege when adjudicating upon the rights of individuals outside the house. This disagreement has given rise to constitutional conflict: *Stockdale* v *Hansard* (1839) 9 Ad & E 1; *Case of the Sheriffs of Middlesex* (1840) 11 Ad & E 273.

MPs as representatives of outside interests

If a member agrees to represent an outside interest group in Parliament, is a threat by that group to remove support from the member a breach of privilege?

a) It is improper for a member to enter into any arrangement fettering his complete independence by undertaking to press some particular point of view on behalf of an outside interest whether for reward or not: *Case of WJ Brown MP* (1947).

b) It is improper to attempt to punish a member financially because of his actions as a member: *Case of the Yorkshire Area Council of National Union of Mineworkers* (1975).

Privileges of the House of Lords

The privileges of the House of Lords are similar to those enjoyed by the House of Commons.

The Nolan Report

The Nolan Report recommended that the House should:

a) require agreements and remuneration relating to parliamentary services to be disclosed;

b) expand the guidance on avoiding conflicts of interests;

c) introduce a new code of conduct for members;

d) appoint a Parliamentary Commissioner for standards;

e) establish a new procedure for investigating and adjudicating on complaints in this area about members.

Controversy has arisen amongst Members of Parliament as to:

a) the extent to which Parliamentarians should enjoy outside interests; and

b) whether consultancies and other paid work should be reviewed by a body other than Parliament.

7.3 Key cases and statutes

- *Beach* v *Freeson* [1972] QB 14
  Communications between MPs and ministers may only enjoy qualified privilege

- *Bradlaugh* v *Gossett* (1884) 12 QBD 271
  Right of the House of Commons to control its own proceedings and regulate its internal affairs

- *Case of the Sheriffs of Middlesex* (1840) 11 Ad & E 273
  Right of Parliament to adjudicate on matters of privilege

- *Church of Scientology of California* v *Johnson-Smith* [1972] 1 QB 522
  Comments made in Parliament not evidence in court

- *Pepper* v *Hart* [1993] 1 All ER 42
  Extracts from *Hansard* admissible to aid interpretation

- *Rivlin* v *Bilainkin* [1953] 1 QB 485
  Words spoken in precincts of the House of Commons may not be privileged

- *Stockdale* v *Hansard* (1839) 9 Ad & E 1
  Right of Parliament to adjudicate on matters of privilege

- *Stourton* v *Stourton* [1963] P 302
  Freedom from arrest

- *Wason* v *Walter* (1869) LR 4 QB 73
  At common law fair and accurate reporting of parliamentary proceedings protected by qualified privilege

- Bill of Rights 1689, art 9 – freedom of speech and debates or proceedings in Parliament

- Defamation Act 1996, s13 – MP can waive privilege when pursuing a defamation action

7.4 Questions and suggested solutions

QUESTION ONE

The House of Commons has too wide a jurisdiction to punish contempts and breaches of privilege.

Discuss.

University of London LLB Examination
(for External Students) Constitutional law June 1984 Q5

General Comment

This is a straightforward essay question requiring the student to show the relationship of Parliament to the courts as regards parliamentary privilege.

Skeleton Solution

Parliamentary privilege – courts decide what privileges exist – Parliament deals with breaches of such privileges.

Suggested Solution

Parliamentary privilege is part of the law and custom of Parliament evolved by the two Houses in order to protect their freedom to conduct their proceedings without improper interference by the sovereign, the courts, or the public. The privileges enjoyed by the House of Commons include those 'ancient and undoubted privileges' claimed by the Speaker at the beginning of each new Parliament such as freedom of speech in debate, freedom from civil arrest and freedom of access via the Speaker to the sovereign. There are also those privileges enjoyed by the House in its corporate capacity such as the right to regulate its own composition and the right to regulate its own proceedings. These special rights, powers and immunities conferred by parliamentary privilege are justified as being essential for the conduct of the business and the maintenance of the authority of the House.

Parliamentary privileges are part of the common law in so far as their existence and validity are recognised by the courts. But they are enforced not by the courts but exclusively by Parliament. By virtue of its inherent right to control its own proceedings and maintain its dignity, the House of Commons in protecting its privileges may punish those who violate them or commit contempt of the House. Breach of privilege consists of either an abuse of a particular privilege by a member or any conduct which interferes with one of the privileges of Parliament. Contempt is a much wider concept and consists of any conduct which tends to bring the House into disrepute or detract from its dignity. No matter whether the offence is styled a breach of privilege or a contempt, or both, the penal powers of the House are the same. Offenders may be reprimanded or admonished by the Speaker. Members may be suspended or expelled. Officials of the House may be dismissed and any member or stranger may be committed to prison for the duration of the Parliamentary session. However, in discussing the jurisdiction of the House to punish for breach of privilege and contempt a distinction must be drawn between the two.

In the past questions of privilege have been a source of considerable conflict between the Commons and the courts. Indeed, the House still asserts that it is the absolute and sole judge of the extent of its own privileges and has invoked its historical status as part of the High Court of Parliament in claiming that its judgments are not examinable by any other court. But this is a claim to which the courts do not fully accede. While the courts recognise the control which the House has over its own proceedings, in *Stockdale* v *Hansard* (1839) 9 Ad & E 1 the court maintained the right to determine the nature and the limits of parliamentary privilege when adjudicating upon the rights of individuals outside the House. The court also affirmed that the Commons cannot create new privileges by resolutions of the House, only by statute. Therefore, while the jurisdiction of the House of Commons to punish for breaches of privilege is wide, in the sense that the privileges are enforced exclusively by the House, nevertheless there are limitations, notably the court's power to determine whether the privilege arises and if so its scope and effect. In such cases privilege forms a part of the common law and is subject to it.

But while the House cannot by resolution enlarge the scope of its own privileges, it has not closed the categories of contempt. Therefore, while the courts may assert their jurisdiction to decide the existence and extent of privileges of the House, what constitutes a contempt of the House is essentially a matter which only the House can decide. If a contempt issue arises relating to the internal proceedings of the House, the courts will decline to interfere, and whether in relation to matters inside or outside the House, the courts have always recognised the power of the House to imprison for contempt. It is accepted today that where the cause of committal stated in the return to the writ is insufficient in law, the court may review. But if no cause for committal other than the simple statement of contempt of the House is shown in the return, the court will not make further inquiry into the reasons for the committal. Therefore the jurisdiction of the House of Commons to punish for contempt is very wide. The House has power to commit persons for contempt for whatever conduct it adjudges to amount to contempt, provided that the cause of the contempt is not stated.

QUESTION TWO

Jones is an MP for the constituency of Westhampton which for some time has suffered from a deterioration in relations between the police and the immigrant community. Recently Jones received a letter from a constituent complaining that he had been beaten up by one PC Plod for no reason whatsoever other than the fact that he was black. (This allegation was completely untrue.) Jones decided this was an opportunity to get to grips with the race relations problem and wrote three letters: one to a minister in the Home Office; one to the Westhampton Weekly; and one to the Community Relations Officer of the Local Authority. All the letters repeated the allegation as if it was pure fact. Jones also repeated the allegation in a question to the Secretary of State for the Home Office made during parliamentary question time and the question was reported in the Daily Garble the next day. Jones has also recently been offered a post with the Equality for Immigrants Association in which he is to be paid £5,000 per annum and he is expected to always support measures furthering the interests of the Association.

PC Plod has recently issued writs against the constituent, the Daily Garble and Jones complaining he has been libelled. Furthermore, the Speaker of the House has become aware of the offer of employment made by the EIA.

Discuss the foregoing in the light of the law relating to parliamentary privilege.

Written by the Editor

General Comment

A typical question on the major aspect of parliamentary privilege, namely freedom of speech, requiring a discussion of the relationship of the privilege with the tort of defamation.

Skeleton Solution

Introduction: outline nature and basis of parliamentary privilege – letter from constituent: probably not absolutely privileged – letters from Jones: which ones fall within meaning of 'proceeding in Parliament'? – question in house: *Church of Scientology* v *Johnston-Smith* (1972) – Daily Garble report: probably attracts qualified privilege; s7 Defamation Act 1954; *Cook* v *Alexander* (1974) – the offer of employment: *Case of DFS Henderson MP* (1945); *Case of WJ Brown MP* (1947).

Suggested Solution

In order for MPs to function properly they must be able to carry out their duties freely and without fear of being sued for defamation. Such protections come within the ambit of parliamentary privilege. This question raises two particular privileges as far as Jones is concerned: freedom of speech and freedom from interference. It is also in the public interest that constituents in their complaints to Members of Parliament and newspapers reporting parliamentary matters should also receive a degree of protection from the possibility of being sued for libel. This question also demands a discussion of the extent to which such persons are protected by qualified privilege.

Turning firstly to the letter to Jones from the constituent, in *R* v *Rule* [1937] 2 KB 375 the appellant wrote a letter to the MP containing defamatory statements about a police officer and a magistrate. It was held that such a letter may attract qualified privilege, ie so long as the author was not motivated by malice he could not be sued for defamation. Further in *Rivlin* v *Bilainkin* [1953] 1 QB 485 it was suggested that if such a letter concerned matters currently being discussed by Parliament it might be absolutely privileged. On the facts of the instant case since the allegation by the constituent is completely untrue it is difficult to see how he can be said not to be acting maliciously and, therefore, he is likely to be held liable to PC Plod.

As regards the actions by Jones, whether he is absolutely privileged depends on whether they fall within the meaning of 'proceedings in Parliament'. Clearly the question raised in the House of Commons must be a 'proceeding in Parliament' and would be privileged: *Church of Scientology* v *Johnston-Smith* [1972] 1 QB 522. In the *Attorney-General for Ceylon* v *De Livera* [1963] AC 103 Viscount Radcliffe stated that it was not only proceedings on the floor of the House that were covered by the expression 'proceedings in Parliament'. His Lordship considered that an MP was protected whenever he was carrying out his 'real' or 'essential' functions as an MP.

It would seem that the letter to the Minister for the Home Office would come within the 'real' or 'essential' functions of Jones and, therefore, be privileged. Support for this can be found in the *Case of GWR Strauss MP* (1957–58) HC 227. In this case Strauss wrote to the Paymaster General about a nationalised industry. The Select Committee held this letter to be privileged although the matter was then referred to the full House of Commons which decided it was not privileged. However, it is now felt that it would be deemed to be privileged.

On the basis of the above, however, it is doubtful whether the letters to the Westhampton Weekly and the Community Relations Officer can be deemed 'proceedings in Parliament' and would not, therefore, be privileged.

The Daily Garble has reported a 'parliamentary proceeding', namely the question in the House. The Defamation Act 1954 preserves the right of newspapers to accurately and fairly report such proceedings. Such reporting attracts qualified privilege and, since there is no suggestion of malice by the Daily Garble, it will be protected from the defamation action by PC Plod: *Cook v Alexander* [1974] QB 279.

Finally, the offer of employment by the Equality for Immigrants Association has to be considered. Jones is to be paid £5,000 for always supporting measures that further the interests of the Association. Two cases fall to be considered in deciding whether this arrangement would be in breach of the privilege against interference.

In the *Case of DFS Henderson* (1945) Henderson asked an MP for help in his negotiations with the Ministry of Agriculture. He offered to pay 100 guineas to the MP's local association if the negotiations were successful. Was this a bribe and, therefore, a contempt of Parliament? It was held that since the payment was not to the MP personally and also because the MP's permission to make such a payment was sought beforehand that there was no contempt. However, such a practice was deemed to be generally objectionable. And in the *Case of WJ Brown* (1947) the MP had been elected General Secretary of the Civil Service Union on condition that it did not affect his political independence and that he did not have to represent the views of the union. Brown fell out with the Union who voted to remove him as its General Secretary. Brown complained that the Union was trying to interfere with his independence as an MP and was, therefore, in contempt. It was held that Brown had voluntarily placed himself in his position and the actions of the Union could not amount to a contempt.

In Jones' case he clearly is receiving a direct payment and, further, is limiting his political independence because he would have to vote in support of measures in the interests of the EIA whether he agreed with them or not. It is likely, therefore, that the Speaker would report him to the Committee on Standards and Privileges if he accepted the employment and that he would be held to be in contempt. Whilst the Committee has powers to expel and fine Members of Parliament it is often the case that MPs are let off with little more than a stern warning.

QUESTION THREE

'The sole justification for the present privileges of the House of Commons is that they are essential for the conduct of its business and the maintenance of its authority.' (Sir Barnett Cocks)

Discuss.

University of London LLB Examination
(for External Students) Constitutional Law June 1989 Q3

General Comment

An essay question requiring a critical discussion of how far parliamentary privileges are justified today.

Skeleton Solution

Introduction – original necessity for privilege and examples of privileges. – examine privileges in detail pointing out whether they remain essential – freedom of speech – freedom from civil arrest – right to regulate composition and proceedings and to punish those in contempt or breach of privilege – conclusion.

Suggested Solution

Many of the privileges of Parliament have their origins in the sixteenth and seventeenth centuries at a time when the House of Commons was striving to prove its independence and to prevent interference with its members and proceedings by the Monarch and others outside Parliament. The privileges were originally developed to safeguard the position of MPs individually and that of the House as a whole. Today the privileges established during these centuries still exist but a select committee in 1967 commented that some were no longer required as they had become obsolete and suggested reforms, which have still not been implemented.

At the beginning of each new Parliament the Speaker claims 'ancient and undoubted privileges' which consist of freedom of speech in debate, freedom from civil arrest and freedom of access via the Speaker to the sovereign. The Commons also enjoys privileges in its corporate capacity such as the right to regulate its own composition, the right to take exclusive cognisance of matters arising within the precincts of the House and the right to punish both members and non-members for breach of privilege and contempt.

Perhaps the most important of the privileges of the Commons is that of freedom of speech. It was enshrined in the Constitution by art 9 of the Bill of Rights 1689 and provides 'The freedom of speech and debates or proceedings in Parliament ought not to be impeached or questioned in any court or place out of Parliament.' Practically this means that no criminal prosecution can be launched nor can any civil action for defamation be commenced in respect of words uttered or written during 'debates and proceedings in Parliament.' There is debate over the meaning of the phrase 'proceedings in Parliament' (*Case of GWR Strauss MP* (1957–58) HC 227) but it seems that for anything said in the House in the course of parliamentary business (such as debates or committee hearings etc) the MP has immunity. Potentially MPs could abuse this privilege by knowingly making false statements in the House but it was considered that this danger was outweighed by the public interest in ensuring that MPs could speak freely when carrying out Parliamentary business. It should be noted that if an MP does abuse his privilege it is open to the House itself to punish him for contempt of Parliament or to expel him from the House as unfit: *Case of Gary Allighan MP* (1947) HC 138.

The privilege of freedom of speech also prevents those outside Parliament attempting to dictate to MPs how they should speak in debate and/or vote. Although it is acknowledged that MPs may maintain business and other interests outside Parliament there is a Register of Members' Interests in which each MP is supposed to declare his other activities. Article 9 has been used to stop such outside commitments being used to force an MP into a particular course of action (see, for example, the 1975 investigation into the sponsoring of MPs by the National Union of Mineworkers).

In these ways the privilege of freedom of speech remains important to the Houses of Parliament.

By contrast the privilege of freedom from civil arrest is obsolete and is long overdue for repeal. It provides that for the forty days before, during a session and for the forty days after it an MP may not be subject to civil (not criminal) arrest. Although this was needed when the usual method of enforcing a debt was to incarcerate the debtor in a debtors' prison which, in the absence of the immunity, could have effectively disenfranchised large numbers of voters it is no longer required when arrest in civil proceedings is rare indeed.

Freedom of access via the speaker to the sovereign is today merely a formality but the Common's powers to regulate its own composition and internal proceedings remain relevant. Election petitions are no longer determined by the Commons itself, but by an election court made up of High Court judges, but the Commons still determines when to move a writ for a by election to fill any vacancies which arise. It may also declare that a member is unfit and expel him from the House. The House regulates its own proceedings and the courts will not take cognisance of these procedures even when these conflict with statute as in *Bradlaugh* v *Gossett* (1884) 12 QBD 271, where an MP was refused permission by the Commons to make his oath of allegiance in a form permitted by statute. The court's refusal to interfere in Parliament's internal procedure is exemplified in *Pickin* v *British Railways Board* [1974] AC 765 where the fact that notices had apparently not been given by promoters of a private Bill so as to satisfy orders of the House of Lords did not lead to the invalidity of the Act of Parliament subsequently passed. This attitude is one aspect of the doctrine of parliamentary sovereignty and there has been criticism of the fact that the courts do not intervene in such cases.

One aspect of Parliament's right to regulate its own conduct is its jurisdiction to punish breach of privilege and contempt of Parliament. Breach of privileges, consists of abuse of privilege by a member or of any conduct by any one MP or non member which interferes with one of the privileges of Parliament. Contempt is a wider concept and consists of conduct which tends to bring the House into disrepute or detract from its dignity. Whether the offence is breach of privilege or contempt, the penal powers of the House are the same. Members may be reprimanded or admonished by the Speaker or Members may be suspended or expelled. Officials of the House may be dismissed or a Member or stranger may be committed to prison for the duration of the Parliamentary Session. The Select Committee on Parliamentary Privileges recommended that the punitive powers of the Commons and Lords be curtailed and although no such reform has been formally made, in practice the Commons seems reluctant to do more than give a reprimand to outsiders found to be in contempt (even where as in 1986 the then Committee of Privileges had recommended that a lobby correspondent be expelled for six months with his paper, *The Times*, being allowed no substitute for that period). The most severe penalty it uses in respect of MPs is suspension.

The procedure by which complaints of breach of privilege or contempt of Parliament are made is open to criticism. At present a member may complain to the Speaker and the Speaker may refer the matter to the Committee on Standards and Privileges. This committee can compel attendance of witnesses and production of documents. Failure to comply is a contempt. The Select Committee on Parliamentary Privileges in 1967 recommended that persons directly concerned in the Committee's investigation should have the right to attend the hearings, make submissions, call and examine witnesses. Also legal aid, with leave of the Committee, should be granted. These recommendations were not implemented.

Furthermore even when the Committee on Standards and Privileges has reached its conclusion on the evidence that decision is not binding on the House which may reject it (eg *Strauss* (above)). This state of affairs can hardly be justified in cases where the Commons might take a harsher point of view without hearing the evidence. However, normally the Commons as a whole take a more lenient view than the Committee.

It does seem that this area is ripe for reform but such reform is unlikely to materialise in the near future as it is not seen by political parties as a priority.

QUESTION FOUR

What reforms, if any, should be made to the privileges of the House of Commons?

University of London LLB Examination
(for External Students) Constitutional Law June 1991 Q5

General Comment

It is desirable to set out the main privileges and then deal with the more significant privileges in detail. Most of the answer will be concerned with the privilege of free speech as this is currently the most contentious. In some cases it is desirable to point out that privileges need not be reformed because they are not being abused in practice.

Skeleton Solution

List the main privileges – explain freedom of speech, possible abuses, reform of its scope – consider freedom from arrest (little need for this any more) – other privileges considered briefly.

Suggested Solution

The principal privileges claimed from the Crown for the Commons are freedom of speech in debate, freedom from arrest, freedom of access to Her Majesty whenever occasion shall require, the right to have the most favourable construction placed upon all their proceedings, the right of the House to regulate its own composition, the right to take exclusive cognisance of matters arising within the precincts of the House, the right to punish both members and non-members for breach of privilege and contempt, and the right of impeachment.

Freedom of speech

Freedom of speech is of fundamental importance to the freedom and indeed the power of Parliament. If members could be attacked by the public or the executive for speaking their minds they might be so intimidated as not to be able to carry out their deliberative and legislative functions properly. The right is guaranteed in art 9 of the Bill of Rights 1689 which provides:

> 'The freedom of speech and debates or proceedings in Parliament ought not to be impeached or questioned in any court or place out of Parliament.'

The effect of art 9 is that no member may be made liable in the courts for words spoken in the course of parliamentary proceedings. If a member were to be sued for defamation in respect of something said during the course of parliamentary proceedings, the writ should be struck out as declaring no cause of action. If the matter did come to trial the court must hold that the member is protected by absolute privilege in the law of defamation. This protection extends to both civil and criminal liability. Nor can what is said in Parliament be used to support a cause of action in defamation where the MP is a defendant (see further *Church of Scientology v Johnson-Smith* [1972] 1 QB 522). But, as a result of the enactment of s13 of the Defamation Act 1996, an MP can now waive parliamentary privilege and pursue an action in defamation that requires him or her to adduce as evidence statements made during proceedings in Parliament.

It has not been seriously suggested that the parliamentary privilege of free speech be removed, otherwise than at the behest of the member in question, but reliance upon it by members has from time to time been criticised. The danger is that members will make statements in the House under the cloak of privilege that they would not dream of repeating outside. The reputations of others can be damaged without any right of compensation. The MP Geoffrey Dickins was heavily criticised when he threatened to reveal the name of a doctor who had allegedly raped an eight-year-old girl, but against whom the police had declined to take proceedings due to lack of evidence. As was pointed out, the danger in such cases is that the individual named may have his career ruined by such statements, without ever having been convicted of the alleged offence in a court of law. It is submitted that such abuses of privilege are best dealt with, not by reforming the scope of the privilege, but by relying upon the Speaker of the House to properly regulate the conduct of debate in the House. It is conceded, however, that one aspect of this privilege that could be clarified is the scope of the expression 'proceedings in Parliament'. Remarks made in debate, discussions in committee, parliamentary questions and answers, and votes are clearly within the definition. Other words spoken within the precincts of Parliament unconnected with parliamentary proceedings are not protected. There are 'grey areas' however, as illustrated by the so-called *Strauss* affair (see *Case of GWR Strauss MP* (1957–58) HC 227), which concerned a letter written by Strauss, a Labour MP, to the Paymaster General complaining about the way in which the London Electricity Board disposed of their scrap cable. The Paymaster General denied responsibility on the ground that the matter concerned day to day administration rather than policy, and he passed the letter to the Board. The Board took exception to Strauss' allegations and threatened to sue him for libel unless he withdrew and apologised. Strauss raised the threat as a question of privilege and the matter was referred to the what was then the Committee of Privileges. The Committee reported that in writing his letter Strauss was engaged in a proceeding in Parliament for the purposes of art 9 and that the Board, in threatening to sue, were in breach of parliamentary privilege. However when the Report of the Committee was debated in the House, on a free vote it rejected the findings of the Committee. The House resolved that Strauss' letter was not a proceeding in Parliament: see further *Rost v Edwards* (1990) The Times 16 February.

Freedom from arrest

Immunity from arrest is now of little importance and in 1967 the Committee on Parliamentary Privilege appointed to review the law of parliamentary privilege recommended its abolition. The immunity only applies to civil arrest and extends not only while Parliament sits, but also for 40 days before and after. The immunity does not protect members from arrest on criminal charges, nor from detention under regulations made under the Defence of the Realm Acts in time of war. In 1940, for example, the Commons Committee of Privileges was of opinion that there had been no breach of privilege when Captain Ramsay, a member, had been detained under regulations made under the Emergency Powers (Defence) Act 1939. There is little basis for the continued existence of the privilege.

The right of the House to regulate its own composition

Within the scope of this privilege fall a number of matters which are important as matters of principle, but which are of little significance in everyday terms. The privilege, which encompasses the right to determine disputed elections, the right to determine by resolution when a writ for the holding of a by-election shall be issued, the right to determine whether a member is qualified to sit in the House, and the right to expel a member whom it considers unfit to sit, has been used sparingly. Provided these powers are not used oppressively, it is submitted that they are not in need of any substantive reform.

The right to punish for breach of privilege and contempt

The House has the power to maintain its privileges and to punish those who break them or commit contempt of the House. All breaches of privilege are contempts of the House but not all contempts involve the infringement of the existing privileges of the House. Contempt of the House is a very wide concept. Perhaps the most questionable aspect of this system is the fact that the House sits as victim, prosecutor and judge when dealing with offenders. It is noteworthy that in proceedings before the European Commission on Human Rights it was held that the jurisdiction of the Maltese House of Representatives, to punish those alleged to have been in breach of its privileges, contravened art 6(1) of the European Convention on Human Rights.

QUESTION FIVE

Critically assess the respective roles of the House of Commons and the courts in regulating Parliamentary privilege.

University of London LLB Examination
(for External Students) Constitutional Law June 1993 Q8(b)

General Comment

A wide-ranging question, requiring the examinee to look at privilege from the angles of the House of Commons (by character prejudiced angles) and of the courts (by character independent angles). But assessment of those angles should take place in the context of the historical development of privilege, which at least gives a kind of rational basis to Parliament's exclusive claims in several important areas. Critical analysis should be supported by reference to appropriate academic research.

Skeleton Solution

Definition of parliamentary privilege and problems of control – internal proceedings of the House and risk of abuse of collective power – roles of Speaker and Standards and Privileges Committee – manner of hearing for alleged contemnors – scope of privilege of free speech under art 9 Bill of Rights 1689 – internal discipline and absence of judicial review – agueness of concept of 'proceedings in Parliament' and case for and against codification.

Suggested Solution

Parliamentary privilege is part of the common law which grants certain exemptions from the law to MPs in order that they may perform their functions. By its nature privilege is difficult to subject to normal processes of parliamentary and judicial review. There is the added complication that parliamentary privilege was won after an historic conflict between the legislature and an absolute monarchy (the latter at times supported by the judges). This explains the traditional sensitivity of the relationship between the legislature and the judiciary on the matter of privilege, raising fears for the rule of law.

Dicey argued for equality under the law, but the internal proceedings of the House of Commons are not subject to judicial review. Control, if any, must be exercised by the Commons itself, principally through the Speaker and the Select Committee on Standards and Privileges. The danger is that the House, collectively, may act as judge and jury in its own cause on a matter concerning an individual MP's rights to represent the constituency which elected him, eg as in the House's expulsion for political reasons of the radical Charles Bradlaugh: *Bradlaugh* v *Gossett* (1884) 12 QBD 271. Since no judicial review is available over such a decision, the only remedy for an expelled member is to petition the House which expelled him: *Case of the Sheriffs of Middlesex* (1840) 11 Ad & E 273.

The House also claims exclusive rights to punish 'strangers' (non-MPs) for breaches of MPs' individual privileges and for contempt of the whole House. These are dealt with either by rulings from the Speaker or by reference to the Committee on Standards and Privileges, consisting of 15 MPs from all parties chosen for their expertise in parliamentary law and their long experience of the life of the Commons. But MPs not on the Committee as well as academic observers, have expressed fears about the degree of discretion delegated to the Speaker and the Committee by the whole House. The methods used to deal with 'offenders' are far removed from 'due process of law'.

For example, the accused may be arrested by the Sergeant-at-Arms (the enforcement officer of the House) and brought before a private hearing of the Committee. The accused has no right to legal representation and may be cross-examined by a panel of QCs. The accused has no right to call evidence or to cross-examine the witnesses against him. The Committee reports to the whole House on whether the offence is proven and, if so, what penalty (including, in theory, imprisonment) should be imposed. There is no right of appeal to the courts against conviction or sentence and no opportunity for judicial review over the way the decision was reached.

It is not surprising that authorities such as the late Professor de Smith condemned privilege hearings as a 'travesty of justice' in which biased MPs acted as judges in their own cause. He argued cogently that, with a modern independent judiciary, such privileges were not necessary and that the House's jurisdiction over punishable contempts and breaches of privilege should be transferred to the courts so that these matters are subject to due process of law.

Similarly it has been argued that the House no longer needs the absolute rights to freedom of speech granted in respect of 'proceedings in Parliament' by art 9 of the Bill of Rights 1689. Such freedom has the potential to become a licence to defame, to be used irresponsibly by publicity-seeking members. Whilst the House, through the Speaker, has the power under its internal standing orders to discipline members who abuse the right, it appears that the House has been very reluctant to exercise such discipline, at least over an MP who criticises the conduct of outsiders. When an MP criticises the behaviour or integrity of a fellow MP this is usually taken more seriously and the speaker will demand a retraction and issue warnings about the need for 'parliamentary language in respect of the honourable members of this House'. Some MPs, eg Labour MPs Brian Sedgemore and Tam Dalyell in the 1980s, were suspended from sittings of the House because of their refusals to retract accusations against particular MPs (who were also government ministers).

Patricia Leopold ([1981] PL 30) suggests that the House should introduce new safeguards on this matter, eg new conventions which oblige MPs to give advance notice to the person they intend to criticise, and to use all other methods to establish the truth of particular rumours/allegations before ventilating them under the cover of privilege. Others have argued that the absolute privilege under art 9 should be replaced by the defence of qualified privilege, giving MPs the same degree of protection as given to everyone else by the law of defamation.

The fact that MPs can now waive parliamentary privilege in order to pursue actions for defamation where they seek to adduce as evidence their statements made during the course of parliamentary proceedings (see s13 Defamation Act 1996) has also been criticised. Opponents of the change have warned against upsetting the delicate balance of the unwritten constitution, and have pointed out that it might result in Parliament surrendering its collective privilege at the behest of one member. It was also envisaged that conflicts between Parliament and the courts could arise where it was alleged in the course of an MP being cross-examined that he or she had lied to the House of Commons. The contrary view, expressed by Lord Hoffmann during the passage of what became the 1996 Act, is that, whilst there is an obvious public interest in maintaining absolute privilege in respect of proceedings in Parliament, there is (arguably) no obvious corresponding public interest in allowing absolute privilege to those commenting upon the way in which members discharge their functions in the House.

Further difficulties remain in respect of determining the scope of the concept of 'proceedings in Parliament': see the inability of the Judicial Committee of the Privy Council to reach a decided view on this point in the reference arising from the *Strauss* case: see *Case of GWR Strauss MP* (1957–58) HC 227. Only a bold judge would feel able to give the benefit of any doubt to the citizen when faced with a claim to privilege, eg Popplewell J in declaring that the Register of MPs' Interests was not privileged in *Rost* v *Edwards* (1990) The Times 16 February. Miss Leopold ([1990] PL 475) commends this 'robust' attitude but argues that the matter is too important to be left to haphazard development of the common law, contending that the area of privilege requires codification on lines of Australia's Parliamentary Proceedings Act 1987.

In this regard it should be noted that s13(5) of the Defamation Act 1996 does attempt such a codification for the purposes of that provision and defines proceedings in Parliament as encompassing:

a) the giving of evidence before either House or a committee;

b) the presentation or submission of a document to either House or a committee;

c) the preparation of a document for the purposes of or incidental to the transacting of any such business;

d) the formulation, making or publication of a document, including a report, by or pursuant to an order of either House or a committee; and

e) any communication with the Parliamentary Commissioner for Standards or any person having functions in connection with the registration of members' interests.

Chapter 8

The Executive: Responsible Government

8.1   Introduction

8.2   Key points

8.3   Key cases and statute

8.4   Questions and suggested solutions

8.1 Introduction

The executive includes the monarchy, ministers, central government, the civil service, armed forces and the police. The monarchy is bound by convention and executive functions are largely exercised by ministers. With the advent of the Cabinet, policies decided by government form the basis of legislation passed by Parliament. The Prime Minister enjoys enormous powers because of his position as head of the Cabinet.

8.2 Key points

The Prime Minister

Formal position of the Prime Minister

a) The office of Prime Minister is a de facto institution recognised by statute but governed mainly by convention.

b) The office of Prime Minister is invariably held together with the office of First Lord of the Treasury: Ministerial and Other Salaries Act 1975.

c) On the creation of the Civil Service Department in 1968 the Prime Minister became Minister for the Civil Service.

Choosing a Prime Minister

a) The choice of Prime Minister is a matter for the Queen alone in the exercise of the sovereign's personal prerogative.

b) By convention however the Queen should choose that person who is able to command the support of the majority in the House of Commons.

Functions of the Prime Minister

a) Formation of the government. Ministers are appointed by the Queen on the advice of the Prime Minister. All ministers must be or become members of one or other House of Parliament. There may be up to 95 holders of ministerial office in the House of Commons: House of Commons Disqualification Act 1975.

b) Formation of the Cabinet. The Prime Minister has effectively unrestricted choice in terms of appointment, subject only to the need to ensure that the Cabinet represents the spread of opinion within the parliamentary party.

c) Presiding over Cabinet meetings. The Prime Minister presides over full Cabinet meetings and also over meetings of the most important committees of the Cabinet. The Prime Minister decides the agenda for Cabinet meetings and controls discussion within the Cabinet. At the conclusion of a Cabinet meeting no formal vote is taken on the policy decided; it is for the Prime Minister to sum up the consensus opinion. The Cabinet Secretariat is directly responsible to the Prime Minister and the allocation of functions between Cabinet, committees of the Cabinet and individual departments is controlled by him.

d) The organisation and control of central government. The Prime Minister decides how government functions should be allocated between departments and may create, amalgamate or abolish government departments. The Prime Minister may also take an interest in the affairs of particular departments and intervene personally in major issues and take decisions without consulting Cabinet.

e) Powers of patronage. By convention the Prime Minister advises the Queen on the granting of peerages and other honours and on appointments to certain high offices of state.

f) Advising the sovereign. The Prime Minister is the main channel of communication between the Cabinet and the sovereign, and it is his duty to keep the Queen informed on matters of state.

g) Presentation and defence of government policy. Prime Minister's interventions in debate always attract media attention. The Prime Minister also controls government communications and the dissemination of information.

The Cabinet

Composition of the Cabinet

The number of ministers in the Cabinet is the sole choice of the Prime Minister. Usually it comprises between 18 and 23 members. The composition of the Cabinet is also a matter for the Prime Minister's discretion. However, by convention and custom certain ministers are always members of the Cabinet.

Conventions relating to Cabinet government

a) The Queen must act on the advice of her ministers.

b) The Cabinet must always tender unanimous advice.

c) The Cabinet must obtain and maintain a majority in the House of Commons on all major matters of policy.

d) The Cabinet must produce a 'Queen's Speech' at the opening of each session of Parliament, stating the legislation which it proposes during that session.

e) The 'mandate' doctrine requires the government's statement in the Queen's speech to be consistent with the policy on which they were elected.

Cabinet committees

A complicated system of Cabinet committees exists to facilitate the discussion and formulation of policy options and to co-ordinate the activities of the various government departments, with regard to policy.

The Cabinet Secretariat

In 1917 a Secretary to the Cabinet was appointed to service Cabinet and Cabinet committee meetings, take minutes and circulate details of conclusions reached in Cabinet. The Secretariat is headed by the Permanent Secretary to the Cabinet Office who is directly responsible to the Prime Minister.

Prime Minister's Policy Unit

The Prime Minister maintains a Policy Unit in Downing Street, independent of the Cabinet Office.

Cabinet secrecy

As all ministers must support government policy it is desirable that the process by which such policy decisions are made be kept secret, unless the Prime Minister decides otherwise, therefore secrecy is attached to discussions in Cabinet, Cabinet papers and the proceedings of Cabinet committees.

Prime Ministerial or Cabinet government?

a) The Cabinet is the engine house of government. Administrative action is co-ordinated and legislative initiatives sanctioned in the Cabinet. Cabinet can therefore exert significant control over Parliament.

However, the special position enjoyed by the Prime Minister has led some authorities to the conclusion that Cabinet government has now given way to Prime Ministerial government.

A Prime Minister is, however, dependent on the support of Cabinet members which once withdrawn makes continued office untenable. This was the position when Margaret Thatcher resigned following the party vote on the leadership contest. It had originally been her intention to continue to the final ballot but she was advised against this action by ministers.

b) The power of Prime Minister relative to the Cabinet depends upon several factors:

   i)   The personality of the particular Prime Minister.

   ii) The standing of the Prime Minister both in Parliament and in the Party.

   ii) Whether the Prime Minister is minded to take full advantage of the conventional powers available to the holder of the office.

Collective responsibility

The doctrine of collective responsibility involves two rules:

a) The rule that the government must resign if it loses the support of the House of Commons.

   The Prime Minister and his ministers are collectively responsible to Parliament for the conduct of national affairs. If the Prime Minister loses support in Parliament he must resign or seek a dissolution of Parliament.

b) The rule that the government must speak with one voice.

   i)   All members of the government share in the collective responsibility of the government, and ministers may not publicly criticise or dissociate themselves from the government policy.

   ii) A Cabinet minister who feels unable to agree with his colleagues should resign.

   iii) The rule is closely related to that of Cabinet secrecy. As all ministers must support government policy it is desirable that the process by which such policy decisions are made be kept secret.

   iv) The rule increases party discipline and unity within the government and also serves to strengthen the authority of the Prime Minister in relation to his colleagues.

Agreements to differ

Occasionally it may be politically impossible for the Cabinet to maintain a collective front.

a) The National government 1932. The Liberal members of the National government only agreed to remain in the government on condition that they were allowed to speak and vote against it on the question of the imposition of tariffs.

b) The Labour government 1975. The Labour Cabinet 'agreed to differ' on the question of the United Kingdom's continued membership of the European Community.

Individual responsibility

Ministers are responsible to Parliament for their own actions, omissions and mistakes as well as for those of the officials in their departments. Normally criticism should be directed at the minister rather than at any civil servant who may be at fault. This principle is said to help preserve the anonymity, and therefore the objectivity and efficiency, of the Civil Service.

Ministerial responsibility for departmental maladministration

Two questions arise from the minister's departmental responsibility:

a) Is the minister obliged to accept responsibility for every piece of maladministration within his department?

b) If maladministration is found to have occurred is the minister under a duty to resign?

Situations in which a minister must accept responsibility

In a debate on the Crichel Down Affair 1954, the Home Secretary stated his views as to when a minister must accept responsibility and not blame his civil servants:

a) A minister must protect a civil servant who has carried out his explicit orders.

b) A minister must defend a civil servant who acts properly in accordance with the policy laid down by the minister.

c) Where an official makes a mistake or causes some delay, but not on an important issue of policy and not where a claim to individual rights is seriously involved, the minister acknowledges the mistake and he accepts the responsibility although he is not personally involved.

d) Where action has been taken by a civil servant of which the minister disapproves and has no previous knowledge, and the conduct of the official is reprehensible, there is no obligation on a minister to endorse what he believes to be wrong or to defend what are clearly shown to be errors of his officers. He remains, however, constitutionally responsible to Parliament for the fact that something has gone wrong, but this does not affect his power to control and discipline his staff.

Is there a duty to resign?

There is no suggestion that a minister has to resign if he does accept responsibility. Whether a minister has to resign or not depends upon a variety of political factors including:

a) the temperament of the minister;

b) the attitude of the Prime Minister; and

c) the mood of the party and the tone of the Opposition.

Note the recent tendency to confine responsibility to 'policy' rather than 'operation' of policy.

The courts and ministerial responsibility

While the courts cannot enforce the convention of ministerial responsibility they are prepared to acknowledge its existence: *Carltona Ltd* v *Commissioners of Works* [1943] 2 All ER 560.

8.3 Key cases and statute

- *Attorney-General* v *Jonathan Cape Ltd* [1976] QB 752 (CA)
  Convention of collective responsibility recognised by the courts

- *Carltona Ltd* v *Commissioner of Works* [1943] 2 All ER 560 (CA)
  Judicial recognition of the convention of ministerial responsibility

- *M* v *Home Office* [1993] 3 WLR 433; [1993] 3 All ER 537 (HL)
  Judicial assumption that ministerial responsibility would ensure compliance with court order

- House of Commons Disqualification Act 1975 – limits the number of minister in the House of Commons

8.4 Questions and suggested solutions

QUESTION ONE

Compare and contrast the effectiveness of judicial and parliamentary controls over the exercise of prerogative executive powers by government ministers.

University of London LLB Examination
(for External Students) Constitutional law June 1996 Q6

General Comment

The question involves a detailed discussion of the cases involved in examining the exercise of the prerogative. Candidates should be familiar with the decision of the House of Lords in the so-called GCHQ case and its potential as revealed in subsequent cases.

With reference to parliamentary control in this area some of the knowledge in relation to the role of the Attorney-General may be utilised. Candidates should be familiar with the operation of the prerogative in foreign affairs (acts of State) and how these are or are not controlled by Parliament.

Skeleton Solution

Definition of royal prerogative – who exercises it? – the attitude of the courts to its exercise: *Council of Civil Service Unions v Minister for the Civil Service – ex parte Everett – ex parte Bentley* – prerogative and statutory authority – parliamentary control – the role of the Attorney-General – the prerogative in foreign affairs – conclusion.

Suggested Solution

The royal prerogative consists of those powers that are unique and inherent to the Crown. These powers are in the majority of cases exercised by the Crown in an executive capacity, by which is meant the government. The prerogative is a non-statutory power, which may be described as having a common law source, or recognised by the common law. Its extent is finite and since the seventeenth century it is clear from judicial pronouncements that it cannot be extended. In the words of Lord Diplock in *BBC v Johns* [1965] Ch 32:

'It is 350 years and a civil war too late for the Queen's courts to broaden the prerogative.'

The seminal case, which defined the attitude of the courts to the attempt by the Crown to extend the prerogative, is the *Case of Proclamations* (1611) 12 Co Rep 74. James I sought to create a new offence without seeking parliamentary approval. The court was robust in quashing such a use or misuse of the prerogative. Coke CJ held that: 'the King hath no prerogative, but that which the law of the land allows him'.

Since the *Case of Proclamations* it has become clear that the Crown cannot create a new offence or in other ways punish its subjects except by an Act of Parliament.

The seventeenth-century pronouncement by Coke CJ in relation to the courts determining the extent of the prerogative has survived intact, and if the British Constitution has any fundamentals then this might be one of them. It was not, however, until relatively recently that the courts felt confident enough to challenge the exercise of the prerogative by the executive. Dicey *Law of the Constitution* (10th edn, 1959) argued that the prerogative may be seen as an arbitrary power in the sense that once the courts have determined its existence they will no longer utilise their jurisdictional powers to examine the adequacy of the grounds upon which it has been exercised. A change in judicial attitudes was foreshadowed by Lord Denning in *Laker Airways v Department of Trade* [1976] 3 WLR 537 and was expanded upon by the House of Lords in the leading case of *Council of Civil Service Unions v Minister for the Civil Service* [1985] AC 374.

This latter case centres on the government intelligence institution known as GCHQ, a public service institution under the Foreign and Commonwealth Office. As a result of civil service industrial action the government, acting under an Order in Council issued by virtue of the prerogative, sought to ban trade union membership for those working at the institution. This was done without any prior consultation. The prerogative power involved was the power to regulate the Home Civil Service.

The House of Lords was presented with the question as to whether the exercise of the prerogative could be examined in the courts. The Lords answered in the affirmative though this did not apply to all the prerogative powers and not under all circumstances. Lord Diplock held that judicial review had developed to a stage where one could classify under three heads the grounds upon which administrative action was subject to control by judicial review: illegality; irrationality; and procedural impropriety. There was in this case procedural impropriety, as the unions had not been consulted before the ban was imposed. Their Lordships were, however, agreed, following earlier precedents, that procedural impropriety must give way to national security.

The importance of the case lies not, however, upon its particular facts but rather its potential. The House of Lords was unanimous in holding that the prerogative is capable of judicial review in its exercise; the difference of opinion centred around how the courts were to determine which prerogatives were so capable. Lord Scarman emphasised the subject matter, while Lord Roskill argued that certain prerogatives, such as the making of treaties and the defence of the realm, were not in their nature amenable to judicial review.

The decision in the GCHQ case has been followed by other judgments, for example, rendering the issuance or non-issuance of passports subject to judicial review (*R v Secretary of State for Foreign and Commonwealth Affairs, ex parte Everett* [1989] 1 All ER 655), and even a willingness to urge the Home Secretary to 'think again' in his refusal to exercise his prerogative of pardon: *R v Secretary of State for the Home Department, ex parte Bentley* [1994] 4 All ER 442. Nor will the courts refrain from holding a minister of the Crown to be personally liable in his official capacity for contempt of court: *M v Home Office* [1993] 3 WLR 433.

The courts have also been active in examining the relationship between the prerogative and statutes as a source of power. In *Attorney-General v De Keyser's Royal Hotel Ltd* [1920] AC 508 the House of Lords emphasised that the courts will not permit the use of the prerogative when a statute covers the same area. The Crown is obliged to use the statute even if the terms are less advantageous to it. What exactly happens to the prerogatives in these circumstances is unclear, but Lord Atkinson was of the opinion that the prerogative went into abeyance. A statute may of course abolish the prerogative, as with the Crown Proceedings Act 1947, rather than just covering the same area. The case of *De Keyser's Royal Hotel* presumes that the Crown has a monopoly of power. In an area where this is not the case, the Court of Appeal has been willing (*R v Secretary of State for the Home Department, ex parte Northumbria Police Authority* [1988] 1 All ER 556) to hold that a statutory power and a prerogative power may co-exist covering the same subject matter (the issuance of riot gear to the police) but only where they are exercised by separate bodies – the police authority and the Home Secretary.

The courts have taken a more robust attitude when discussing this relationship in other areas. In *R v Secretary of State for the Home Department, ex parte Fire Brigades Union* [1995] 2 WLR 1 the Home Secretary had attempted to use the prerogative to amend the workings of the Criminal Injuries Compensation Scheme, which had itself been set up under the royal prerogative. By a majority the House of Lords ruled that this was unlawful. There was an alternative scheme from the Criminal Justice Act 1988 already on the statue book (but not yet in force), and the Home Secretary could neither abuse his power to introduce that by deciding never to do so, nor could he frustrate the will of Parliament by introducing a scheme so different to that which they had approved.

Parliamentary control over the governmental exercise of the prerogative varies in effectiveness depending upon the subject matter. As has been mentioned, the signing of treaties is a prerogative act and whether they are ever discussed or approved by Parliament often depends upon the will of the executive. If, however, a treaty is to have domestic effect (as with European Community and Union treaties), then an Act of Parliament must be passed. A declaration of war is also a prerogative power and, for instance, the declaration of war against Germany in 1939 was carried out without parliamentary approval. The Crown does not, however, have any independent source of revenue, and if Parliament were to oppose the military action then the government would run out of money.

Individual office holders in the exercise of their prerogative functions are not in some cases answerable to the courts but are answerable to Parliament. The Attorney-General in performing his role as a quasi-judicial officer of the Crown is not answerable to the courts, but is answerable to Parliament, and theoretically could be asked to resign after a vote of no confidence. Similarly, moves by the court notwithstanding, the Home Secretary is answerable to Parliament for his acts or omissions in not granting a prerogative of mercy or pardon.

The above is, of course, dependent upon the workings of the House of Commons, and if the government of the day can maintain a majority in any vote of confidence then the office holder will survive. Other prerogatives, such as the granting of honours, are not open to parliamentary scrutiny neither are those involving defence of the realm.

One may conclude that while the courts are now robust in examining the prerogative, and more particularly its exercise, parliamentary control is hindered by the impact of the party system upon the workings of the House of Commons in particular. There is a word of warning, though. One should not draw far-reaching conclusions from particular events. On the facts of the GCHQ case the trade unions failed in their case but the potential of the House of Lords' decision was there for all to see. Similarly, the perceived weakness of Parliament in controlling the prerogative exercise by ministers could be reversed if minority governments were to become the norm rather than the exception.

QUESTION TWO

'The doctrine of individual and collective responsibility requires greater clarification if members of government are to be confined within the rule of law.'

Discuss.

University of London LLB Examination
(for External Students) Constitutional law June 1997 Q5

General Comment

The question clearly calls for an explanation of the doctrines of collective and ministerial responsibility, and the concept of the rule of law, but the link between responsible government and the rule of law must be explored as well. The impact of recent developments such as the Nolan Committee recommendations, and the Scott Report also needs to be considered.

Skeleton Solution

What is collective responsibility? – what is ministerial responsibility? – what is meant by the rule of law? – what is the relationship between these doctrines? – are there clear rules? – what dangers exist? – what attempts have been made at clarification?

Suggested Solution

There are two main constitutional conventions that govern the activities of government ministers, namely collective responsibility and individual ministerial responsibility. The convention of collective responsibility is traditionally evidenced by two separate conventions: that the government must resign if it loses the support of the House of Commons; that the government must speak with one voice. In practice this means that ministers must support each other in public, and support agreed Cabinet policy. Individual ministerial responsibility has, traditionally, two aspects: the individual responsibility of ministers to Parliament for decisions taken in their departments, whether by themselves or by their civil servants; and responsibility for the conduct of private life, to the extent that it might impinge upon a minister's ability to discharge his or her functions effectively.

What is the relationship between these doctrines of responsibility and the rule of law? The traditional view of the rule of law is that the law should be certain (as opposed to arbitrary), and that no one should be above the law, in the sense that all should be equally subject to the rule of law. The difficulty in confining the doctrines of responsible government within the concept of the rule of law lies, initially at least, in the fact that the doctrines are not rooted in law at all, but in convention. Conventions are the custom and practice of government that pertain in those areas where no statute law or common law applies. Conventions often reflect 'efficient' constitutional practice and are borne out of pragmatism, for example the convention that a government should resign if it loses a vote of 'no confidence' in the House of Commons. If a government were to ignore this convention it could remain in office, but it would not be in power, as it would have lost the ability to determine the legislative programme of the House of Commons, hence the need to request a dissolution of Parliament. On the other hand, even though conventions are not, in the technical sense, laws, one should look at the way in which ministers regard them. If conventions are observed as if they are laws, then there is a strong argument that, in a sense, conventions come within the scope of the rule of law.

Given that responsible government is, therefore, largely a matter of convention, as opposed to law, much depends on how certain these conventions are. As regards collective responsibility the position is tolerably clear. Constitutional practice indicates that ministers do resign when they cannot agree with their colleagues. Michael Heseltine's resignation over the Westland affair is an example. Where, however, the disagreements threaten to split the Cabinet there is the possibility that there might be an 'agreement to differ'. In 1932 the Liberal members of the National government only agreed to remain on condition that they were allowed to speak and vote against it on the question of the imposition of tariffs. In 1975, the Labour Cabinet agreed to differ on the question of the United Kingdom's continued membership of the EEC. It could be argued that a new convention is emerging to the effect that collective responsibility applies except where the Prime Minister of the day allows it to be relaxed. This, however, is such a flexible notion that most would say it goes against the argument that collective responsibility is actually governed by any rules, and therefore confined by the rule of law. Perhaps the more pertinent question to ask is whether or not the doctrine of collective responsibility needs to be clarified any further. There is much to be said for a flexible doctrine that can adapt to the political situation facing any particular government, for example disagreement amongst ministers over the decision to join a single European currency. This is all the more so where the opposition appears split on the same issue.

How clear are the conventions relating ministerial responsibility? In theory, ministers are responsible to Parliament for their own actions, omissions and mistakes as well as for those of the officials in their departments. In its classical form, the convention is that criticism should be directed at the minister rather than at any civil servant who may be at fault, and that in cases where there has been serious mismanagement of a department's affairs, it is the minister who resigns. This convention reflects the theory that individual civil servants are meant to remain anonymous, so as to promote the objectivity and efficiency, of the Civil Service. The Crichel Down affair is an oft-cited example of this convention in operation. In more modern times one might point to the resignation of Lord Carrington over the invasion of the Falkland Islands by the Argentinians. Increasingly, however, ministers have adopted the view that they should not be criticised for shortcomings of which they are not aware, and which they could not reasonably have been expected to discover, or which do not occur as a foreseeable result of their own actions. This is allied to the changes in ministerial responsibility resulting from the transfer of departmental functions to the Next Steps agencies.

Increasingly ministers criticised for departmental failings are drawing a distinction between their policies and the execution of those policies by agency staff. Provided the minister sacks the head of the relevant agency when something goes seriously wrong he will feel that he has discharged his ministerial responsibility: see the action taken by Michael Howard as Home Secretary in sacking the Chief Executive of the Prison Service following a number of escapes from Parkhurst Prison. The weaknesses in the doctrine of ministerial responsibility were further exposed by the 'Arms to Iraq' affair. The Scott Report (1996) indicated that guidelines on arms exports had been relaxed, so as to permit the export of militarily useful equipment to countries such as Iraq; that this information had been withheld from Parliament; and that the government had appeared to be willing to rely on public interest immunity certificates being granted to suppress the evidence concerning the changes to the guidelines with the possibility that innocent persons might have been convicted of breaching them. Sir Richard Scott concluded that the doctrine of ministerial responsibility had not operated effectively to ensure that the House of Commons was kept aware of changes in government policy regarding arms sales, and that the usual mechanisms for enforcing ministerial responsibility, such as parliamentary questions and hearings of select committees, had not adduced accurate answers. In a subsequent report, the Public Service Committee of the House of Commons concluded that ministerial responsibility in the modern constitution was not based on a convention of resignation in the wake of departmental failings, but on one of keeping Parliament fully and accurately informed. In short a minister should really only resign if found to have knowingly lied to Parliament. This emphasises that ministerial responsibility has, to some extent, evolved from being a doctrine concerned with responsibility for departments, to being one concerned with effective accountability in the House of Commons.

As regards the personal conduct of ministers, or those closely connected to them, there is no hard and fast convention regarding resignation. Everything depends on the extent to which they are able to command the respect of colleagues and the public at large. Extra-marital activities that suggest subterfuge and deceit generally lead to resignation because they cast doubt upon the honesty of a minister. If it is a minister whose son is discovered trading in illegal substances however, there would appear to be no reason to resign provided there has been no attempt at a cover-up.

All of this suggests that the doctrine of individual ministerial responsibility is more difficult to reconcile with the notion of the rule of law, because there is so little clarity regarding when a minister should resign or how he should conduct himself. As a response to this, and in the wake of the Nolan Committee Report on Standards in Public Life, the code of practice, known as *Questions of Procedure for Ministers*, has been revised. Essentially it is an attempt to codify the rules relating to ministerial behaviour. Amongst other things it provides that ministers must give accurate and truthful information to Parliament, correcting any inadvertent error at the earliest opportunity, and makes clear that ministers who knowingly mislead Parliament will be expected to offer their resignation to the Prime Minister.

The revised Code provides greater clarity, therefore, but does not answer criticisms regarding the extent to which such matters are confined by the rule of law, as the Code does not have the status of law. It is enforced by the Prime Minister, and the sanctions are a matter for him. Overall, given the extent to which political expediency plays a part in determining the behaviour of ministers, it is difficult to see what tighter legal controls could achieve.

QUESTION THREE

'Parliamentary experience of recent years has demonstrated that collectively Members (of the House of Commons) can exercise the political will necessary to provide the parameters within which the Government can govern, albeit of necessity in a limited and generally negative way.' (Norton)

Discuss.

University of London LLB Examination
(for External Students) Constitutional Law June 1990 Q1

General Comment

A difficult question that requires students to identify ways in which MPs can influence and hold to account the government.

Skeleton Solution

Parliamentary accountability – the extent to which government is truly accountable for its actions: conventions of accountability; committee system; ombudsman; debate, question time – conclusion: separation of powers; legislature's control over the executive.

Suggested Solution

The starting point of the constitution is the representation of the electorate in Parliament, which is the supreme and sovereign law maker. Developed from this is the notion that the electorate thereby makes its preferred choice of government. However, for obvious practical reasons, elections cannot be held every year, nor can referendums be held on all points of importance that arise during a government's term of office. Thus, the accountability of government directly to the electorate is only periodic and it is this situation that gives rise to the fear of the possibility of an 'elective dictatorship', with a carte blanche to govern in whichever way it pleases for the term of its office.

To a certain extent this is an ill-founded fear since the final reckoning will ultimately come with the dissolution of Parliament. Of more concern, however, is the situation that arises where, for the most part, a government's policies and style of government finds general approval, but where particular measures are potentially constitutionally threatening.

In such circumstances, government becomes indirectly accountable to the representatives of the electorate in Parliament and as such Parliament is termed the 'watchdog' of executive action. Since the Commons is the elected chamber and the focus of most political activity, without dismissing the important work of the Lords, it must clearly be the area where the ground rules of governmental activity are laid down.

Thus in purist theory, the political arm of the executive is collectively responsible to Parliament in general and to the House of Commons in particular. The idiomatic traditions of Parliament provide the forum for the supervision of government. The experience of recent years has brought much attention to bear on how effective these complex constraints and restrictions are when the Commons is effectively dominated by the party that holds office.

Before considering in detail the general parliamentary restrictions on government activity, it must be made clear that the mere fact that a party commands a majority in the House does not guarantee a majority of votes. Even where the whip system that urges members to comply is in strict operation, a member cannot be forcibly compelled to vote with the government. Although the price of such rebellion might be suspension from the parliamentary party, such defiance often has a profound political consequence and may be the prompt for revision of legislation when the action is taken in concert.

As well as such purely political considerations, the application of conventions relating to the accountability individually and collectively of ministers establishes a further set of checks that are enforced through Parliament. The intense political embarrassment caused by ministerial or departmental misfeasance usually finds its focus in parliamentary questions or debates, where, on serious issues, the choice of either a convincing explanation or resignation is expected to be forthcoming.

Similarly, where decisions are made at Cabinet level, ministers are held collectively to account to Parliament. As De Smith observes, if a minister dissents he should resign first, and then publicly distance himself from the subject in contention. However, the purist theory lacks a little in substance, since a suspension of the convention is possible and the government attitude seems to be enshrined not a little in Mr Callaghan's remark that 'I certainly think the doctrine should apply, except in cases where I announce that it does not.' This indeed indicates the extent of the 'flexibility' of our unwritten constitution.

Parliament, if it feels so inclined, may censure the government with a motion of no confidence where the government is held to be collectively responsible. Of convention, such a motion, if it were successful, would prompt the resignation of the government. In recent years, however, Mrs Thatcher was censured on specific issues without subsequently leaving office. Once again it is the 'flexible' constitution at work. The significance of such a motion is to be viewed more in terms of a political tactic and a method of attracting media attention.

A more direct and effective control of government is the need for parliamentary approval for the financing of government initiatives. Since Parliament holds the country's purse strings, the government must inspire enough confidence in the Commons, at least to provide funding for new policies. The structure of government finance is necessarily complex, but the parliamentary system is structured so as to cope with these rigours. Central to this system is the Public Accounts Committee, which, although reflecting the parliamentary representation of the parties, has such a non-partisan reputation that it is, by convention, chaired by a member of the opposition. Although it primarily seeks out financial irregularities, it also monitors extravagant spending and imprudent contractual transactions.

Extensive powers of discovery and enquiry were conferred on the Treasury and Civil Service Committee, which was set up in 1979, to the extent that scrutinising Treasury policy is within the Committee's brief. In such ways Parliament tacitly defines the parameters within which the executive can finance its policies.

Aside from these financial controls, the standing orders and procedures of the Commons provide adequate opportunities for confrontation of the government by the opposition and their own backbenchers on contentious issues. Debating opportunities on the Queen's speech, budget and on opposition days, motions of censure and others and emergency debates take on more significance with the eye of the country fixed on television.

The committee system now mirrors the departmental organisation of central government with the setting up of select committees to examine the expenditure, administration and policy of various designated government departments. Their powers are the same as those of the Treasury and Civil Service Committee and are brought together under the auspices of the Liaison Committee. The force of the House's authority and powers to punish for contempt are behind these committees.

The teeth of the Defence Select Committee were tested during the 'Westland Affair' (1986) when it sought to discover the names of civil servants who were responsible for the leaking of a letter from the Solicitor General. Although the government achieved a compromise, the Committee never conceded that in law there were any governmental restraints on the exercise of its functions.

The departmental select committee system is generally regarded as a forum for more in-depth and informed discussion than is available elsewhere in Parliament. Furthermore, their unanimous, but often powerfully critical reports, such as that of the Foreign Affairs Committee on government proposals to raise fees for overseas university students, have certainly had effects on executive policy. However, the paucity of free debating time means that only a handful of the reports have had full discussion on the floor of the House of Commons.

Parliament's role as the arena for airing criticism of the government has been significantly augmented by the advent of television cameras. Certainly the parliamentary proceeding that most captivates the imagination of the electorate is

Question Time, when the government at least appears to be under the most stringent attack. The extent to which the request for oral or written answers to questions to any minister is actually laying down the parameters of government, rather than political point scoring, is somewhat questionable. However, it is clear that the electoral fortunes of a party or MP may be decided in the cut and thrust of these brief sessions, something of which the government is clearly aware. However, De Smith's view that 'a question to a minister is rather a method of ventilating a grievance than of securing a remedy' is perhaps the most realistic approach.

In addition to the practical limitations of parliamentary questions as a method of scrutinising the government, certain questions may be refused if they lie outside the sphere of competence of a minister. Answers may not be forthcoming if the matter is sub judice, or simply because an answer would cost more than £250, the current ceiling for expenditure on parliamentary answers.

A final method available to members to ensure the maintenance of the standards of government is by directing the Parliamentary Commissioner for Administration to investigate alleged maladministration. However, this function is one that is seldom exercised collectively, and therefore merits no detailed discussion.

Thus, having explored the way in which members might scrutinise the executive, we must assess the truth of Norton's assertions. In our parliamentary system, strong reliance is placed upon adherence to conventions. The effect of disapproving motions relating to conventions of responsibility cannot be denied; resignations in the 1988–89 parliamentary session underline this. However, the change in attitude towards, for example, the motion of censure, demonstrates that reliance on convention as a method of executive control is unsatisfactory, particularly when a government commands a sizeable majority in the Commons.

Equally, there are limits on the extent to which control of the government can be exercised by intermittent rebellions of backbench members, who stand to lose their status within the parliamentary party and with the electorate.

Financial control holds out the most practical promise as delineating the parameters of government, but once again is subject to the control of the majority party in the House, which is almost always subject to strict party discipline.

It is therefore in the arena of the debating floor and during Question Time, which, due to its high media profile, is of great significance in terms of public opinion, that the democratic check on the executive finds its strongest weapon. Where MPs collectively know that public opinion supports them against government policy, even backbenchers of the party in power may find a reservoir of courage to criticise and rebel.

Conversely, the committee system is increasingly being regarded as the part of the Commons where much of the serious work goes on. With its smaller and more informed membership, and its greater opportunities for detailed and lengthy scrutiny, as well as the tendency of committees to be less partisan or concerned with political point scoring, this forum has become in many ways a powerhouse of the democratic process. Opportunities exist not only to criticise, but also to make searching enquiries of the way in which the process of government is carried on.

It is difficult to envisage, however, what Norton's conception of a positive way of providing the parameters within which government can govern would amount to. Obviously, the doctrine of the separation of powers prevents excessive interference by the legislature in executive functions. Thus, the positive function of members must be to maintain and enforce the constitutional safeguards against abuse of executive power. Since these safeguards are largely in the nature of conventions, then following the general view that they are adhered to since their breach would result in political embarrassment, Parliament's only significant function is to heighten the electorate's awareness of government threats to the constitution. It is arguable that this role is better performed by the media, although it cannot compel ministers to account. More importantly parliamentary committees can extract information in a way that need not be as self-consciously populist as the methods employed on the floor of the House of Commons.

In the final analysis, any weaknesses or limitations in the methods available to members who wish to lay down the parameters for good government have to be put down to the inherent weaknesses of our constitution. Additionally, it must be remembered that excessive interference in executive functions by the legislature is constitutionally undesirable.

QUESTION FOUR

To what extent, if at all, is it true to say that the conventions of individual and collective ministerial responsibility are twins and yet incompatible?

University of London LLB Examination
(for External Students) Constitutional Law June 1986 Q6

General Comment

This question involves discussion of the conventions of collective and individual responsibility and comment upon the inter-relationship between them, in particular the overlaps which seem to exist in their application.

Skeleton Solution

Introduction – the doctrine of responsible government – collective responsibility: the content and application of, and the justification for, the convention – individual responsibility: the content and application of, and the justification for, the convention – the possibility for conflict in the application of collective and individual responsibility.

Suggested Solution

Democracy requires that those who govern should be responsible to those whom they govern. The convention of ministerial responsibility seeks to achieve this aim. It has two aspects. Firstly, the collective responsibility of the government as a whole to Parliament and, secondly the individual responsibility of ministers to Parliament for decisions, taken in their departments, whether by themselves or by their civil servants.

The doctrine of collective responsibility involves two rules. Firstly, it is accepted that the government must resign if it loses the support of the House of Commons. The Prime Minister and his ministers are collectively responsible to Parliament for the conduct of national affairs. If the Prime Minister loses support in Parliament he must resign or seek a dissolution of parliament. The rule does not mean that the government must resign whenever it is defeated on any issue. There has to be a clear-cut defeat for the government on a matter of policy.

Second, the doctrine of collective responsibility involves the rule that the government must speak with one voice. All members of the government share in the collective responsibility of the government, and ministers may not publicly criticise or dissociate themselves from government policy. The essence of collective responsibility is that the Cabinet should be seen to be in agreement: a Cabinet minister who feels unable to agree with his colleagues should resign. The constitutional justification for the rule is that the answerability of the government to Parliament would be severely impaired if individual ministers were able to say that they personally did not agree with decisions taken in Cabinet. Ministers, including non-Cabinet members, are normally bound therefore not to differ publicly from Cabinet decisions nor to speak or vote against the government in Parliament. The rule increases party discipline and unity within the government, strengthens the government in Parliament and reinforces the secrecy of decision making within the Cabinet thereby minimising public disagreement between both ministers and departments of state. It also serves to strengthen the authority of the Prime Minister in relation to his colleagues.

The convention of individual responsibility requires that ministers are responsible to Parliament for their own actions, omissions and mistakes as well as for those of the officials in their departments. This principle is said to help preserve the anonymity and therefore the objectivity and efficiency of the civil service. Thus, government Bills are introduced into Parliament by the departmental ministers, who are responsible for the proposals they contain. In debates concerning the work of individual departments, the minister concerned is expected to reply to the criticisms raised and usually seek to defend the department. Ministers are also expected to meet the reasonable requests of members for information concerning their departments and answer questions relating to their departments at question time.

It can be seen therefore that in many respects the relationship between individual and collective responsibility is very close and to this extent they may be viewed as twins. However, there is also in some respects a high degree of incompatibility between the two. For instance, if responsibility for making of policy decisions lies collectively with the whole government, is it not inconsistent to hold the departmental minister individually responsible for the implementation of that policy? Many of the decisions announced by a minister will have been taken or approved in Cabinet or by Cabinet committees and to this extent the doctrine of collective responsibility will attach to them. Similarly, while a departmental minister may have the authority to make decisions relating exclusively to the sphere for which he is responsible, on many matters he may have to consult with other departments, for example the Treasury. Should that minister then be held responsible for the consequences? Conversely, if a minister is facing censure in Parliament as a result of his departmental policies, he may be individually responsible and accountable to Parliament, but he can nevertheless expect to receive the support of his governmental colleagues by bringing collective responsibility into play.

Of course, both individual and collective responsibility are rules of convention governed largely by political expediency and in consequence their practice may bear little relation to their theory. While their theory therefore may give an impression of incompatibility, the practical application of these conventions, looked at in their political context and judged on their particular facts, may explain the apparent incompatibility.

QUESTION FIVE

'If a mistake is made in a government department the minister is responsible even if he knew nothing about it.' 'A minister cannot be blamed for a mistake made if he did not make it himself.'

Consider these contrasting views.

University of London LLB Examination
(for External Students) Constitutional Law June 1989 Q4

General Comment

A straightforward question on individual responsibility.

Skeleton Solution

Discuss individual responsibility giving examples which are relevant – a lot depends on the attitude of PM of the day – contrast Crichel Down criteria with recent examples of resignations.

Suggested Solution

In any democratic state it is a requirement that the people who govern should be responsible to those whom they govern. In the UK, for instance, responsibility is collective ie the government as a whole is responsible to Parliament and responsibility is individual ie individual ministers are responsible to Parliament for decisions taken by them or their civil servants in their departments. The principle of individual ministerial responsibility developed historically before the doctrine of collective responsibility. Collective and individual responsibility are rules of convention and as such are flexible concepts since conventions are rules of political practice regarded as binding by those to whom they apply but everyone recognises that they are subject to exceptions. Neither of the two quotations is an accurate statement of the requirements of individual ministerial responsibility, which it is well nigh impossible to formulate in a way which indicates in every case what the outcome will be for a minister who has made a mistake or whose department has in some way failed.

A minister is responsible for his or her personal acts whether or not he or she is a member of the Cabinet. Responsibility will also include general conduct in the relevant department and any acts or omissions done in the name of the department. The responsibility may be legal or political or a combination of these. It seems that the meaning of responsibility and the persons or bodies to whom it is owed will vary according to the circumstances.

One of the practical expressions of individual ministerial responsibility is that a minister is required to answer questions in Parliament with regard to the conduct of officials in his department although questions may be disallowed because of the sub judice rule or because of national security. It is true that a minister need not accept responsibility if an official has committed a dishonest act, exceeded his authority or disobeyed instructions. He cannot, however, totally absolve himself and he will be required to explain in public what has happened. In this sense the minister will – whether he is to blame or not – have to 'carry the can'. The minister must also, of course, when required, explain government policy in relation to his department. In the event that the minister's replies fail to satisfy MPs or the Lords a motion to reduce the minister's salary or to censure him may result, but because of party discipline these are rare. In order to consider the truth or otherwise of the quotations it is now necessary to consider some precedents in detail categorising them, if possible, under one of the quotations.

Perhaps one of the clearest examples of a minister resigning because of a mistake, even though he knew nothing of it at the time it occurred, is that of Sir Thomas Dugdale who resigned as Minister of Agriculture as a result of the Crichel Down Affair in 1954: In doing so he took responsibility for alleged maladministration by senior civil servants without his knowledge. Some commentators have sought to explain this resignation on the basis that compulsory purchase was involved, (a matter about which the electorate were extremely sensitive at the time) but it certainly stands as a most stringent example of the 'rule' in force, particularly since the maladministration affected only one family and was a matter of embarrassment rather than one where severe loss either financial or in terms of physical wellbeing was concerned.

Lord Carrington's resignation in 1982 as Secretary of State for Foreign Affairs together with those of the other Foreign Office ministers who resigned with him can also be seen as an example of the first quotation in that it could be argued that Lord Carrington was poorly advised during the negotiations with Argentina over the Falkland Islands but personally made no mistake. On the other hand one could argue that he himself was culpable in that the department's failure to predict the invasion was an indication that it was inefficient or ill run and that in his position he should himself have been better informed and better able to foresee the invasion.

In recent times a rather different attitude has been taken in relation to mistakes by civil servants; whereas formerly the minister maintained the anonymity of the civil servant and would take responsibility in certain recent cases the blame has been laid squarely at the feet of civil servants (who have sometimes been disciplined) whilst ministers have felt no compunction to resign. An example of the 'rule' set out in the second quotation is the Maze Prison breakout, which was followed by resignation of civil servants but no ministerial departures.

If the first quotation is correct then a fortiori it would be expected that any minister himself making a mistake would have to take responsibility for it and very likely resign. If one examines some recent resignations and calls for resignation one can see that ministerial mistakes do not necessarily result in resignation.

The second quotation also tends to imply that a minister who personally makes a mistake will be 'blamed'; and the concomitant of this would very likely be resignation. If one examines recent cases one can see that there is no hard and fast rule. Some mistakes by ministers lead to resignations others merely to calls by the Opposition for resignation. Whether a minister survives a mistake seems to depend upon factors such as whether he nevertheless retains the confidence of the Prime Minister and the Cabinet, the view of the backbenchers of his own party and the level of public outcry. For instance Sir Leon Brittan initially survived calls for his resignation as Secretary of State for Trade and Industry over allegations that he had misled the Commons about a letter from British Aerospace to the government during the Westland Helicopter Affair in 1986. His survival was due to the continued support of Prime Minister and Cabinet. However when his behaviour (in authorising a leak to the press of a letter sent by the law officers to Michael Heseltine and then arguably covering up what had been done) came to light, several weeks later not even the Cabinet's support could protect his position when the Conservative backbenchers withdrew their support from him and he was forced to resign. In December 1988 Edwina Currie resigned as a Health Minister after over enthusiastic and somewhat misleading comments on the level of salmonella infection in poultry production. Her fault was to alienate poultry producers who had suffered severe financial loss and the government was forced to mount a costly compensation scheme. The remarks cost Mrs Currie her job but was she simply unlucky? Had there been some other important news story on the day of her remarks perhaps the media and the public would have overlooked them entirely – they would not then have been a 'mistake' and there would have been no resignation.

A further issue to consider in relation to both quotations is the increasing 'agensificisation' of the work of government, which results in the distancing of ministers from the execution of policy. For example, the Home Secretary has increasingly refused to take responsibility for failures within the prison system following the creation of the Prison Service, which was set up as an executive agency to run prisons in the late 1980s. Following a number of high-profile prison escapes, including escapes from Parkhurst, there were calls for the then Home Secretary, Michael Howard, to resign. He, however, argued that the running of prisons was now chiefly the responsibility of the Prison Service, and duly sacked its chief executive Derek Lewis, pointing out that the escapes in question were not the direct result of any Home Office policy for which the Home Secretary was responsible. It is significant that between 1945 and 1995, only five Cabinet ministers have resigned because of the way in which they have discharged their ministerial functions. Much depends on the attitude of the Prime Minister of the day, the Cabinet and backbenchers and the attitude of the public to the particular mistake. The two contrasting views expressed in the question are not (whether taken singly or together) a sufficient explanation of the difficult and subtle convention of individual ministerial responsibility.

Chapter 9

Judicial Review of Administrative Action

9.1   Introduction

9.2   Key points

9.3   Key cases and statutes

9.4   Questions and suggested solutions

9.1 Introduction

Far from being a separate subject, administrative law is a key aspect of constitutional law. At its core is the role played by the judiciary in ensuring that the executive – for these purposes comprising in its 'narrow' sense government ministers, local authorities, tribunals and other statutory bodies – stays within the limits of its powers. The basis of administrative law is the ultra vires doctrine – the common law notion that a public body should not be permitted to exceed the limits placed on its powers either by statute or common law. In this sense it becomes possible to see administrative law for what it really is – a vital aspect of two key constitutional principles: the separation of powers whereby the judiciary can act as a check and balance on the powers of the executive; and the rule of law doctrine whereby no body should be above the law.

The application for judicial review is the means by which administrative law is brought into effect. Any body with sufficient interest in the matter concerned can apply to the courts to have the legality of the executive action tested. Where it is found to be unlawful it can, at the court's discretion, be struck down by means of an order of certiorari – the effect is that the decision in question becomes a nullity.

In the latter part of the twentieth century the judges grew more confidant in their application of the principles of administrative law, however. The scope of judicial review has been extended to subjectively worded powers vested in ministers and to the exercise of prerogative power. The scope of judicial review has also been extended by the courts adopting a creative approach to the concept of what constitutes a 'public' body. That term is no longer limited to statutory bodies but has been extended to encompass any organisation or person exercising a significant power that affects the public at large, particularly where those affected by the exercise of the power would have no other means of seeking legal control of the way in which the power has been exercised.

The incorporation of the Human Rights Act 1998 into domestic law has started to have a significant impact on judicial review. Breach of Convention rights has effectively emerged as a substantive head of ultra vires as the Act makes it unlawful for any public body to act in a way that conflicts with Convention rights. In reviewing administrative action where Convention rights are in play the courts have embraced the jurisprudence of the European Court of Human Rights, hence there has been a shift towards review based on proportionality as opposed to review based on reasonableness: see further *R (Daly)* v *Secretary of State for the Home Department* [2001] 3 All ER 433.

9.2 Key points

The ultra vires principle

The essence of the High Court's jurisdiction is that it has the power to review the actions of an executive or public law body to determine whether or not that body has acted within the scope of its powers (ie acted 'ultra vires'). In general terms action can be ultra vires because it is incompatible with the express limits laid down in an enabling Act or because it is incompatible with the implied limits that attach to the power provided for in the enabling Act. Of the implied limits there are some that relate to the way in which a decision is made (ie the procedure leading up to the decision) and others that relate to the actual decision itself (ie the reasonableness of the decision), although it would be inaccurate to suggest that the two types of implied limit were mutually exclusive. As indicated above, any statutory or common law power exercised by a decision-maker must accord with the requirements of the European Convention on Human Rights – see s6 Human Rights Act 1998 – hence a public body will be acting ultra vires if it violates an individual's Convention rights.

Breach of natural justice

Where a statute lays down a procedure that a public body must follow before exercising its discretion the courts will ensure that such requirements are complied with, to the extent that they are seen as being mandatory. In many cases there is no statutory procedure, or the statute does not cover all aspects of the procedure. Where the statute is silent the courts will look to the common rules of natural justice to determine what is required.

As a general principle *Ridge* v *Baldwin* [1964] AC 40 provides that the extent to which the common law will require procedural safeguards to be complied with will in turn depend upon the nature of the interest at stake. The more significant the rights affected, and the more significant the impact of the decision on the applicant, the more that will be required in the way of fairness at common law. For these purposes interests are not just traditional property rights: see *Leech* v *Deputy Governor of Parkhurst Prison* [1988] 1 All ER 485. The courts are less likely to intervene on behalf of an applicant who merely seeks a privilege: *R* v *Gaming Board for Great Britain, ex parte Benaim and Khaida* [1970] 2 QB 417. Again, bear in mind that where an individual's civil rights are involved art 6 of the Convention will have to be borne in mind, as it lays down various procedural requirements, such as the absence of bias, commensurate with a fair procedure.

Legitimate expectation

Today the courts will often assess the applicant's entitlement to protection by the rules of natural justice by asking whether or not he has a 'legitimate expectation' of fairness. Four different bases for legitimate expectation can be identified.

a) Where the litigant asserts a substantive right, in the form of an entitlement that should not be denied him: see *R v Secretary of State for the Home Department, ex parte Khan* [1985] 1 All ER 40.

b) Where the applicant's interest lies in some ultimate benefit that he hopes to attain or, possibly, retain. This classification can be traced back to decisions such as *Schmidt v Secretary of State for Home Affairs* [1969] 2 Ch 149 and *R v North and East Devon Health Authority, ex parte Coughlan* [2000] 3 All ER 850.

c) Where the legitimate expectation is used to refer to the fair procedure itself, ie the applicant claims to have a legitimate expectation that the public body will act fairly towards him.

d) Where a particular procedure, not otherwise required by law, has to be followed as a result of a previous promise or course of dealing: see *Attorney-General of Hong Kong v Ng Yuen Shiu* [1983] 2 All ER 346.

Aspects of a fair procedure

There are no set rules on what constitutes a fair procedure at common law – much depends upon the context within which the decision-making process is being conducted. The following points frequently arise, however.

a) Notice of the hearing should be given: see *Glynn v Keele University* [1971] 1 WLR 487. Clearly the more that is at stake for the applicant, the greater the obligation to give notice of the case to be met: see *R v Secretary of State for the Home Department, ex parte Mohammed Al Fayed* [1997] 1 All ER 228.

b) A hearing need not entail an oral hearing: see *Lloyd and Others v McMahon* [1987] 2 WLR 821 and *R v Secretary of State for the Home Department, ex parte Doody and Others* [1993] 3 WLR 154.

c) Fairness may require that the applicant is permitted the right to cross-examine witnesses if a hearing is held: see *R v Army Board of the Defence Council, ex parte Anderson* [1991] 3 All ER 375 and *University of Ceylon v Fernando* [1960] 1 All ER 631.

d) Legal representation should normally be permitted if a hearing is held, but is not always required in order to satisfy the requirements of natural justice. Again much depends on whether the hearing is disciplinary in nature, and the consequences for the applicant if the hearing goes against him: see *R* v *Secretary of State for the Home Department, ex parte Tarrant* [1984] 1 All ER 799.

e) There is no absolute duty to provide reasons for decisions at common law, however the courts increasingly regard the giving of reasons as an aspect of good administrative practice: see *R* v *Secretary of State for the Home Department, ex parte Doody and Others* (above). A useful summary of the current law was provided by Sedley J in *R* v *Higher Education Funding Council, ex parte Institute of Dental Surgery* [1994] 1 All ER 651.

The rule against bias

The rule against bias is a common law doctrine that provides that no man should be a judge in his own cause. Where an applicant can provide the court with evidence of actual bias, the court should be willing to quash the decision in question, subject to any statutory considerations. Apart from actual bias, two types of apparent bias can occur:

a) Financial interest. *Dimes* v *Grand Junction Canal Proprietors* (1852) 3 HL Cas 759 provides that anything other than a remote and negligible financial interest in the subject matter of a dispute will always disqualify the decision-maker.

b) Apparent bias. This can be based on arrange of matters such as political interest, family links, business connections, avowed prejudices etc: see *R* v *Sussex Justices, ex parte McCarthy* [1924] 1 KB 256 and *R* v *Bow Street Metropolitan Stipendiary Magistrate, ex parte Pinochet Ugarte (No 1)* [1998] 4 All ER 897.

Whether or not such connections or interests will disqualify a decision-maker on the grounds of bias will depend upon the application of the test for bias: see *Porter* v *Magill; Weeks* v *Magill* [2002] 1 All ER 465. The correct test to be applied to determine whether or not there was a reasonable apprehension of bias was the modified form of the test in *R* v *Gough* [1993] AC 646, approved by the court in *Re Medicaments and Related Classes of Goods (No 2)* [2001] 1 WLR 700, whereby the court should first ascertain all the relevant circumstances and then ask whether those circumstances would lead a fair-minded and informed observer to conclude that there was a real possibility that the tribunal was biased.

Reasonableness

A decision may be ultra vires because it is in itself unreasonable. This is a broad concept covering decisions that are so wrong-headed that no sane person could have arrived at the conclusion (eg *Williams* v *Giddy* [1911] AC 381 and *Backhouse* v *Lambeth London Borough Council* (1972) 116 SJ 802), decisions based on irrelevant considerations, decisions where relevant considerations have not been taken into account and, increasingly, decisions that are ultra vires on the grounds of proportionality.

The modern basis for the test for reasonableness in English administrative law is derived from the Court of Appeal's decision in *Associated Provincial Picture Houses Ltd v Wednesbury Corporation* [1948] 1 KB 223 – the test to be applied is whether or not the public body has acted in a manner that no reasonable authority would have. Lord Diplock, in the course of his speech in *Council of Civil Service Unions* v *Minister for the Civil Service* [1984] 3 All ER 935 preferred to use the term 'irrationality' to describe what had hitherto traditionally been regarded as Wednesbury unreasonableness. He stated (at p951):

> 'By "irrationality" I mean what can by now be succinctly referred to as "*Wednesbury* unreasonableness"... It applies to a decision which is so outrageous in its defiance of logic or of accepted moral standards that no sensible person who had applied his mind to the question to be decided could have arrived at it. Whether a decision falls within this category is a question that judges by their training and experience should be well equipped to answer, or else there would be something badly wrong without judicial system ... "Irrationality" by now can stand on its own feet as an accepted ground on which a decision may be attacked by judicial review.'

a) The doctrine of proportionality provides that action will be unlawful if it is disproportionate in its effect, or relative to what is required. The doctrine might, for example, be invoked where a punishment is out of all proportion to the wrongdoing alleged: see *R* v *Barnsley Metropolitan Borough Council, ex parte Hook* [1976] 1 WLR 1052. In *R* v *Chief Constable of Sussex, ex parte International Trader's Ferry Ltd* [1999] 1 All ER 129 Lord Slynn noted that even if the Chief Constable's decisions survived scrutiny on the basis of the domestic law concept of *Wednesbury* reasonableness, it was not necessarily the case that they would also be lawful within the context of Community law, where a key question was whether they were proportionate to the problem they sought to deal with.

b) Proportionality is also a feature of the jurisprudence of the European Court of Human Rights and is increasingly featuring in applications for judicial review where the Human Rights Act 1998 is being relied upon. In *R (Daly)* v *Secretary of State for the Home Department* [2001] 3 All ER 433 Lord Steyn observed (comparing the traditional *Wednesbury* approach to review and the approach of a reviewing court applying principles of proportionality):

> 'Most cases would be decided in the same way whichever approach is adopted. But the intensity of review is somewhat greater under the proportionality approach ... the doctrine of proportionality may require the reviewing court to assess the balance which the decision-maker has struck, not merely whether it is within the range of rational or reasonable decisions.'

The proportionality test may go further than the traditional grounds of review inasmuch as it may require attention to be directed to the relative weight accorded to interests and considerations. It is clear that the intensity of review in a public law case will depend on the subject matter in hand – the more fundamental rights are affected by a decision, the more justification will have to be provided by the decision-maker.

c) If Convention rights are interfered with the court will first ask whether the interference was necessary – ie could the public body have achieved its legitin aims adopting means that caused less interference with the applicant's rights? fact that a policy, of necessity, interferes with Convention rights does not automatically mean that action taken in pursuance of that policy is therefore lawful: see comments of Schiemann LJ in *R* v *Secretary of State for the Home Department parte Isiko* (2001) The Times 20 February. If the interference is shown to be necessary the court will go on to consider the question of proportionality – did the interference go further than was necessary to achieve the legitimate aims of the public body? In considering this second question the court will be considering whether the public body has struck a fair balance between the legitimate aims of the impugned administrative action on the one hand, and the affected person's Convention rights on the other. Allowing the public body an appropriate margin of appreciation, the court would intervene if the weight accorded to the legitimate aims was unfair and unreasonable: see further *R (Samaroo)* v *Secretary of State for the Home Department* (2001) The Times 18 September. As indicated above the 'proportionality' approach inevitably leads the court into a closer examination of the factual basis for the actions of a public body, and hence the merits of the decision – although in a sense they will be doing what they have always done, ie looking to see whether the decision-maker has given sufficient weight to relevant factors, or too much weight to irrelevant factors. The role of the court in judicial review proceedings has not become one of substituting its view for that of the primary decision-maker, but it does have an enhanced role in assessing the legality of the decisions of public bodies where Convention rights are in issue.

d) The courts will intervene if a public body fails to take into account relevant considerations prior to exercising a statutory discretion: see the key case of *Padfield* v *Minister of Agriculture* [1968] AC 997 where the Minister was held to have abused his discretion by not acting in accordance with the aims and objects of the parent Act, the Agricultural Marketing Act 1958. Similarly, if there is evidence that a public body has taken irrelevant considerations into account the courts can strike the decision down: see *Sydney Municipal Council* v *Campbell* [1925] AC 388; *R* v *Hillingdon London Borough Council, ex parte Royco Homes Ltd* [1974] QB 720; and *R* v *Ealing London Borough Council and Others, ex parte Times Newspapers Ltd* (1986) 85 LGR 316. Public bodies such as local authorities have to exercise care regarding the extent to which the exercise of discretion can be impugned on the basis that it is motivated by political dogma or even political correctness: see *R* v *Somerset County Council, ex parte Fewings* [1995] 3 All ER 20, where the Court of Appeal held (by a majority) that a resolution passed by the respondent authority prohibiting stag hunting on certain land within its ownership was unlawful.

e) A public body must have regard to its financial resources when exercising discretion, but only to the extent that resources were intended by Parliament to be a relevant consideration – determining whether or not this is the case can be extremely complex. Compare *R* v *Gloucestershire County Council, ex parte Barry* [1997] 2 WLR 459 with *R* v *East Sussex County Council, ex parte Tandy* [1998] 2 All ER 769.

The application for judicial review

The procedure for an application for judicial review is as laid down in RSC O.53 and s31 of the Supreme Court Act 1981. The following points should be noted:

Is the respondent a public law body?

In *O'Reilly* v *Mackman* [1983] 2 AC 237 the House of Lords held that if the applicant sought to challenge the decision of a public body on an issue of public law the challenge would have to proceed as an application for judicial review – to proceed by way of action would be an abuse of process causing the action to be struck out. A public law body would typically be one that derived its powers from statute – but not necessarily. In *R* v *Panel on Take-overs and Mergers, ex parte Datafin plc* [1987] 2 WLR 699 the court held that the Panel could be reviewed even though it exercised no statutory or prerogative powers, and was not even based on a private contract or constitution. What mattered was that it wielded enormous de facto power to take decisions affecting the public and, significantly, there was no other means by which those affected by the decisions could have challenged them in the courts.

Is the issue a public law issue?

Following *Davy* v *Spelthorne Borough Council* [1984] AC 262 it will not be an abuse of process to proceed by way of action in respect of a private law issue provided the public law issue was merely tangential to the main purpose of the litigation. There are signs that the courts are taking a more flexible approach to the issue: see *Roy* v *Kensington and Chelsea and Westminster Family Practitioner Committee* [1992] 1 AC 624 and *Trustees of the Dennis Rye Pension Fund and Another* v *Sheffield City Council* [1997] 4 All ER 747.

A more flexible approach

The introduction of the new Civil Procedure Rules (CPR) has had a significant impact on the argument about which procedure should be used when proceeding against public bodies. In *Clark* v *University of Lincolnshire and Humberside* [2000] 3 All ER 752 the respondent university contended that C's action was an abuse of process, and that she should have proceeded by way of an application for judicial review – the time limit for which had long since passed. Allowing C's appeal Sedley LJ observed that under the new CPR the courts did not have to counter perceived abuses of process by resort to strict (procedural) exclusionary rules which might in themselves cause unfairness. Just as on a judicial review application the court might extend time limits if justice so required, in a civil suit it could now intervene, notwithstanding the currency of the limitation period, if the entirety of circumstances demonstrated that the court's processes were being misused, or if it was clear that because of the lapse of time or other circumstances no worthwhile relief could be expected.

Lord Woolf MR went on to explain that under the CPR:

> '... if proceedings involving public law issues are commenced by an ordinary action under Pt 7 or Pt 8 [of the CPR] they are now subject to Pt 24. Part 24 is important because it enables the court, either on its own motion or on the application of a party, if it considers that a claimant has no real prospect of succeeding on a claim or an issue, to give summary judgment on the claim or issue. This is a markedly different position from that which existed when *O'Reilly v Mackman* was decided. if a defendant public body or an interested person considers that a claim has no real prospect of success an application can now be made under Pt 24. This restricts the inconvenience to third parties and the administration of public bodies caused by a hopeless claim to which Lord Diplock referred ... The distinction between proceedings under O.53 and an ordinary claim are now limited. Under O.53 the claimant has to obtain permission to bring the proceedings so that the onus is upon him to establish he has a real prospect of success. In the case of ordinary proceedings the defendant has to establish that the proceedings do not have a real prospect of success.'

Does the applicant have locus standi?

On the basis of *Inland Revenue Commissioners* v *National Federation of Self-Employed and Small Businesses* [1982] AC 617, whether or not an applicant seeking judicial review has sufficient interest is to be regarded as a mixed decision of fact and law for the courts to decide on legal principles. The issue should be considered when the application for leave to apply for judicial review is made and, if granted, reconsidered when the actual hearing of the application takes place. There is increasing evidence that the courts are coming to value the role played by certain pressure groups in making applications for judicial review: see *R* v *Secretary of State for Foreign and Commonwealth Affairs, ex parte World Development Movement Ltd* [1995] 1 WLR 386 where significant matters included the need to uphold the rule of law, the fact that no other organisation was likely to launch such a challenge, and the key role played by the applicants in giving advice, guidance and assistance regarding aid.

Is the application out of time?

Applications for judicial review must be made without delay, and at any rate within three months of the action complained: see RSC O.53 r4. Section 31(6) of the Supreme Court Act 1981 provides that the court may refuse an application for judicial review if there has been undue delay, particularly if permitting the application would be likely to cause substantial hardship to, or substantially prejudice the rights of, any person or would be detrimental to good administration. See further *R* v *Stratford-upon-Avon District Council, ex parte Jackson* [1985] 1 WLR 1319 and *R* v *Criminal Injuries Compensation Board, ex parte A* (1999) The Times 26 March.

What remedies are available?

a) A quashing order (formerly referred to as 'certiorari') – effect is to quash the decision of an inferior body.

b) A prohibiting order (formerly referred to as 'prohibition') – an order directed at an inferior body, compelling it to refrain from a course of action, in effect the public law equivalent of an injunction.

c) A mandatory order (formerly referred to as 'mandamus') – an order directed at an inferior body, compelling it to act in accordance with duties to which it is subject.

An applicant for judicial review can also apply for the 'private' law remedies of injunction, declaration and damages. All remedies are at the discretion of the court, and regard will be had to the conduct of the applicant, the availability of other remedies, and the consequences of granting the remedy sought.

9.3 Key cases and statutes

When to use judicial review

• *Clark* v *University of Lincolnshire and Humberside* [2000] 3 All ER 752 (CA)
Flexibility in determining appropriate procedure

• *Davy* v *Spelthorne Borough Council* [1984] AC 262; [1983] 3 All ER 278 (HL)
Public/private dichotomy

• *O'Reilly* v *Mackman* [1983] 2 AC 237; [1982] 3 All ER 1124 (HL)
Whether body amenable to judicial review

• *Poplar Housing Association* v *Donoghue* (2001) The Times 21 June (CA)
Public body for the purposes of the Human Rights Act 1998

• *R* v *Disciplinary Committee of the Jockey Club, ex parte The Aga Khan* [1993] 1 WLR 909; [1993] 2 All ER 853
Public body for the purposes of the Human Rights Act 1998

• *R* v *Panel on Take-Overs and Mergers, ex parte Datafin plc* [1987] 2 WLR 699; [1987] 1 All ER 564 (CA)
Public body for the purposes of the Human Rights Act 1998

• *Roy* v *Kensington and Chelsea and Westminster Family Practitioner Committee* [1992] 2 WLR 239; [1992] 1 All ER 705 (HL)
Whether public law issue

Standing

- *Inland Revenue Commissioners* v *National Federation of Self-Employed and Small Businesses Ltd* [1982] AC 617 (HL)
  Whether pressure group has locus standi

- *R* v *Secretary of State for Foreign Affairs, ex parte World Development Movement Ltd* [1995] 1 All ER 611
  Whether pressure group has locus standi

Delay

- *R* v *Criminal Injuries Compensation Board, ex parte A* (1999) The Times 26 March (HL)
  When court can exercise discretion to allow application out of time

- *R* v *Dairy Produce Quota Tribunal, ex parte Caswell* [1990] 2 AC 738 (HL)
  When court can exercise discretion to allow application out of time

Grounds for review

Express statutory requirements

- *R* v *Secretary of State for the Home Department, ex parte Jeyeanathan* [1999] 3 All ER 231 (CA)
  Whether statutory requirements directory or mandatory

Common law fairness – duty to act fairly

- *McInnes* v *Onslow Fane* [1978] 1 WLR 1520; [1978] 3 All ER 211
  Categories of procedure determining application of natural justice

Legitimate expectation

- *Attorney-General of Hong Kong* v *Ng Yuen Shiu* [1983] 2 AC 629 (PC)
  Legitimate expectation arising from undertaking

- *Council of Civil Service Unions* v *Minister for Civil Service* [1985] AC 374; [1984] 3 All ER 935 (HL)
  Right to be heard before existing right removed

- *R* v *Devon County Council, ex parte Baker* [1995] 1 All ER 73 (CA)
  Legitimate expectation arising from undertaking

- *R* v *North and East Devon Health Authority, ex parte Coughlan* [2000] 3 All ER 850 (CA)
  Legitimate expectation arising from undertaking

Rules of natural justice – right to a fair hearing

- *Lloyd* v *McMahon* [1987] AC 625; [1987] 2 WLR 821 (HL)
  Whether an oral hearing required

- *R* v *Higher Education Funding Council, ex parte Institute of Dental Surgery* [1994] 1 All ER 651
  Whether reasons required

- *R* v *Secretary of State for the Home Department, ex parte Tarrant* [1985] QB 251
  May be unreasonable to prohibit legal representation

- *Ridge* v *Baldwin* [1964] AC 40; [1963] 2 All ER 66 (HL)
  Natural justice depends on rights affected

The rule against bias

- *Dimes* v *Grand Junction Canal* (1852) 3 HL Cas 759 (HL)
  Financial interest

- *Director General of Fair Trading* v *Proprietary Association of Great Britain* (sub nom *Re Medicaments and Related Classes of Goods (No 2)*) [2001] 1 WLR 700 (CA)
  Correct test to be applied

- *Locabail* v *Bayfield* [2000] 1 All ER 65 (CA)
  Bias based on some connection with, or preference for, one of the parties

- *Porter* v *Magill*; *Weeks* v *Magill* [2002] 1 All ER 465
  Correct test to be applied

Improper/ulterior purpose

- *Congreve* v *Home Office* [1976] QB 629; [1976] 1 All ER 697 (CA)
  Power given for one purpose not to be used for another

- *Padfield* v *Minister of Agriculture* [1968] AC 997 (HL)
  Political motivation for not acting is unlawful

Relevant and irrelevant factors

- *Pickwell* v *Camden London Borough Council* [1983] 1 All ER 602
  Weight to be given to competing factors

- *R* v *East Sussex County Council, ex parte Tandy* [1998] 2 All ER 769
  Resources not relevant in determining what was a 'suitable education' for an individual pupil

- *R* v *Gloucestershire County Council, ex parte Barry* [1997] 2 WLR 459
  Relevance of resources in determining the needs of a chronically sick and disabled persons – statute permitted reference to resources

- *R* v *Secretary of State for the Home Department, ex parte Venables and Thompson* [1997] 3 All ER 97 (HL)
  Relevance of public opinion in parole decision

- *R v Somerset County Council, ex parte Fewings* [1995] 1 WLR 1037; [1995] 3 All ER 20 (CA)
  Legality of hunting ban

- *Roberts v Hopwood* [1925] AC 578 (HL)
  Ratepayers versus employees' interests

- *Wheeler v Leicester County Council* [1985] 2 All ER 1106 (HL)
  Political considerations irrelevant in granting permission to use land

The rule against delegation (delegatus non potest delegare)

- *Carltona v Commissioner of Works* [1943] 2 All ER 560 (CA)
  Civil servant acts in the name of the minister

- *R v Secretary of State for the Home Department, ex parte Oladehinde* [1990] 3 WLR 797; [1990] 3 All ER 393 (HL)
  Civil servant acts in the name of the minister

- *Vine v National Dock Labour Board* [1957] AC 488 (HL)
  Judicial function not to be delegated

The rule against fettering discretion by policy

- *British Oxygen Co Ltd v Minister of Technology* [1971] AC 610 (HL)
  Policy legal but must be flexible

Irrationality/unreasonableness

- *Associated Provincial Picture Houses v Wednesbury Corporation* [1948] 1 KB 223; [1947] 2 All ER 680 (CA)
  Ultra vires to act as no reasonable public body would act

- *R v Cambridge District Health Authority, ex parte B* [1995] 1 WLR 898; [1995] 2 All ER 129 (CA)
  Courts will not intervene in rationing of resources

Human rights and judicial review

- *R v Chief Constable of Sussex, ex parte International Trader's Ferry Ltd* [1999] 1 All ER 129
  House of Lords applying the doctrine of proportionality to judge the legality of action taken by the Chief Constable in policing animal rights protests

- *R v Pierson* [1997] 3 All ER 577
  Home Secretary's decision to increase tariffs for life-sentence prisoners quashed by the courts because it contravened the principles of legal certainty and non-retrospectivity

- *R v Secretary of State for the Environment, Transport and the Regions, ex parte Holding and Barnes plc ('Alconbury')* [2001] 2 All ER 929
  Planning process lawful – bias intended

- *R (Daly)* v *Secretary of State for the Home Department* [2001] 3 All ER 433.
  Difference between proportionality and reasonableness as grounds for review

Ousting the jurisdiction of the courts

- *Anisminic* v *Foreign Compensation Commission* [1969] 2 AC 147 (HL)
  Only ultra vires decisions fall outside ouster clauses

Statutes

- Human Rights Act 1998 – creates a new head of ultra vires – acting in breach of Convention rights

- Parliamentary Commissioner Act 1967 – established Parliamentary Commissioner for Administration

- Supreme Court Act 1981 – places the post-1977 procedural reforms on a statutory basis

9.4 Questions and suggested solutions

QUESTION ONE

Discuss, giving examples, the extent to which the courts distinguish between statutory and prerogative powers in judicial review of administrative action.

University of London LLB Examination
(for External Students) Constitutional Law June 1995 Q5

General Comment

This question requires detailed knowledge of the way in which judicial review cases have operated to distinguish between these differing forms of powers. A general discussion of judicial review will not be perceived as answering the question accurately. The student must be careful to structure the answer between the two sides to the question and to introduce some detailed discussion of case law.

Skeleton Solution

Prerogative powers: *Council of Civil Service Unions* v *Minister for the Civil Service* – *BBC* v *Johns* – *Malone* v *Metropolitan Police Commissioner*.

Statute: express and implied limitations – *Wednesbury* unreasonableness – *Ridge* v *Baldwin*.

Suggested Solution

The prerogative is that body of powers and immunities of the Crown which is residual and which is now largely exercised by government ministers on behalf of the Crown.

The prerogative itself derives from the common law and therefore can be fettered or abolished by statute.

The notion that the exercise of prerogative power could be subject to judicial review is a comparatively recent phenomenon. Before the decision in *Council of Civil Service Unions* v *Minister for the Civil Service* [1985] AC 374 (the GCHQ case), the courts restricted their review of the prerogative powers to questions of whether or not a particular prerogative power existed, or whether or not a prerogative power had been supplanted by a statutory power. The traditional view would consider first whether or not the act complained of was an exercise of the prerogative. If the act was found to be such an exercise of power, the courts would decline the jurisdiction to challenge its use. For example, in *Malone* v *Metropolitan Police Commissioner* [1979] Ch 344 the courts recognised the right of the Crown to intercept postal communications as part of the prerogative, but declined to adjudicate on the legality of the way in which this had been done. Further, in *BBC* v *Johns* [1965] Ch 32 it was confirmed that only those powers recognised by the common law would be upheld in the courts. Famously, Diplock LJ held that 'it was 350 years and a civil war too late for the Queen's courts to broaden the prerogative'. The House of Lords in *Gouriet* v *Union of Post Office Workers* [1978] AC 435 rejected a contention that a decision of the Attorney-General not to lend his name to proceedings against a trade union could be reviewed by the courts. In so doing, the House of Lords overturned a decision of Lord Denning in the Court of Appeal, which had found the court competent to review that decision. In *Laker Airways* v *Department of Trade* [1977] 2 All ER 182 Lord Denning argued similarly that the courts could interfere where the executive exercised prerogative powers improperly.

The breakthrough made by the GCHQ case was the recognition by the House of Lords that the actual exercise of prerogative powers itself could be subject to the ultra vires doctrine. The facts of the case arose from a decision by the Foreign Secretary to ban trade unions from the Government Communication Headquarters at Cheltenham. This decision was taken without any prior consultation. The applicant trade union sought judicial review of the decision as an exercise of the government's prerogative powers.

The House of Lords decided that because a power exercised in the sphere of public law was derived from the common law, it did not mean that it should be immune from review. Lord Diplock held that judicial review had developed to the extent where one could classify the grounds for review under three heads: illegality, irrationality, and procedural impropriety. The existence of any of these three would found a justiciable issue.

The right to review the power, however, was qualified. Where the decision was made with reference to the defence of the realm, it would not be reviewable. Therefore, the extent to which the prerogative can be reviewed by the courts is similar to executive acts based upon statutory sources. As in *R* v *Secretary of State for Home Affairs, ex parte Hosenball* [1977] 1 WLR 766, there are principles of public policy which will be applied to the review of a power exercised by the executive, whether that is a statutory or a prerogative power.

Where a power is derived from statute a reviewing court will essentially be engaged in an exercise of statutory interpretation. Statutes will contain express and implied limitations relating to the exercise of the discretion delegated to the decision-maker by Parliament. Where the limitation is expressed in the statute the court will have to determine whether the limitation is mandatory – ie no deviation is permitted, or whether it is directory, meaning that a more flexible approach can be taken. In *R v Secretary of State for the Home Department, ex parte Jeyeanthan* [1999] 3 All ER 231 Lord Woolf MR summarised the correct approach to distinguishing between mandatory and directory provisions in statutes thus: (i) first assess the legislative intention – will substantial compliance suffice?; (ii) if there is non-compliance can it be waived, has it been waived, should it have been waived?; and (iii) what was the consequence of non-compliance (assuming it could have been or was waived)?

Statutory powers are also subject to implies limitations – they must be exercised reasonably and fairly. These are the two great concepts in judicial review that have been developed by the courts in the post-1945 era to bring the executive under closer judicial control. The test for reasonableness is derived from *Associated Provincial Picture Houses Ltd v Wednesbury Corporation* [1948] 1 KB 223 – the test to be applied is whether or not the public body has acted in a manner that no reasonable authority would have. The origins of the modern approach to fairness can be seen in *Ridge v Baldwin* [1964] AC 40.

In conclusion, therefore, it can be said that the same approaches are taken to reviewing the exercise of both statutory and prerogative powers. The point of departure is the issue of justiciability. If the courts conclude that a prerogative power challenge is essentially a policy issue, such as the disposition of troops, or signing a treaty, they will decline jurisdiction and leave the issue to be dealt with through the conventions of responsible government.

QUESTION TWO

To what extent are and should the rules of natural justice be flexible?

University of London LLB Examination
(for External Students) Constitutional Law June 1995 Q8

General Comment

This question gives scope to the candidate to expound on the role of natural justice in constitutional and administrative law in general terms. The candidate must therefore attempt to structure an answer by using case law material to illustrate a particular point of view or to canvass the alternative possible points of view.

Skeleton Solution

General introduction – need for flexibility – analysis of bias rules – highlight inflexible and flexible rules – contrast with fair hearing – give specific examples – right to an oral hearing – legal representation – legitimate expectation – conclusion.

Suggested Solution

Natural justice is concerned with procedural impropriety. It is one of the principles of administrative law that certain powers must be exercised in accordance with natural justice. There are too many variables to allow a precise and uniform code of procedure and this has led to what are sometimes felt to be inconsistencies in approach. The truth of the matter is that the requirements of natural justice, or what fairness requires, will vary according to the context in which the decision making power is being exercised.

A distinction can perhaps be drawn between the rules of natural justice as they apply to the concept of bias, where they are somewhat inflexible, and the rules of natural justice as they apply to the so-called 'fair hearing' rule, where a much more fluid approach is taken.

If a party to a hearing can establish actual bias on the part of a decision-maker a reviewing court will regard that decision-maker as automatically disqualified on the grounds of bias. Most cases in public law, however, are concerned with apparent bias. If the complainant can identify a pecuniary interest on the part of the decision-maker in relation to the matter under consideration this will be fatal to the validity of the decision: see *Dimes v Grand Junction Canal Proprietors* (1852) 3 HL Cas 759. Even this apparently inflexible rule is subject to a number of qualifications, however. Where a pecuniary interest is so minimal or indirect as to be of negligible significance, it will not be used as justification for invalidating a decision: *R v Rand* (1866) LR 1 QB 230. Second, the operation of the rule against pecuniary interest may be affected by statute – an Act of Parliament might provide for a procedure where the decision-maker has an interest in the subject matter. Provided such a provision does not offend against the right to a fair hearing guaranteed by art 6 of the ECHR it will stand: see *R v Secretary of State for the Environment, Transport and the Regions, ex parte Holding and Barnes plc; R v Same, ex parte Alconbury Developments Ltd and Others; Secretary of State for the Environment, Transport and the Regions v Legal and General Assurance Society Ltd* [2001] 2 All ER 929, where the House of Lords upheld the legality of the Secretary of State's role in planning process, even though he had an interest in the outcome of planning appeals. His involvement was important, as he was responsible for the application of government policy in planning decisions.

The situation is perhaps less clear in cases of non-pecuniary interest, although Lord Browne-Wilkinson in *R v Bow Street Metropolitan Stipendiary Magistrate, ex parte Pinochet Ugarte (No 2)* [1999] 1 All ER 577 expressed the view that the rationale disqualifying a judge in pecuniary interest cases applies just as much if the judge's decision will lead to the promotion of a cause in which the judge is involved together with one of the parties.

In *Locabail (UK) Ltd v Bayfield Properties Ltd; Locabail (UK) Ltd v Waldorf Investment Corporation; Timmins v Gormley; Williams v Inspector of Taxes; R v Bristol Betting and Gaming Licensing Committee, ex parte O'Callaghan* [2000] 1 All ER 65. the court sought to offer some general guidance on factors that might or might not lead to a finding of bias in those cases where disqualification was not otherwise automatic. It was thought that no sensible objection could ever be based on factors such as religious persuasion, ethnic origin, gender, age, class, means or sexual orientation. The court doubted whether a challenge could ever succeed on the basis that the adjudicator had a particular social or educational background, employment history, political associations, was a member of any social, sporting or charitable bodies, or had Masonic associations. Also regarded as unimportant were previous judicial decisions, extracurricular utterances and membership of the same Inn, circuit or local Law Society. By contrast it was felt that a real danger of bias might arise where there was a friendship or personal animosity between the judge and a member of the public involved in a case, or if the judge had doubted the credibility of a party in previous proceedings in outspoken terms suggesting that he was unable to approach a party's evidence with an open mind, or if for any other reason there were real grounds for doubting the judge's ability to ignore extraneous considerations and bring an objective judgment to bear on the issues before him.

The test to be applied for bias in non-pecuniary cases does now seem to be settled. In *Porter* v *Magill; Weeks* v *Magill* [2002] 1 All ER 465 the House of Lords held that a court should first ascertain all the relevant circumstances and then ask whether those circumstances would lead a fair-minded and informed observer to conclude that there was a real possibility that the tribunal was biased. This now seems to apply equally to judicial and quasi-judicial proceedings.

As indicated above there is much greater flexibility regarding other aspects of a fair ing. Does natural justice require an oral hearing? It all depends. In *Lloyd* v *McMahon* [1987] 2 WLR 821 Lord Keith stated suggested that it would be easy to envisage cases where an oral hearing would clearly be essential in the interests of ess, for example where there was a dispute as to fact. Lord Mustill in *R* v *Secretary te for the Home Office, ex parte Doody and Others* [1993] 3 WLR 154, in relation to whether or not a prisoner sentenced to mandatory life imprisonment should be given the opportunity to make representations prior to the Home Secretary's determination of the minimum period to be served, observed that the standards of fairness were not immutable. They might change with the passage of time, both in the general and in their application to decisions of a particular type. He emphasised that the principles of fairness were not to be applied identically by rote in every situation. What fairness demanded depended on the context of the decision.

Does fairness require that legal representation should be permitted? Again there is no straight answer. Where an individual's reputation or livelihood is at stake there may be a much stronger argument in favour of legal representation: see *Pett* v *Greyhound Racing Association* [1969] 1 QB 125. All that can be said with any certainty is that where a hearing can have serious consequences for those concerned, the denial of legal representation might not only be unfair but also irrational: see *R* v *Secretary of State for the Home Department, ex parte Tarrant* [1984] 1 All ER 799 – breach of natural justice to deny the prisoner legal representation, given the grave nature of the charge and the consequences for the prisoner of his being found guilty.

Finally, consider the issue of 'legitimate expectation' and its use in determining whether or not the courts should intervene on the grounds of breach of natural justice.

In *R v Devon County Council, ex parte Baker and Another*; *R v Durham County Council, ex parte Curtis and Another* [1995] 1 All ER 73 Simon Brown LJ identified four broad categories of case in which the concept might be relevant.

First, those cases where the litigant asserts a substantive right, in the form of an entitlement that should not be denied him: see *R v Secretary of State for the Home Department, ex parte Khan* [1985] 1 All ER 40. Second, where the applicant's interest lies in some ultimate benefit which he hopes to attain or, possibly, retain. In *R v Rochdale Metropolitan Borough Council, ex parte Schemet* (1992) 91 LGR 425 the applicants successfully established a 'category 2' claim in respect of the local authority's decision to abandon its policy of paying the travelling expenses of children attending schools maintained by a neighbouring authority. Third, there are those cases where the concept of legitimate expectation is used to refer to the fair procedure itself, ie the applicant claims to have a legitimate expectation that the public body will act fairly towards him. Finally, there are those cases where a particular procedure, not otherwise required by law, has to be followed as a result of a previous promise or course of dealing: see *Attorney-General of Hong Kong v Ng Yuen Shiu* [1983] 2 All ER 346.

What the above examples illustrate is that the rules of natural justice can be enormously difficult to pin down. This, it is submitted, is deliberate. The courts want to retain as much flexibility as possible in order to do what appears to be fair in any particular case. There is a trade off here between certainty and justice. What can be observed is that, in general terms, the rules of natural justice will apply more stringently where the rights affected are more fundamental.

QUESTION THREE

Section 2 of the (fictitious) National Health Act 1996, provides that Area Health Authorities 'are under a duty to maintain adequate hospital beds and services to ensure the protection and maintenance of the health of residents in the area'.

In January 1996, the (fictitious) Western Area Health Authority, in an effort to cut costs, decided to close two hospital wards usually reserved for elderly patients requiring long-term care, and a ward containing ten beds reserved for patients in need of either pre- or post-operative intensive care.

In April 1996, Mrs Jones, who is elderly and has no living relatives to care for her, was admitted to the Wellbeing Hospital, a National Health Service hospital in the Western area. In June, however, Mr Smith, a hospital administrator, notified Mrs Jones that she would have to leave hospital within a week, even though she could not care for herself.

In February 1996, Toby, who is six years old, was found to be suffering from a rare bone marrow disease. The Wellbeing Hospital has refused to admit Toby for urgent surgery because of the shortage of beds. His mother, Mrs Brown, has been told that he will have to wait 'for up to three months' for the necessary surgery. She has consulted another doctor, who is a family friend, who has advised her that the delay in treatment could seriously affect Toby's chances of a full recovery from the disease.

Advise Mrs Brown and Mrs Jones as to whether they are entitled to seek a remedy by way of an action for judicial review, and as to the likely outcome of any judicial review proceedings.

University of London LLB Examination
(for External Students) Constitutional Law June 1996 Q8

General Comment

This question involves judicial review. There are a number of issues present in the problem and the candidate should be aware of substantive administrative law and the procedure necessary to obtain a judicial review of an administrative action. The subject necessary involves a consideration of a significant amount of case law. It is normally not necessary or desirable to examine the facts of the cases.

Skeleton Solution

Which procedure – 'sufficient interest' – basis of the claim of Mrs Jones – statutory interpretation, illegality – irrelevant considerations – ignoring relevant considerations – reviewability of spending decisions – whether duty or discretion.

Basis of the claim of Mrs Brown – similar considerations – *Wednesbury* unreasonableness – human rights issues.

Suggested Solution

The Health Authority is a public body – empowered by statute and in receipt of public funds – hence there will be no dispute as to the appropriate procedure to be followed by both Mrs Brown and Mrs Jones. The decisions taken by the Health Authority can only be challenged by way of an application for judicial review.

Both applicants will have to establish that they have sufficient standing to apply – ie that they have locus standi. The Supreme Court Act (SCA) 1981 states that the court will not grant leave for an application for judicial review unless the applicant has 'sufficient interest' or locus standi, ie the applicant must have an interest in the matter for which the application is being made. This is described in *Inland Revenue Commissioners* v *National Federation of Self-Employed and Small Businesses* [1982] AC 617 as 'an interest over and above that of the general public', a categorisation which the courts have expanded and been flexible in determining. Locus standi is determined at two stages of judicial review proceedings. First, when leave to apply is sought and, second, when the court examines the merits of the case: see eg *R* v *Oxford, ex parte Levey* (1996) The Independent 30 October.

In the present case Mrs Brown would appear to have sufficient interest, as she is the mother of Toby. The courts are relatively pragmatic in defining locus standi and, as Lord Diplock argued in the *National Federation* case, there is considerable room for evaluation of this concept. There was a clear demonstration of this in *R* v *IBA, ex parte Whitehouse* (1984) The Times 14 April in which the Divisional Court was prepared to grant Mary Whitehouse locus standi in her attempt to review a decision of the Independent Broadcasting Authority (IBA), on the ground that she was a sole licence holder. In cases involving a matter of public concern the courts are prepared to be open to suggestion with relation to locus standi. In the present instance the attempt to ration surgical care is of obvious public interest and the mother is likely to obtain leave to bring the case. As to Mrs Jones, the courts are also likely to grant her leave as she is certainly going to suffer if she is dismissed from the hospital.

Having established that the two individuals may seek a judicial review upon the basis of their standing, upon what grounds may they challenge their respective decisions?

Mrs Jones

First, we turn to consider the case of Mrs Jones. She is told that she must leave the hospital within a week even though she is unable to care for herself. Section 2 of the (fictitious) statute states that health authorities 'are under a duty to maintain adequate hospital beds and services and to ensure the protection and maintenance of the health of the residents in the area'. Whether or not the authority has acted unlawfully in taking the decision to close the wards on financial grounds will depend on how the courts interpret the statutory duty. In *R* v *Gloucestershire County Council, ex parte Barry* [1997] 2 WLR 459 the House of Lords held that a local authority was entitled to take into account its own resources in determining the manner in which the needs of chronically sick and disabled persons should be met, although resources would not have been relevant in determining what those needs were. By contrast, in *R* v *East Sussex County Council, ex parte Tandy* [1998] 2 All ER 769 the House of Lords held that a local education authority had acted unlawfully in reducing its expenditure on home tuition for special needs pupils because of a lack of resources. The statute in question placed the authority under a duty to provide 'suitable education' for children with special needs. It was held that the availability of resources was an irrelevant consideration in determining what was a 'suitable education' for an individual pupil. The House of Lords reached this conclusion by reference to the fact that other sections of the Act did refer to the efficient use of resources, hence the inference that resources were not relevant in this case.

In the present case Mrs Jones will argue that the duty to provide adequate beds is one that cannot be taken by reference to the availability of resources. It is submitted, however that she will be unsuccessful on this basis. As Lord Browne-Wilkinson noted in *Tandy*, the reasonableness of how a local authority spends scarce financial resources becomes extremely difficult to review once it is within the bounds of reasonableness. The courts are very reluctant to second-guess a local authority in the way in which it spends its limited resources: see also *R* v *Cambridge District Health Authority, ex parte B* [1995] 2 All ER 129.

An alternative, and possibly more promising argument for Mrs Jones, is that she had a legitimate expectation of being accommodated in NHS care having been admitted in April 1996 – especially as she has no one else to care for her. If any express indications were given to her that this would be the case then her argument is that much stronger. Otherwise the legitimate expectation would have to be based on the implied undertakings. The case in point is *R v North and East Devon Health Authority, ex parte Coughlan* [2000] 3 All ER 850. The applicant had been severely injured following a road accident in 1971. She was placed in the long-term care in NHS accommodation and was given an assurance that this would be her home for life. The respondent authority subsequently decided to close Mardon House and transfer the applicant to the care of the local authority. Regarding the promise made to the applicant that she would have a home for life at Mardon House, Lord Woolf MR expressed the view that the undertaking gave rise to a legitimate expectation on the part of the applicant that she would not be moved to another location against her wishes. Although the authority was not irrevocably bound by the undertaking, there was no overriding public interest that justified the court in allowing the authority to resile from it. Further, Lord Woolf observed that the Human Rights Act 1998 could be relevant. Article 8 of the European Convention on Human Rights (ECHR) provides for a right of respect for an individual's home. The action of the respondent authority in deciding to close Mardon House amounted to a breach of art 8 that was not justified by the provisions of art 8(2). These arguments, with suitable adaptation can be invoked by Mrs Jones.

Finally, Mrs Jones may be able to argue that the WAHA has failed in its discretion in deciding to close the two hospital wards reserved for elderly patients. This is a blanket decision not based upon the needs of the patients and not protecting the health of the residents in the area. If a policy is adopted which effectively prevents the relevant institution from examining the merits of individual cases this will prevent the authority from exercising its discretion and render the decision ultra vires: *British Oxygen Co v Minister of Technology* [1971] AC 610.

Mrs Brown

Mrs Brown, on behalf of her son, will have strong grounds to challenge the decision of Wellbeing Hospital. First, is the hospital entitled to refuse the admission of Toby as it appears to be based upon a reason that goes against the statutory duty? While as has been pointed out, the courts are reluctant to become involved in matters of opinion over the allocation of resources, this action appears to be in clear violation of the statutory duty to maintain adequate hospital beds.

Mrs Brown will have a stronger case in arguing that the decision is unreasonable, as it will seriously affect Toby's chance of a full recovery. Unreasonableness is a word which occupies a considerable amount of space when discussing administrative law decisions and is based on the seminal case of *Associated Provincial Picture Houses Ltd v Wednesbury Corporation* [1948] 1 KB 223. In the course of his judgment Lord Green MR held:

> '... if a decision on a competent matter is so unreasonable that no reasonable authority could ever have come to it then the courts can interfere ...'

He did, however, emphasise the caveat that to prove a case of that kind would require something overwhelming, a decision such that no reasonable body of persons could have come to. In this instance Mrs Brown might be able to show that as Toby's chance of recovery is going to be seriously affected then the decision is unreasonable, but the Court of Appeal in *Wednesbury* did emphasise that they should be slow to substitute their own judgment for that of the authority making the decision. In addition, as the doctor giving Mrs Brown his opinion is a family friend the court might question the impartiality of the advice. Mrs Brown will be well advised to seek a separate opinion from a medical practitioner who has no personal or family relationship.

Finally, Mrs Brown could argue that the Health Authority, in not providing more prompt treatment, is violating Toby's right to life, or exposing him to inhumane treatment – arts 2 and 3 of the ECHR are relevant here. There will be argument here as to whether or not arts 2 and 3 rights are engaged in a case such as this, and whether or not any margin of appreciation should be allowed to the authority in determining how to allocate its resources. The courts are likely to be influenced by the fact that forcing the authority to spend money on Toby will mean depriving someone else of treatment. It seems unlikely; therefore, that the courts would want to intervene in an issue such as this unless the authority's decision really was in defiance of all logic.

QUESTION FOUR

To what extent does the Parliamentary Commissioner for Administration fulfil a valuable constitutional role in relation to administration? What reform, if any, would you advocate to his role and jurisdiction?

University of London LLB Examination
(for External Students) Constitutional Law June 1999 Q6

General Comment

A relatively straightforward question on the Parliamentary Commissioner (PCA). The point to note is that the examiner is not asking candidates to write everything they know about the PCA. Comments have to be focused towards the thrust of the question. What useful constitutional purposes does the PCA serve, and how would you reform the role to make it yet more useful? The work of the Select Committee must be adverted to here. Some specific examples of the PCA's achievements should be included to bring the answer to life.

Skeleton Solution

Background to the PCA – relationship with judicial review – compare and contrast – advantages of using the PCA compared to the courts – complaints to MPs – what has the PCA achieved – provide examples – look at possible reforms – build upon the recommendations of the Select Committee – publicity – jurisdiction – enforcement – clarification of role – summary and conclusion.

Suggested Solution

Complaining to the Parliamentary Commissioner for Administration (PCA) represents a remedy available to citizens within the United Kingdom constitution. He is an officer of Parliament, investigating complaints of maladministration brought against government departments and other quangos, but he is also independent, having the same security of tenure as a High Court judge.

To what extent can it be said that he fulfils a valuable constitutional role in relation to the administration?

To answer that question one has to have a grasp of the complimentary relationship that exists between the jurisdiction of the PCA, judicial review and the traditional role of the MP. Judicial review is concerned with challenging allegedly ultra vires action in the courts. The heads of ultra vires are well known. Lord Diplock in *Council of Civil Service Unions* v *Minister for the Civil Service* [1985] AC 374 summarised them as irrationality, illegality and unfairness. There are, however, many administrative failings that a citizen may wish to complain about that do fall within the scope of judicial review. The ultra vires doctrine is concerned with whether or not action is lawful. Administration can be slow, or sloppy, or negligent without actually being 'unlawful' in the technical sense in which that word is used in the sphere of judicial review. The jurisdiction of the PCA is broadly described as being the investigation of complaints of maladministration. This concept is not defined in the Parliamentary Commissioner Act 1967, but the late Richard Crossman, in his so-called 'catalogue', described it as involving rudeness, ineptitude, delay, wrong advice and loss of documents. Hence the PCA can deal with complaints relating to matters that might otherwise have no legal remedy. Indeed the PCA will normally decline to investigate a complaint if it appears that it concerns any action in respect of which the person aggrieved has or had right of appeal, reference or review to or before a tribunal, or has a remedy by way of proceedings in any court of law. An exception can be made if the PCA is nevertheless satisfied that, in the particular circumstances, it is not reasonable to expect the complainant to have pursued some alternative remedy. For example, in *Congreve* v *Home Office* [1976] QB 629 the plaintiff successfully applied for a declaration that the Home Office had acted illegally in revoking the television licences of those who had renewed their licences early to avoid paying the new higher fee. In fact, the action of the Home Office had already been condemned in a special report by the PCA, illustrating the overlap between the powers of the courts and the role of the PCA in policing maladministration.

There may be matters that a citizen feels aggrieved about that do not warrant expenditure on litigation – the PCA procedure can be invoked for the cost of a postage stamp. Also the PCA may be able to secure a remedy that is more appropriate that those obtainable through an application for judicial review. For example, a complaint may result in a form being made more comprehensible, or a process being speeded up. As the investigation is conducted by the PCA no effort is required on the part of the complainant to prepare a prima facie case, unlike the application for judicial review.

The time limit for bringing a complaint at 12 months is more liberal than the three months allowed under RSC O.53.

One of the most valuable aspects of the PCA's role is that when he carries out an investigation he works from within the administration, rather than as an outsider trying to determine what has occurred. Under s5(5) of the 1967 Act it is for the PCA to use his discretion to determine the manner in which a complaint should be investigated. The PCA adopts an investigatory approach to complaints, if possible promoting a friendly settlement between the private individual and government department. The PCA is at liberty to obtain information from such persons and in such manner, and make such inquiries, as he thinks fit. Although his methods can be informal the PCA has powers similar to those of the High Court as regards securing the presence of witnesses and the production of documents, hence he may be able to obtain information unavailable to a constituency MP pursuing a complaint on behalf of a constituent.

What has the PCA achieved in concrete terms? At the micro level the PCA has, over the years, undoubtedly persuaded government departments to improve the quality of administration generally – the many instances cited in the annual reports laid before Parliament attest to this. Many of these small investigations have a 'ripple' effect, whereby one complaint and investigation can lead to a general administrative change that benefits thousands of other citizens in the same situation.

The key high profile achievements include the report on the failure of the Home Office to review the convictions of over 1,500 prisoners who had been sentenced to imprisonment on the strength of the discredited evidence of Home Office forensic scientist Dr Alan Clift. The PCA severely criticised the department for not acting more quickly in the light of what he described as an 'unprecedented pollution of justice'. Similarly high profile was the Barlow Clowes investigation into the granting of credit licences by the Department of Trade and Industry which led, eventually, to the payment of compensation (over £150 million) to those who had lost their investments because of the company's fraudulent activities. Other reports published during the last decade give details of compensation awarded to poultry farmers following a finding of maladministration on the part of the Ministry of Agriculture; criticisms of the planing blight caused by the handling of the Channel tunnel rail link project; and criticisms of the operation of certain aspects of the work of the Child Support Agency.

Arguably the most famous victory for the PCA arose out of the Sachsenhausen case. An Anglo-German Agreement of 1964 provided for £1 million to be paid in compensation to UK citizens who suffered from Nazi persecution during the Second World War. Distribution of this money was left to the discretion of the UK government. The Foreign Office withheld compensation from 12 persons who had been held in detention within the Sachsenhausen concentration camp. Pressure from many MPs failed to get this decision reversed and a complaint of maladministration was referred to the PCA, even though by this time the whole of the £1 million had been distributed to other claimants. After extensive investigations the PCA reported that there were defects in the administrative procedures and an additional £25,000 was made available in order that the complainants might receive the same rate of compensation as successful claimants on the fund.

These high profile cases and the rather more mundane ones serve as a salutary reminder to civil servants that they can be investigated from within the system, and help to maintain a level of public confidence in the administration of government.

How might the role and jurisdiction of the PCA be reformed? The matter was considered by the Select Committee on the Parliamentary Commissioner and its report was published at the end of 1993, *The Powers, Work and Jurisdiction of the Ombudsman* (HC 33–1 (1993)).

Most would agree that greater publicity would be an improvement. It would appear that the general public is still woefully ignorant of the PCA's existence. Complaints rarely exceed 2,000 pa. The need for increased awareness of the PCA's work, not least amongst MPs, was highlighted by the Select Committee, which proposed the circulation of an informal newsletter containing details of the PCA's caseload.

From time to time it has been suggested that the PCA ought to be given some coercive powers. There have been instances where PCA findings have been ignored, most notably in the case of the collapse of the Court Line holiday company, where the PCA criticised the minister concerned for leading the public into believing that the company was sound and that they should continue to book holidays with them. Many members of the public suffered financial loss when the company went into liquidation, but the government department denied any fault on its part.

At present the PCA cannot investigate complaints of maladministration of his own volition, he can only respond to complaints from members of the public. It may be that he could play a more effective role as an administrative watchdog if he was able to instigate inquiries himself. The continued existence of the 'MP filter' has been subject to criticism on the basis that some MPs may adopt a policy of automatically referring complaints to the PCA, and because it may serve to distance the PCA from the public. The Select Committee recommended that the current system be retained, partly because it attached some constitutional significance to the role of the MP in dealing with constituents' complaints, but also because it meant that MPs would be aware of the types of complaints being made about the executive by the public. A further concern was the likely impact on the resources of the PCA's office if the filter was removed. Where complaints are received direct from members of the public there is, in any event, nothing to prevent the PCA from submitting them to Members of Parliament so that they cans be re-submitted to him.

The Select Committee suggested that the PCA should be given an inclusive jurisdiction, ie the 1967 Act should be amended to provide that the PCA can investigate all complaints other than those relating to matters specifically excluded. In particular it was felt that commercial contracts and personnel matters should be included in his remit. The government rejected this proposal, indicating that more could be done via publicity to ensure that the public had a higher level of awareness as to the role of the PCA. The level of complaints rejected because they fall outside the jurisdiction of the PCA indicates that more needs to be done to educate the public in respect of the PCA's role.

Section 12(3) of the 1967 Act provides that nothing in the Act authorises or requires the PCA to question the merits of a decision taken without maladministration by a government department or other authority in the exercise of a discretion vested in that department or authority. This could be revised to avoid confusion, or to make the jurisdiction of the PCA clearer. The section is now seen as meaning that the PCA cannot actually question the merits of a decision taken without maladministration, although he can investigate maladministration in administrative processes and the decisions resulting therefrom. Perhaps he ought to be permitted to question the merits of a decision where appropriate?

In summary the PCA treads a careful course between the constitutional giants of judicial review and ministerial responsibility. To date he has provided a valuable adjunct to both those mechanisms as a means of improving the administration and bringing it to account. Increasing his profile and jurisdiction could help him achieve yet more.

QUESTION FIVE

Critically assess the means by which and extent to which the law and procedure of judicial review ensures a satisfactory balance between the requirements of effective administration under the law and individual rights.

University of London LLB Examination
(for External Students) Constitutional Law June 1998 Q8

General Comment

There is a grave danger with questions of this nature that the candidate will misread the question and proceed to give an account of the process of judicial review. What is required is a critical analysis of two particular aspects, the procedure and the substantive law. A good answer will attempt to show: the limitations of judicial review; the way in which the process has evolved to provide procedural protection to public bodies; and the impact of the Human Rights Act 1998.

Skeleton Solution

Explanation of judicial review – constitutional significance – examination of procedure – *O'Reilly* v *Mackman* – relaxation of rules – advantages for the applicant – major advantages for public bodies – outline the grounds for review – illustrate the ways in which the courts can prevent review – problems of proof – the discretionary factor – impact of Human Rights Act 1998 – conclusion.

Suggested Solution

Judicial review is, in theory, one of the most important mechanisms in the United Kingdom constitution for ensuring that public bodies act within the scope of their powers. The ultra vires principle holds that any action taken by an administrative agency that results in it exceeding its powers will be unlawful and invalid. In other words administrative bodies must act within the limits of the powers given to them, and in that sense are subject to the rule of law as imposed by means of judicial review. The courts can therefore ensure that there are known limits to the powers of administrative agencies, rather than administrative agencies having arbitrary powers over individuals. The courts can also uphold the rule of law by ensuring that the law applies equally to all. Indeed the significance of judicial review lies in the fact that it is a process by which the ordinary citizen can, in principle, challenge the legality of any action in the public law sphere, even that taken by a minister of the Crown. In doing so, to what extent does it achieve a proper balance between the interests of the individual and the interests of administrative agencies?

Turning first to the procedure of judicial review, it is probably true to say that it has favoured the interests of public bodies at the expense of individual citizens. Prior to the decision of the House of Lords in *O'Reilly v Mackman* [1983] 2 AC 237, a citizen seeking to challenge the decision of a public body effectively had the choice of either applying for judicial review, or proceeding by way of action (possibly originating summons). In that case the House of Lords laid down the procedural rule that, subject to a number of exceptions, if a litigant sought to challenge the decision of a public body in respect of an issue of public law, it would be regarded as an abuse of process to proceed by way of action. Effectively the application for judicial review procedure under RSC O.53 had to be used. Lord Diplock observed that, following the changes to the procedure for applying for judicial review introduced in 1977, many of the procedural handicaps that would previously have led a complainant to avoid having to apply for a prerogative order if at all possible had since been removed. In particular he observed that: discovery was now available; interrogatories could now be administered; deponents could now be cross-examined on affidavits; a claim for damages could be added to the application; and a declaration or injunction could now be included in an application for review.

In Lord Diplock's view there were no longer any compelling reasons for permitting a litigant to proceed by way of action in a public law matter. All of this suggests that the judicial review procedure was somehow reformed with the interests of individual litigants in mind. It is submitted that nothing could be further from the truth. Again, it is Lord Diplock's speech that provides the evidence for this view. The judicial review procedure actually provides public bodies with a number of important safeguards. Applications for review have to be made without delay, usually within three months of the action complained of. Compare with the six-year time limit on some actions by writ. It was important that a public body should know quickly of any significant challenge to the legality of its actions in public law so that third-party interests were not adversely affected. These restrictions have been relaxed to some extent in the wake of the Civil Procedure Rules (CPR) that give the courts more discretion regarding the disposal and transfer of cases. In *Clark* v *University of Lincolnshire and Humberside* [2000] 3 All ER 752 Sedley LJ observed that under the CPR the courts did not have to counter perceived abuses of process by resort to strict (procedural) exclusionary rules which might in themselves cause unfairness. Just as on a judicial review application the court might extend time limits if justice so required, in a civil suit it could now intervene, notwithstanding the currency of the limitation period, if the entirety of circumstances demonstrated that the court's processes were being misused, or if it was clear that because of the lapse of time or other circumstances no worthwhile relief could be expected.

The requirement that those seeking review should have to possess 'sufficient interest' in the matter to which their application relates, and should have to obtain leave to apply for review, provides an important 'filter'. By the very nature of their activities public bodies are likely to attract the attention of so-called 'cranks and busybodies'. If a public body is on the receiving end of legal proceedings it must at least put in a defence to stop the process no matter how vexatious and ill-starred the action. Public bodies might thus incur considerable expense in legal costs. With judicial review, however, the applicant must obtain leave – effectively establishing a prima facie case for review. The leave hearing is ex parte in the sense that the respondent public body may not be represented. The application can be dismissed without the public body having to instruct lawyers at all – the court will do the job on its behalf.

As noted above, although the so-called rule in *O'Reilly* v *Mackman* has since been relaxed somewhat, it is still the case that, if in doubt as to the correct procedure, litigants would be advised to opt for judicial review, despite the constraints that it imposes. What is perhaps more significant is that despite the increase in judicial review cases over the last 30 years, the number of applications is still relatively low. This is partly explained by the fact that, in many cases, statute provides an alternative form of challenge, such as an appeal to a minister or tribunal, rendering judicial review inappropriate. It is a matter of speculation, however, as to how many potential litigants are deterred by the time limits, the cost implications or the need to establish standing.

Turning to the actual law of judicial review, by which it is assumed the question is referring to the grounds for review, it can be said that here the courts have striven to develop a body of rules that seek to ensure that administrators act within the scope of the law. The system is not without its shortcomings however. The three broad grounds of ultra vires were usefully summarised by Lord Diplock in *Council of Civil Service Unions* v *Minister for the Civil Service* [1984] 3 All ER 935 as being irrationality, illegality and procedural impropriety. The result is that a citizen can apply for judicial review to challenge the decision of a public body, or body making decisions affecting the public, on the basis that it has not applied the law properly, has 'taken leave of its senses', or has not adhered to the rules of natural justice. Where ultra vires action is identified the decision can be struck down. This all sounds very encouraging and reassuring, but regard must be had to the way the system actually operates in practice.

First, judicial review can only be effective if an application is made. There may be many ultra vires decisions that go unchallenged because those affected are ignorant, impecunious, or simply accept the actions of administrators unquestioningly. Second, the courts may decline to intervene because what is being challenged is a policy issue, the legality of which the courts cannot comment upon. Hence in *R v Cambridge District Health Authority, ex parte B* [1995] 1 WLR 898 the court held that it would not review the budgeting decision taken by a health authority refusing to provide treatment due to lack of resources. The courts will also decline to intervene if they characterise an impugned decision as involving principally a question of fact. In *Puhlhofer v Hillingdon London Borough Council* [1986] 1 All ER 467 the House of Lords held that it was for a local housing authority to determine whether applicants had been provided with 'suitable accommodation'. A closer reading of the judgments will reveal, however, that the House of Lords was concerned that if it allowed the application for judicial review to proceed local authorities might face a huge increase in the number of judicial review cases. An application for judicial review may also be unsuccessful if the court determines that the decision in question falls into the 'non-justiciable' category. The speeches in *Council of Civil Service Unions v Minister for the Civil Service* (above) identify those matters traditionally considered to fall outside the scope of justiciability, including the conduct of foreign affairs, disposition of troops, appointment of ministers and so forth. Courts are particularly reluctant to intervene where a minister claims to have acted to protect national security. In *R v Secretary of State for the Home Department, ex parte Cheblak* [1991] 1 WLR 890 Lord Donaldson MR argued that where the courts declined to review a decision of a minister on the grounds of national security, the constitutional safeguard was supplied by ministerial responsibility to Parliament. The Scott Report, which revealed the extent to which ministers had withheld information from Parliament in respect of arms sales, perhaps casts doubt upon this view.

In the area of human rights there has been a significant shift in favour of the individual as opposed to the public body. Prior to the enactment of the Human Rights Act 1998 the European Convention on Human Rights was merely a persuasive source of law to be referred to where domestic legislation was arguably ambiguous. Post-October 2000, when the Act came fully into force, failure to comply with the Convention has become a ground for applying for judicial review in its own right. Furthermore, the courts have indicated that where Convention rights are in issue a more vigorous approach will be taken to the review of administrative action. As Lord Steyn explained in *R (Daly) v Secretary of State for the Home Department* [2001] 3 All ER 433, the intensity of review is greater under the doctrine of proportionality, which may require the reviewing court to assess the balance which the decision-maker has struck, not merely whether it is within the range of rational or reasonable decisions. The more fundamental rights are affected by a decision, the more justification will have to be provided by the decision-maker.

In conclusion it must be conceded that judicial review has been developed by the judiciary as an exceptionally important constitutional safeguard for individual rights. There is, however, no room for complacency in this regard, and it must be accepted that even under the current system, there are many instances where meritorious cases go unresolved.

Chapter 10

The European Convention on Human Rights

10.1   Introduction

10.2   Key points

10.3   Key cases and statute

10.4   Questions and suggested solutions

10.1 Introduction

The civil liberties enjoyed by citizens of the United Kingdom have, traditionally, been described as 'residual'. What is meant by this is that citizens have been free to do as they please provided their actions have not contravened the law. This position can be contrasted with the position in countries with a written constitution where individual freedoms are usually 'positive', ie defined and protected in a Bill of Rights.

Legislation which curtails freedom includes, for example, public order legislation, laws on obscenity, laws to protect national security and so on. By the same token some legislation confers rights, eg race relations and sex equality. Traditionally the courts have viewed their role as being to protect liberty. Note, however, that under the doctrine of parliamentary sovereignty the government is often able to pass primary legislation that cannot be challenged by the courts. Civil liberties groups complain from time to time that such measures make significant inroads into traditional freedoms.

The incorporation of most aspects of the European Convention on Human Rights in the form of the Human Rights Act 1998 has started to change the whole philosophy of civil rights in the United Kingdom. There are now directly enforceable legal rights to privacy, family life, freedom of expression and public association.

10.2 Key points

Why is a Bill of Rights important?

The common law is inadequate to protect human rights; it lays down negative as opposed to positive rights. For example, there is no positive common law right to freedom of speech but merely a number of rules about what cannot be said, ie defamation, obscenity etc.

Whilst rights are given to the individual by the common law and statute, an individual would have to search through a host of cases and statutory provisions to find out what his civil rights were; much better for such rights to be contained in one document which would be fixed in the mind of each citizen, eg the basic rights contained in the American constitution are known by most United States' citizens.

The United Kingdom lacks a written constitution. In countries with such a written constitution the courts are free to strike down legislation which is in breach of the constitution. In the United Kingdom the concept of parliamentary sovereignty means that Parliament can do no wrong; so long as an Act receives the approval of both Houses of Parliament and the assent of the monarch the courts are bound to apply it even if it does interfere with what elsewhere would be basic civil liberties.

The apparent reluctance of the courts to trespass on the right of Parliament to enact any such legislation as it sees fit further suggests that Parliament ought to be constrained by a document that sets out and protects basic human rights.

The European Convention on Human Rights

The United Kingdom was one of the original signatories to the European Convention on Human Rights, which entered into force in September 1953, but it was not until the Human Rights Act 1998 was enacted that the Convention became directly enforceable as part of the United Kingdom's domestic law.

The rights protected are:

Article 2: Right to life

Article 3: Prohibition of torture

Article 4: Prohibition of slavery and forced labour

Article 5: Right to liberty and security

Article 6: Right to a fair trial

Article 7: No punishment without law

Article 8: Right to respect for private and family life

Article 9: Freedom of thought, conscience and religion

Article 10: Freedom of expression

Article 11: Freedom of assembly and association

Article 12: Right to marry

There are a number of protocols to the European Convention on Human Rights that states can sign up to as they see fit. The First Protocol, to which the United Kingdom is a signatory, provides for peaceful enjoyment of possessions. A number of articles contain express exemption provisions. For example, arts 11(2), 8(2), 9(2) and 10(2). States can apply for a derogation in time of war or public emergency – the United Kingdom applied for a derogation in respect of art 5(3) in the light of the terrorist problem in Northern Ireland: see *Brannigan and McBride* v *United Kingdom* (1993) 17 EHRR 539.

Enforcing these rights at Strasbourg

Since November 1998, under the procedure introduced under Protocol 11, there has been a permanent European Court of Human Rights, replacing the previous structure of Commission and Court. The new Court comprises 40 judges (one from each member state) allocated to committees (three judges to each committee), chambers (comprising seven judges) and a Grand Chamber of 17 judges. The Court is assisted by a single Registry. The revised procedure involves an applicant filing his application with the Court's Registry, which assigns it to a chamber and a judge rapporteur who has responsibility for overseeing the progress of the application. A committee, or tribunal, of judges considers the admissibility of the application and, provided at least one of the three considers it to be admissible, the ruling is communicated to the member state against whom the application has been made. An application will only need to be referred to the Grand Chamber in exceptional cases.

How the Convention is enforced in the United Kingdom

How are Convention issues be brought before the courts?

The 1998 Act does not expressly create a new procedure for raising alleged violations of Convention rights. Section 7(1) envisages that individuals will be able to bring proceedings (or a counterclaim) against a public body in the appropriate court or tribunal 'as may be determined in accordance with rules': s7(2). Section 7(9) provides that these rules are to be made by the Lord Chancellor. Alternatively, litigants will be allowed to 'rely on the Convention right or rights concerned in any legal proceedings' (s7(1)(b)), legal proceedings including, for these purposes, 'proceedings brought by or at the instigation of a public authority; and … an appeal against the decision of a court or tribunal': s7(6)(a) and (b). Only the 'victim' of the alleged unlawful act is permitted to bring proceedings or rely on the Convention in legal proceedings: s7(1). It is clear that many of the cases involving reliance on Convention rights will take the form of applications for judicial review, given that the Act is of direct application to public bodies (see below). The result is that a narrower test for locus standi will be applied in applications alleging a breach of Convention rights, as compared to applications for review generally.

Who can be the subject of these proceedings?

By virtue of s6(1) it becomes unlawful for a public authority to act (or fail to act – see s6(6)) in a way which is incompatible with a Convention right. A public body for these purposes includes a court or tribunal, and 'any person certain of whose functions are functions of a public nature, but does not include either House of the [United Kingdom] Parliament or a person exercising functions in connection with proceedings in the [United Kingdom] Parliament': s6(3). The term 'Parliament' as used in s6(3) does not include the House of Lords in its judicial capacity. By contrast the Scottish Parliament and the Welsh Assembly, as subordinate legislatures, are bound by the 1998 Act. A 'person is not a public authority by virtue only of subsection (3)(b) if the nature of the act is private.' There is evidence, provided by decisions such as *Poplar Housing and Regeneration Community Association Ltd* v *Donoghue* [2001] 4 All ER 604, that the courts will advert to the jurisprudence built up in relation to applications for judicial review in determining whether non-statutory bodies can be regarded as public authorities for these purposes: see for example *R* v *Panel on Take-overs and Mergers, ex parte Datafin plc* [1987] 2 WLR 699. One can assume that bodies such as the BBC, the Church of England and other religious bodies, universities, the governing bodies of various sports associations, self-regulatory bodies, and any organisation that has taken over what was previously a public law function, such as running prisons, could come within the scope of 'public authority' for the purposes of the Act, as regards their public law functions. The press remains outside the scope of the 1998 Act, hence in privacy cases the courts themselves have become the public bodies under a duty to develop domestic law so as to ensure adequate protection of art 8 rights: see further *Douglas* v *Hello! Ltd* [2001] 2 All ER 289.

How should the courts approach a Convention claim?

A court or tribunal called upon to do so, must interpret primary legislation and subordinate legislation 'in a way which is compatible with the Convention rights': s3(1). This duty applies whether the legislation was enacted before or after the coming into force of the Human Rights Act 1998. Section 2(1) of the 1998 Act makes it clear that any court or tribunal determining a question arising in connection with a Convention right must take into account: any judgment, decision, declaration or advisory opinion of the European Court of Human Rights; any opinion of the Commission given in a report adopted under art 31 of the Convention; any decision of the Commission in connection with arts 26 or 27(2) of the Convention, or any decision of the Committee of Ministers taken under art 46 of the Convention, 'whenever made or given, so far as, in the opinion of the court or tribunal, it is relevant to the proceedings in which that question has arisen.'

Note that there is a divergence of judicial opinion as to how far this power of interpretation should be used. In *Poplar Housing and Regeneration Community Association Ltd* v *Donoghue* [2001] 4 All ER 604 Lord Woolf CJ cautioned against judges using the power to re-write legislation – what he described as straying over the line into the area of legislating. By contrast, Lord Steyn in *R* v *A* [2001] 3 All ER 1 showed his willingness to ride roughshod over the 'niceties' of legislation to achieve a reading compatible with the Convention's demands.

What remedies will be available?

A court dealing with an application for judicial review of subordinate legislation would be able to declare it to be ultra vires if it was found to incompatible with the Convention rights. The courts have no such power in relation to primary legislation, however. Indeed s3(2)(b) expressly provides that the section 'does not affect the validity, continuing operation or enforcement of any incompatible primary legislation'. Further the section cannot be relied upon to invalidate incompatible subordinate legislation if '(disregarding any possibility of revocation) primary legislation prevents removal of the incompatibility': s3(2)(c). Where an irreconcilable issue of compatibility arises before the House of Lords, the Judicial Committee of the Privy Council, the Courts-Martial Appeal Court, or the High Court or the Court of Appeal, that court will be empowered to grant a declaration of incompatibility. In relation to subordinate legislation the power to make such declarations will arise provided (disregarding any possibility of revocation) the primary legislation concerned prevents removal of the incompatibility. Where such a declaration is made it does not 'affect the validity, continuing operation or enforcement of the provision in respect of which it is given; and ... is not binding on the parties to the proceedings in which it is made': s4(6). Whilst the 1998 Act does not provide for any new judicial remedies (other than the declaration of incompatibility), a court finding that a public authority as acted unlawfully within the terms of s6 'may grant such relief or remedy, or make such order, within its powers as it considers just and appropriate': s8(1).

Remedial action by ministers

Where a declaration of incompatibility has been made and rights of appeal have been exhausted, abandoned or become time-barred, or it appears to a minister that (in the light of a finding of the European Court of Human Rights) a provision of legislation is incompatible with obligations under the Convention, a minister may, if he considers that there are compelling reasons for so doing, make orders to amend the relevant legislation to the extent that considers necessary to remove the incompatibility: see s10(1) and (2).

Pre-enactment procedures

Section 19 of the 1998 Act places the relevant minister in charge of a Bill under a duty to 'make a statement to the effect that in his view the provisions of the Bill are compatible with the Convention rights', or to make a statement to the effect that 'although he is unable to make a statement of compatibility the government nevertheless wishes the House to proceed with the Bill.' Such statements must be made before the second reading of a Bill, must be in writing and should be published in such manner as the minister considers appropriate.

Is the European Convention on Human Rights the most desirable Bill of Rights?

The European Convention on Human Rights is over 50 years old. It was mooted and designed in the years immediately following the end of the Second World War. Can it really be said to be relevant to what is today a very different world?

It is drafted in very general terms. United Kingdom judges are used to specifically worded statutes that they can and do interpret literally. Will United Kingdom judges be able to deal with such generally worded provisions that will require more than a mere literal interpretation? Even if they are will they be accused of 'making' law and thereby come into conflict with the legislature?

The nature of the rights protected under the Convention is open to question. For example the right to 'liberty and security of the person' (art 5) is expressly subject to a number of exceptions allowing, for example, the lawful detention of persons for the prevention of infectious diseases, of persons of unsound mind, of alcoholics, of vagrants and of drug addicts. Article 11 which protects the 'right of freedom of assembly' etc is subject to restrictions – in particular governments can argue 'national security' as a legitimate reason for denying such a freedom. Finally, art 15 allows a government in time of war or other public emergency to ignore certain of the Convention's provisions. What is a public emergency can be a very subjective matter!

Should the Human Rights Act 1998 have been protected by entrenchment?

Given the doctrine of parliamentary sovereignty entrenchment of domestic legislation in the United Kingdom is problematic. Generally Parliament cannot bind its successors. Accordingly it cannot pass 'unrepealable' Acts: see *Vauxhall Estates* v *Liverpool Corporation* [1932] 1 KB 733 and *Ellen Street Estates Ltd* v *Minister of Health* [1934] 1 KB 590. Thus, in theory, it would be impossible to pass a Bill of Rights which could be 'entrenched' for evermore.

The courts could have been given the express power to disapply legislation found to be incompatible with Convention rights, but this would have represented a constitutional resettlement for which the Labour government responsible for the Human Rights Act 1998 had no political mandate. See as an example of this approach the Canadian Charter of Rights and Freedoms whereby the Canadian courts have been given the power to disapply incompatible legislation, unless the legislation in question expressly states that it is to apply notwithstanding any such incompatibility. The Labour government opted not to copy the approach taken following the incorporation of the Treaty of Rome (as it then was), whereby the European Communities Act 1972 operates to make certain aspects of European Community law directly part of domestic law, as this was a prerequisite of EU membership whilst becoming a signatory to the European Convention on Human Rights created no such obligations.

The Human Rights Act does, however, fall into that category of legislation recognised at common law as 'constitutional'. As Lord Hoffmann explained in *R* v *Secretary of State for the Home Department, ex parte Simms; Same, ex parte O'Brien* [1999] 3 All ER 400, this means that, in the absence of express language or necessary implication to the contrary, the courts presume that even the most general words used in primary Acts are intended to be subject to the basic rights of the individual. Hence the Human Rights Act 1998 can be regarded as entrenched to the extent that it will not be accidentally or impliedly repealed as far as the courts are concerned. Only express repeal can amend or remove the Act.

10.3 Key cases and statute

* *A* v *United Kingdom* Case 100/1997/884/1096 (1998) The Times 1 October (ECHR)
  Beating of child – violation of art 3

* *D* v *United Kingdom* (1997) The Times 12 May
  Deportation as a breach of art 3

* *Douglas* v *Hello! Ltd* [2001] 2 All ER 289
  Article 8 right to privacy and breach of confidence

* *H* v *Mental Health Review Tribunal* (2001) The Times 4 April
  First declaration of incompatibility granted under the Human Rights Act 1998

* *Halford* v *United* Kingdom (1997) The Times 3 July
  Right to privacy

* *Hatton* v *United Kingdom* (2001) The Times 8 October
  Right to family life

* *Poplar Housing and Regeneration Community Association Ltd* v *Donoghue* [2001] 4 All ER 604
  Limited power of interpretation under s3 of the Human Rights Act 1998

* *R* v *A* [2001] 3 All ER 1
  Courts to use interpretive power under s3 Human Rights Act 1998 to the full

* *R* v *Secretary of State for the Environment, Transport and the Regions, ex parte Holding and Barnes plc; R* v *Same, ex parte Alconbury Developments Ltd and Others; Secretary of State for the Environment, Transport and the Regions* v *Legal and General Assurance Society Ltd* [2001] 2 All ER 929
  Impact of Human Rights Act 1998 on the planning appeals system

* *R* v Secretary of *State for the Home Department, ex parte Simms; Same, ex parte O'Brien* [1999] 3 All ER 400
  Human Rights Act 1998 – a constitutional statute not subject to implied repeal

* *R (Daly)* v *Secretary of State for the Home Department* [2001] 3 All ER 433
  Impact of Human Rights Act 1998 on grounds for judicial review

* *R (Pretty)* v *Director of Public Prosecutions* [2002] 1 All ER 1
  Right to life

- *Steel and Others* v *United Kingdom* (1998) The Times 1 October
  Public order laws – whether compliant with Convention

- *Venables* v *News Group Newspapers Ltd* [2001] 1 All ER 908
  Article 8 right to privacy

- Human Rights Act 1998 – incorporates the European Convention on Human Rights

10.4 Questions and suggested solutions

QUESTION ONE

How, following the enactment of the Human Rights Act 1998, does English law uphold
the requirements of the European Convention on Human Rights?

Adapted from University of London LLB Examination
(for External Students) Constitutional Law June 1997 Q6

General Comment

This question requires an examination of the status of the European Convention on
Human Rights in English law. The position during the pre-incorporation period needs
to be explained. Examples of the extent to which the courts were prepared to take the
Convention into account as a persuasive source of law should also be referred to. The
question also requires some examination of how much of the Convention is
incorporated into domestic law and the extent to which it is entrenched.

Skeleton Solution

Overview of the present position – pre-incorporation – current status – use as a source
of law – extent to which the common law upholds rights in any event – how compliance
with ECJ rulings is ensured – effect of Human Rights Act 1998.

Suggested Solution

The European Convention on Human Rights (ECHR) was incorporated into domestic
law by virtue of the Human Rights Act 1998. The short answer to the question set,
therefore, might appear to be that the ECHR is now part of domestic law with the force
of statute and that is the end of the matter. This would, however, be a somewhat over-
simplistic analysis.

It is useful to begin by examining what incorporation was meant to achieve. Prior to
incorporation the ECHR was seen by domestic courts as an international treaty to
which the United Kingdom was a signatory. The ECHR therefore created international
obligations imposed on the United Kingdom as regards other sovereign states. It was
not part of domestic law because it had not been incorporated, ie enacted as an Act of
Parliament. Domestic courts applied the Convention to resolve ambiguities in domestic
legislation, invoking the rule of statutory interpretation that it is presumed that

Parliament would not have legislated in contravention of the United Kingdom's international obligations without clearly flagging that fact. Beyond this, however, the courts were reluctant to give effect to the ECHR in any sense in which it might be said to override domestic law. In *Uppal v Home Office* (1978) The Times 11 November the court rejected the argument that deportation would be a breach of the right to respect for family life under art 8 of the Convention, holding that obligations in international law which were not enforceable as part of English law could not be the subject of declaratory judgments. A request for a declaration that art 8 had been violated by police tapping telephone calls was also famously rejected by the court in *Malone v Metropolitan Police Commissioner* [1979] Ch 344. In *R v Home Secretary, ex parte Bhajan Singh* [1976] QB 198 Lord Denning MR observed that the executive should have regard to the Convention in exercising its discretion because it was, in his view, only a statement of the principles of fair dealing, but the House of Lords made clear in *R v Secretary of State for the Home Department, ex parte Brind* [1991] 2 WLR 588 that a public body, in exercising its discretion, was not bound, in law, to take the Convention into account. In arriving at this conclusion the House of Lords recognised that to have accepted such a contention would have amounted to the incorporation of the Convention via the 'back door'. Some decisions of the domestic courts have been highly debatable in their refusal to take into account the Convention.

How has incorporation changed this state of affairs? The Human Rights Act 1998 is a cleverly drafted piece of legislation. A Bill of Rights is a fundamental constitutional document that would normally form part of the 'higher' law of a written constitution. If the ECHR had been given such status it would have involved a constitutional revolution in the United Kingdom, which operates on the basis of parliamentary sovereignty in the context of an unwritten constitution. Instead the Human Rights Act 1998 walks a tightrope between empowering the judges to bend domestic law so as to ensure compliance with the ECHR, and ensuring that Parliament retains the sovereignty to legislate as it sees fit.

How does achieve this balancing act? Section 2(1) of the Human Rights Act 1998 makes it clear that any court or tribunal determining a question arising in connection with a Convention right must take into account: any judgment, decision, declaration or advisory opinion of the European Court of Human Rights; any opinion of the Commission given in a report adopted under art 31 of the Convention; any decision of the Commission in connection with arts 26 or 27(2) of the Convention, or any decision of the Committee of Ministers taken under art 46 of the Convention, 'whenever made or given, so far as, in the opinion of the court or tribunal, it is relevant to the proceedings in which that question has arisen.' Hence, all ECHR law is immediately made a primary and binding source of law when rights protected by the Convention are in play. Note however the clever conjunction of the duty and the phrase 'take into acconut' – this is not the same as 'must directly apply without modification'. Domestic courts retain the power to advert to ECHR case law and determine that it is not applicable to the case in point.

The more striking duty is that created by s3(1) of the 1998 Act which provides that a court or tribunal called upon to do so, must interpret primary legislation and subordinate legislation 'in a way which is compatible with the Convention rights.'

If this task appears to be impossible, in the sense that the provision cannot be read in a way that achieves compatibility with the ECHR, the higher courts have the power to grant a declaration of incompatibility. The Court of Appeal made the first such declaration in *H* v *Mental Health Review Tribunal* (2001) The Times 4 April – the court was unable to construe the burden of proof provisions relating to applications to the Tribunal in a manner consistent with art 5.

The fact that any domestic legislation pre or post the Human Rights Act 1998 will be read in the context of the ECHR creates as dilemma for the judges. If a domestic statute appears to be incompatible with the requirements of the Convention should the judge exercise the power of interpretation under s3, or simply issue a declaration of incompatibility? The debate is as to whether the courts should adopt a 'narrow' interpretive approach – with the result that limited powers of interpretation may leave the court with no option but to conclude that a statue is incompatible with the Convention and grant a declaration accordingly – or a 'broad' interpretative approach – whereby the need to issue declarations of incompatibility is avoided by a radical and dynamic reading of a statute that ensure compliance with the Convention – even though the meaning given to the statutory provision is the precise opposite of what Parliament appears to have enacted.

Strong support for the broad approach is to be found in the speech of Lord Steyn in *R* v *A* [2001] 3 All ER 1, where it was held that provisions in the s41(3)(c) of the Youth Justice and Criminal Evidence Act 1999 (prohibiting questioning of a complainant regarding her previous sexual history with the defendant in rape trials) had to be read so as permit such questioning in order to ensure compliance with the fair trial requirements under art 6. In Lord Steyn's view s3 of the Human Rights Act 1998 places the courts under a strong interpretative obligation to ensure the conformity of primary legislation with the Convention even if there is no ambiguity in the language of the statute. Critics have argued that this very pro Convention approach, whilst ensuring that the ECHR has full effect in domestic law, involves judges in straying across the line from interpretation to legislating – the domain of Parliament. In *Poplar Housing and Regeneration Community Association Ltd* v *Donoghue* [2001] 4 All ER 604 Lord Woolf CJ expressed the view that s3 of the Human Rights Act 1998 does not entitle a court to legislate – as he saw, it if it is necessary in order to obtain compliance to radically alter the effect of legislation this indicates that more than interpretation is involved.

Many of the cases involving Convention rights will be brought as applications for judicial review – not surprising given that the Human Rights Act 1998 places public bodies under a duty to abide by the ECHR. The courts have responded to this by effectively recognising breach of the Convention as a new head of ultra vires. In *R (Daly)* v *Secretary of State for the Home Department* [2001] 3 All ER 433 the House of Lords noted that the stringency with which the power of judicial review was exercised by the courts would intensify where more fundamental human rights were concerned. In effect a public body is required to provide more by way of justification where it exercises its powers so as to impinge upon the Convention rights. The 'proportionality' basis for review under the jurisprudence of the ECHR is thus more taxing for the public body than the traditional domestic grounds of review such as those based on reasonableness. A court will need to be satisfied that any interference with protected rights is justified in the public interests in a free democratic society.

Two other developments can be seen as very significant in the way in which the ECHR is now given effect in domestic law. The first relates to the fact that the Human Rights Act 1998 only creates obligations for public bodies. Private bodies, such as companies publishing newspapers, are technically outside the ambit of the Act, and therefore are not under a duty to observe rights such as privacy. The courts have embraced the culture of the Convention by seeing themselves as public bodies obliged to uphold Convention rights. The result is that the Human Rights Act 1998 does have application in litigation between private parties. The court will be under an obligation to develop the common law in conformity with the spirit of the Convention. Hence the courts have developed the common law relating to breach of confidence to build a doctrine of privacy offering some protection for private individuals whose personal details are published by the media: see *Douglas* v *Hello! Ltd* [2001] 2 All ER 189.

The second key development is the recognition at common law that certain statutes, such as the Human Rights Act 1998 are 'constitutional' in the sense that they deal with fundamental constitutional principles and human rights. The Human Rights Act 1998 is not entrenched, but as Lord Hoffmann explained in *R* v *Secretary of State for the Home Department, ex parte Simms; Same, ex parte O'Brien* [1999] 3 All ER 400, fundamental rights cannot be overridden by general or ambiguous words. In the absence of express language or necessary implication to the contrary, the courts will presume that even the most general words in primary legislation are intended to be subject to the basic rights of the individual. In effect statutes like the Human Rights Act 1998 cannot be impliedly repealed. If Parliament wants to amend or repeal the Human Rights Act 1998 it must plainly say so and take the political consequences that flow from this.

In conclusion, therefore, it is true to say that an elegant compromise has been reached whereby the ECHR has been as firmly entrenched in domestic law as it could be, short of engaging in a complete constitutional upheaval involving a move towards a written constitution and the demise of parliamentary sovereignty as we know it.

QUESTION TWO

Consider the view that the Human Rights Act 1998 falls short of providing a constitutional guarantee of rights and freedoms.

University of London LLB Examination
(for External Students) Constitutional Law June 1999 Q5

General Comment

For candidates who have done their homework on the Human Rights Act 1998 this should be a relatively straightforward question. There are, as ever, dangers that candidates will simply resort to reciting the terms of the Act. This is not what is required here. Note the key phrase 'constitutional guarantees'. The question is inviting you to consider how the Act has attempted to enshrine the Convention rights in the constitution, whilst at the same time not disturbing the delicate balance of power between the courts, the executive and the judiciary. The question therefore provides an opportunity to revisit some constitutional fundamentals in the process of looking at the way in which the Act will operate.

Skeleton Solution

Examine the nature of constitutional guarantees – typical devices such as entrenchment and procedural preconditions – note the absence of these measures with the Human Rights Act 1998 – consider political guarantees – obligations placed on the courts – remedies – remedial action – who can complain? – who can be the object of the complaint? – link with judicial review – criticisms of the cautious approach of the Act – absence of any Human Rights Commission – concluding thoughts.

Suggested Solution

The enactment of the Human Rights Act 1998, which came fully into effect in October 2000, marked something of a sea change in the way in which civil rights are protected under the domestic law of the United Kingdom. Out went the old Diceyian notion of individual rights being adequately protected by the common law as and when necessary, with the emphasis on the negative right to do anything not expressly prohibited by law. In came the concept of positive rights, such as the right to privacy, freedom of expression, peaceful assembly and the right to family life.

The issue to be explored is the extent to which these rights have become constitutionally guaranteed. The first point to make is that the Human Rights Act 1998 is not part and parcel of some wider constitutional resettlement. The Labour government that introduced the legislation was committed to 'bringing rights home'. The emphasis was very much on no longer having to go to Strasbourg to claim redress; on not 'washing our dirty linen in public'. It was never the purpose of the 1998 Act to achieve any seismic shift in the balance of power within the constitution. Indeed the framers of the Bill were at pains to ensure that it could work with the grain of existing constitutional arrangements and not against it.

Parliamentary sovereignty still rules therefore. The Human Rights Act 1998 is not entrenched in any way. It is at the mercy of any incoming government committed to repealing it. It has no more status than the Theatres Act 1968 or the Dentists Act 1878. There is no provision in the Act to the effect that it can only be amended provided a certain proportion of members in the House of Commons vote in favour of such a change. The House of Lords is given no special power of veto over a Bill to repeal the 1998 Act. There is no special procedure laid down for reform or abolition, such as requiring a referendum vote in favour of change. If a future Parliament seeks to amend of repeal the Human Rights Act 1998, however, the judges have made it clear that it will have to send a very clear signal in legislative form that this is its intention: see comments of Lord Hoffmann in *R* v *Secretary of State for the Home Department, ex parte Simms; Same, ex parte O'Brien* [1999] 3 All ER 400.

The judges regard the Human Rights Act 1998 as falling within the category of what are known as 'constitutional' statutes. This means that the courts will presume that Parliament does not intend to amend or repeal the Act by 'accident'. In the absence of express language or necessary implication to the contrary, the courts will presume that even the most general words in primary legislation are intended to be subject to the basic rights of the individual. In effect statutes like the Human Rights Act 1998 cannot be impliedly repealed. If Parliament wants to amend or repeal the Human Rights Act 1998 it must plainly say so and take the political consequences that flow from this.

A further protection is provided by the fact that the Human Rights Act 1998 has an 'early warning' system whereby, under s19, the relevant minister in charge of a Bill is under a duty to make a statement to the effect that, in his view, the provisions of the Bill are compatible with the Convention rights, or alternatively that although he is unable to make a statement of compatibility the government nevertheless wishes the House to proceed with the Bill. These statements must be made before the second reading of a Bill, must be in writing and should be published in such manner as the minister considers appropriate. Presumably a statement of non-compliance would only ever be made where the government had already secured derogations or reservations in respect of certain Convention provisions, or had at least indicated that it intended to do so. Otherwise Parliament would be being invited to enact legislation acknowledged to be in breach of the Convention. It begs the question: could a litigant obtain an injunction to prevent the passage of a Bill introduced without s19 being complied with? On the basis of *Pickin* v *British Railways Board* [1974] AC 765, the answer should be 'no'. The matter relates to proceedings entirely internal to the House of Commons.

The real guarantees, if that is the right term in the circumstances, are political. Would any major political party now campaign on a manifesto committed to repealing the Act? How would it be depicted by its opponents? What would be the international consequences of introducing legislation inimical to the United Kingdom's obligations under the European Convention on Human Rights (ECHR)? Non-compliance would have repercussions in terms of participation in the pan-European organs of government such as the Council of Europe. No developed nation wants the pariah status that exclusion from such organisations would result in. The experience of the military regime in Greece during the 1960s is instructive in this regard.

If one accepts, therefore, that the 1998 Act contains no mechanisms for constitutionally guaranteeing rights, attention shifts to what devices, if any, the Act provides for giving a degree of precedence to Convention rights and freedoms. Section 3(1) provides that a court or tribunal called upon to do so, must interpret primary legislation and subordinate legislation 'in a way which is compatible with the Convention rights.' This duty applies whether the legislation was enacted before or after the coming into force of the Human Rights Act 1998. Hence a new rule of construction emerges. Resort is no longer had to the ECHR in cases of ambiguity – domestic legislation must be read subject to it. Further s2(1) of the 1998 Act makes it clear that any court or tribunal determining a question arising in connection with a Convention right must take into account: any judgment, decision, declaration or advisory opinion of the European Court of Human Rights; any opinion of the Commission given in a report adopted under art 31 of the Convention; any decision of the Commission in connection with arts 26 or 27(2) of the Convention, or any decision of the Committee of Ministers taken under art 46 of the Convention, 'whenever made or given, so far as, in the opinion of the court or tribunal, it is relevant to the proceedings in which that question has arisen.' *R v A* [2001] 3 All ER 1 shows how far this can go.

The Act effectively introduces a new 'head' of ultra vires action on which an application for judicial review could be based. The extent to which this becomes an effect 'guarantee' of rights depends very much on the dynamism of the judges in the Divisional Court. A court dealing with an application for judicial review of subordinate legislation would be able to declare it to be ultra vires if it was found to incompatible with the Convention rights. The courts have no such power in relation to primary legislation, however. Indeed s3(2)(b) expressly adverts to the issue of parliamentary sovereignty where it provides that the section does not affect the validity, continuing operation or enforcement of any incompatible primary legislation: see further *R (Daly) v Secretary of State for the Home Department* [2001] 3 All ER 433.

The attempt to provide a (weak) constitutional guarantee of Convention rights arises where the Act states that, in the event of an irreconcilable issue of compatibility arising before the House of Lords, the Judicial Committee of the Privy Council, the Courts-Martial Appeal Court, or the High Court or the Court of Appeal, the court can grant a declaration of incompatibility. Although such a declaration, if granted, would not place a minister under a duty to take remedial action, the political pressure to do so will be intense. The Act goes out of its way almost to prevent any strong enforcement measures from coming into existence by providing that no action will lie against a minister for not laying a proposal for legislation before Parliament or for not making any primary legislation or remedial order. Examples such as this illustrate how the Act seeks to work with the existing arrangements, respecting the separation of powers between the judiciary and the executive. In short it steps back from allowing the judiciary to force the executive to introduce legislation of a specific type. This is entirely sensible. If the House of Commons were to vote against a remedial measure, the courts would look foolish and a constitutional crisis might result with the judiciary, executive and legislature at loggerheads. All of this suggests more clearly than ever before that it is the judiciary that are to be the protectors of minority groups, not a legislature that represents, by definition, the interests of majority groups.

Beyond this the 1998 Act does not provide for any new judicial remedies, in particular there is no new power to award damages simply because Convention rights have been violated. The cautious approach adopted by the framers of the Act is further reflected in the fact that it does not expressly create a new procedure for raising alleged violations of Convention rights. Litigants will simply be able to bring proceedings against a public body in the appropriate court or tribunal, and be allowed to rely on the Convention right or rights concerned in any legal proceedings. The Act does not open up the prospect of pressure groups mounting challenges on an actio popularis basis – only the 'victim' of the alleged unlawful act is permitted to bring proceedings or rely on the Convention in legal proceedings.

To many critics the usefulness of the protection offered by the Act is further limited by the fact that compliance is only required on the part of public bodies. A public body for these purposes includes a court or tribunal, and any person certain of whose functions are functions of a public nature. Significantly it does not include either House of Parliament. The courts are influenced by the jurisprudence built up in relation to applications for judicial review in determining whether non-statutory bodies can be regarded as public authorities for these purposes: see the approach of the court in *Poplar Housing and Regeneration Community Association Ltd* v *Donoghue* [2001] 4 All ER 604.

The courts have been dynamic in developing the concept of the Convention having indirect 'horizontal' effect. Although the 1998 Act does not expressly create any obligation on the part of private individuals to abide by the terms of the Convention, a private action can be pursued on the basis that the court as a public body must develop the common law in a way that is consistent with the protection of Convention rights. Suppose a newspaper has invaded the privacy of an individual. There is no common law right to privacy as such. Article 8 of the Convention is now part of domestic law, but appears only to apply to public authorities, not newspapers. If a court were to strike out proceedings brought by a private individual against a newspaper alleging invasion of privacy as disclosing no cause of action, the court might itself then become the focus of an action for not upholding Convention rights. It remains to be seen how the courts will deal with such claims. In *Douglas* v *Hello! Ltd* [2001] 2 All ER 289 the court responded to this problem by developing the domestic law of breach of confidence so as to extend the protection offered to private individuals regarding intrusive press reporting.

Against these encouraging developments critics of the Human Rights Act 1998 have pointed out that it makes no provision for a Human Rights Commission to oversee compliance with the ECHR, and to bring proceedings in respect of non-compliance. Comparisons have been drawn with the work of the Equal Opportunities Commission and Commission for Racial Equality in overseeing legislation dealing with discrimination on the grounds of gender and ethnicity.

In conclusion, therefore, it is submitted that the Human Rights Act 1998 does not provide any constitutional guarantees, in the purist sense of that term, for the rights listed in the ECHR. What the Act does try to do is to give precedence to Convention rights to the extent that this can be consistent with continuing parliamentary sovereignty.

QUESTION THREE

Why has the European Convention on Human Rights been incorporated into domestic law?

Written by the Editor

General Comment

This question requires a good knowledge of the arguments for and against the adoption of the European Convention on Human Rights as a Bill of Rights.

Skeleton Solution

Introduction – the existing constitutional safeguards for protecting human rights in the United Kingdom – the nature of the European Convention on Human Rights – the arguments in favour of adopting the Convention as a Bill of Rights for the United Kingdom – the effect of the Human Rights Act 1998.

Suggested Solution

The United Kingdom constitution is unwritten in the formal sense and accordingly lays great emphasis on the virtues of the common law and the legislative supremacy of Parliament. It relies heavily on the political process to ensure that Parliament does not override the basic rights and liberties of the subject, nor remove from the courts the adjudication of disputes between the citizen and the state arising out of the exercise of executive power.

The European Convention on Human Rights (ECHR), prepared under the auspices of the Council of Europe, entered into force in September 1953. The Convention is a treaty under international law and its authority derives solely from the consent of those states that have become parties to it. The Convention declares certain human rights that should be protected by law in each state and provides political and judicial procedures by which alleged infringements of these rights may be examined at an international level. Every state party to the Convention has a duty to ensure that its domestic law conforms to the Convention, but a state is under no duty to incorporate the Convention itself within its domestic law.

Those who argued in favour of adopting the Convention as a Bill of Rights for the United Kingdom pointed out that human rights were not adequately protected under then existing United Kingdom law and that further constitutional protection for human rights was therefore necessary. In support of their case they pointed to the ever-increasing role of the state in economic and social affairs and the widespread public disillusionment with the parliamentary process and the 'undemocratic' electoral system which produced a legislature dominated and controlled by the executive. Critics pointed also to the 'incremental' erosion of civil liberties exemplified by measures such as the Criminal Justice and Public Order Act 1994. There was also concern at the record of the United Kingdom under the ECHR and dissatisfaction with the performance of the courts in dealing with disputes between the citizen and the state: see *Malone* v *Metropolitan Police Commissioner* [1979] Ch 344. With the executive every day assuming more statutory powers and in so doing eroding common law liberties, so it was argued that it became more vital to provide safeguards against the abuse of those powers.

This traditional British approach to individual liberties is considered by many to be outdated and incapable of protecting individual rights from executive encroachment. Critics have long advocated the creation of a new Bill of Rights for the United Kingdom. In 1978 a select committee of the House of Lords was established to consider whether a Bill of Rights was desirable and, if so, what form it should take. The committee, while doubting that a Bill of Rights was desirable, nevertheless held unanimously that if there were to be a Bill of Rights, it should be a Bill to incorporate the ECHR into United Kingdom law. Following the May 1997 general election the Labour government carried out its manifesto promise to incorporate the European Convention of Human Rights into United Kingdom law by enacting the Human Rights Act 1998.

If one accepts that some form of Bill of Rights was needed in the United Kingdom, incorporation of the Convention offered the easiest and most acceptable option available to the government. There is no dispute as to the rights protected. The Convention omits economic and social rights, over which considerable political controversy might arise, and is confined to certain basic rights and liberties which the framers of the Convention considered would be generally accepted in the liberal democracies of Western Europe. Incorporation of the Convention will also help avoid the frequent humiliations suffered by the United Kingdom before the European Court of Human Rights when, in the glare of international publicity, it is found in breach of its international obligations under the Convention. 'Foreign' judges will no longer be able to pontificate on the acceptability of United Kingdom law, unless an applicant has exhausted all legal remedies available within the United Kingdom.

Many would argue that, to be fully effective, incorporation would have to enable the British courts to apply the Convention if necessary in preference to existing rules of statute or common law and that this would entail grafting onto the present constitution an added power in the courts to give redress to the individual even against an Act of Parliament. Such an approach would raise issues concerning the relationship of the courts to the political process, including the special difficulties inherent in the attempt by a supreme Parliament to bind itself. In the light of this the government has opted for a compromise by providing in s3(1) of the Human Rights Act 1998 that a court or tribunal called upon to do so, must interpret primary legislation and subordinate legislation in a way which is compatible with the Convention rights. This duty applies whether the legislation was enacted before or after the coming into force of the Human Rights Act 1998.

QUESTION FOUR

What difference, if any, does incorporation of the European Convention on Human Rights into United Kingdom law make to the United Kingdom's constitution?

Adapted from University of London LLB Examination
(for External Students) Constitutional Law June 1987 Q9

General Comment

Although this question is phrased rather generally students should concentrate on the effects of incorporation on the sovereignty of Parliament and the role of the judiciary in interpreting and enforcing a Bill of Rights in the United Kingdom.

Skeleton Solution

Introduction. – the need for a Bill of Rights – the Human Rights Act 1998 – the role of the judges – the impact on parliamentary sovereignty.

Suggested Solution

The incorporation into domestic law of the European Convention on Human Rights (ECHR) by means of the Human Rights Act 1998 comes in the wake of increasing demands for better protection for individual rights in the United Kingdom. The Criminal Justice and Public Order Act 1994 was a controversial measure and seen by many as evidence of the further erosion of freedom of expression and protest under the United Kingdom constitution. In most countries there is a written constitution which is not just a 'sacred' piece of paper but a statement that the people are the ultimate source of power, that the state and its legislature and its civil servants and laws are the servants of the people. It was thought by some that the enactment of a Bill of Rights in the United Kingdom would help to reassert the supremacy of the individual over the state. Does the incorporation of the ECHR achieve these ends?

The answer has to be a qualified 'no'. There are a number of reasons for this. First, the 1998 Act only incorporates certain provisions of the Convention. Second, the United Kingdom courts have not been given the power to override statutes found to be incompatible with the Convention.

A court or tribunal called upon to do so, must interpret primary legislation and subordinate legislation 'in a way which is compatible with the Convention rights': s3(1). This duty applies whether the legislation was enacted before or after the coming into force of the Human Rights Act 1998. Section 2(1) of the 1998 Act further makes it clear that any court or tribunal determining a question arising in connection with a Convention right must take into account: any judgment, decision, declaration or advisory opinion of the European Court of Human Rights; any opinion of the Commission given in a report adopted under art 31 of the Convention; any decision of the Commission in connection with arts 26 or 27(2) of the Convention, or any decision of the Committee of Ministers taken under art 46 of the Convention, 'whenever made or given, so far as, in the opinion of the court or tribunal, it is relevant to the proceedings in which that question has arisen.'

Hence the courts retain their traditional role of applying the law, rather than ruling on the validity of primary legislation. Indeed s3(2)(b) expressly provides that the section 'does not affect the validity, continuing operation or enforcement of any incompatible primary legislation'. Where an irreconcilable issue of compatibility arises before the House of Lords, the Judicial Committee of the Privy Council, the Courts-Martial Appeal Court, or the High Court or the Court of Appeal, that court will be empowered to grant a declaration of incompatibility. Where a declaration of incompatibility has been made and rights of appeal have been exhausted, abandoned or become time-barred, or it appears to a minister that (in the light of a finding of the European Court of Human Rights) a provision of legislation is incompatible with obligations under the Convention, a minister may, if he considers that there are compelling reasons for so doing, make orders to amend the relevant legislation to the extent that considers necessary to remove the incompatibility: see s10(1) and (2). What has emerged, however, is a dilemma facing the judiciary in the higher courts. Should a judge lean in favour of using the interpretive power to ensure compliance of domestic legislation, or should a judge step back from adopting a bold interpretive approach and resort to a declaration of incompatibility? The issue concerns where the dividing line should be drawn between interpreting legislation – a judicial function – and legislating – the role of Parliament. Lord Steyn in *R v A* [2001] 3 All ER 1 firmly advocated the bold interpretive approach. In his view, s3 of the Human Rights Act 1998 places the courts under a strong interpretative obligation to ensure the conformity of primary legislation with the Convention even if there is no ambiguity in the language of the statute. By contrast, Lord Woolf CJ in *Poplar Housing and Regeneration Community Association Ltd* v *Donoghue* [2001] 4 All ER 604 expressed the view that s3 of the Human Rights Act 1998 does not entitle a court to legislate – as he saw it if it is necessary in order to obtain compliance to radically alter the effect of legislation this indicates that more than interpretation is involved.

It could be argued that the 1998 Act is further evidence of the steady erosion parliamentary sovereignty. Although a declaration of incompatibility does place a minister under a duty to take remedial action (see below), the political pressure to do so will be intense. It suggests more clearly than ever before that it is the judiciary that are to be the protectors of minority groups, not a legislature that represents, by definition, the interests of majority groups.

It seems inevitable that the courts are going to have to adopt a new approach to statutory interpretation where Convention rights are concerned, rather than stick rigidly to the traditional 'rules' of interpretation. The tradition of the European Court on Human Rights is to be more flexible and evaluative in its exercise of its interpretative functions. Thus domestic judges will have a more explicit role in assessing the merits of executive decision-making (ie its legitimacy within the context of the ECHR), whereas their role to date, at least in theory, has been limited to scrutinising the legality of executive action by means of judicial review.

In all of this it should be remembered that the Human Rights Act 1998 is still just a domestic Act. It would be open to any future Parliament to repeal it at will. Parliament can still make or unmake any law. There is still no area or subject matter outside the scope of its legislative powers. Parliament still cannot bind its successors and a later Parliament will remain, in theory at least, able to expressly repeal the legislation made by an earlier Parliament. The only limitation at common law is that adverted to by Lord Hoffmann in *R v Secretary of State for the Home Department, ex parte Simms; Same, ex parte O'Brien* [1999] 3 All ER 400. As he explained the Human Rights Act 1998 is to be regarded as a 'constitutional' statute attracting particular protection from the judiciary. In practice this means that the judges will only regard a later Act as amending or repealing the Human Rights Act 1998 if the later Act expressly states that it is to have such an effect. In effect the Human Rights Act 1998 cannot be impliedly repealed. This is not entrenchment, but it makes clear to Parliament that a certain 'manner and form' must be followed if it seeks to change the Human Rights Act 1998.

The real check upon the sovereignty of Parliament in practice remains public opinion. The government always knows that it will have to face a general election within a few years and this stark reality may have a restraining effect upon their legislative proposals and deter any attempted government tampering with the Bill of Rights. Of course these informal restraints are present and operating already to curtail executive power and in this respect the presence of a Bill of Rights will make little difference.

QUESTION FIVE

Was incorporation of the European Convention of Human Rights into domestic law really necessary?

Written by the Editor

General Comment

It is tempting to run through all the well rehearsed arguments for and against incorporation of the Convention on Human Rights, but the examiner wishes the student to concentrate on a particular issue: will individual rights in the United kingdom be better protected following incorporation?

Skeleton Solution

Examination of the common law tradition – Lord Lester's critique – the case for incorporation – counter arguments – the reality of incorporation – how the Human Rights Act 1998 will work – conclusion.

Suggested Solution

In Dicey's exposition of the theory of the rule of law emphasis was placed on the role of the judge as defender of civil liberties; indeed Dicey went as far as to assert that the British constitution, in its aspects relating to basic rights and freedoms, was a judge-made one. Historically Parliament built on the foundations laid by the common law. Since 1952 successive British governments have ratified the European Convention on Human Rights (ECHR) and since 1965 individual United Kingdom citizens have been permitted to petition the European Court of Human Rights at Strasbourg to obtain remedies for breaches of the Convention by United Kingdom governments. Eventually, in 1998, the Convention was incorporated into domestic law with the enactment of the Human Rights Act. It came fully into effect in October 2000.

Why was such incorporation seen as necessary? In a devastating critique, Anthony Lester QC ([1984] PL 46) argued that the United Kingdom had one of the worst records of violations of the European Convention and stated that: 'no other country which belongs to the Convention has been faced with so many cases of such importance'. His catalogue included cases involving inhumane treatment of prisoners generally and of terrorist suspects in particular; inadequate safeguards against invasion of privacy; unfair sex and race discrimination, especially in the fields of employment and immigration law; inhumane punishments for school children (cane in English schools, tawse or strap in Scottish schools); nationalisation without fair compensation; oppressive interference with free speech through the laws of contempt of court and confidentiality; and so the list goes on. In all these examples the government of the day was usually obliged to enact new laws to comply with the rulings of the European Court of Human Rights. As Lester cogently argued, such slow reform could have been avoided if the ECHR had been directly enforceable by United Kingdom judges able (and indeed obliged) to adapt common law and statute law to comply with the jurisprudence of the European Court of Human Rights and the precedents set by that Court.

Although the matter is somewhat academic, given that incorporation of the Convention has now occurred, thought might still be given to whether it was as necessary as Lord Lester and others maintained. At first sight Lester's catalogue of British inadequacies would appear conclusive, but in fact his case is rather misleading. Although it is true that the United Kingdom has the worst record of violations, this should be set in the context that the United Kingdom allowed the right of individual petition as long ago as 1965, whereas others of the 1952 signatories allowed their citizens such access much later, eg France in the early 1980s, so that the inadequacies of the French system are only now coming to light (bearing in mind the typical wait of four to five years before a case reaches judgment at the European Court of Human Rights).

Another factor which could be used to counter Lester's argument is that United Kingdom judges were already taking account of the Convention when interpreting ambiguous common law and statute law: see *Derbyshire County Council v Times Newspapers Ltd* [1993] 2 WLR 449. In the *Derbyshire* case both the Court of Appeal and the House of Lords held that local authorities could not sue for libel in respect of their reputation for administration because otherwise such a right of action would stifle legitimate public criticism of their activities and impose an unnecessary restriction on freedom of expression in a democratic society. Lord Keith, in the leading judgment, managed to reach his conclusion without finding the need to rely upon the European Convention: 'I find it satisfactory to be able to conclude that the common law of England is consistent with the obligations assumed by the Crown under the treaty in this particular field.' Was incorporation of the Convention really necessary when the common law was capable of responding to the challenges placed before it? As Lord Denning often said in his career on the bench, common law is capable of evolving from precedent to precedent so as to move with the times and to meet the needs of society.

Are rights any better protected following incorporation? The answer must be in the affirmative given that it is so much easier for litigants to raise arguments related to Convention rights. Instead of taking a case to Strasbourg a litigant can now bring proceedings (or a counterclaim) against a public body in the appropriate court or tribunal. Alternatively litigants are allowed to 'rely on the Convention right or rights concerned in any legal proceedings': s7(1)(b). By virtue of s6(1) it is now unlawful for a public authority to act (or fail to act – see s6(6)) in a way which is incompatible with a Convention right. A public body for these purposes includes a court or tribunal, and 'any person certain of whose functions are functions of a public nature': see further *Poplar Housing and Regeneration Community Association Ltd* v *Donoghue* [2001] 4 All ER 604.

Section 6(1), therefore, effectively creates a new 'head' of ultra vires as regards applications for judicial review of public bodies. If a public body fails to pay due regard to the terms of the Convention, or indeed the jurisprudence of the European Court of Human Rights, in exercising its discretion, prima facie grounds for review will exist. In particular the notion of proportionality as developed by the European Court of Human Rights becomes a facet of domestic law to which reviewing courts will now be obliged to have regard: see further *R (Daly)* v *Secretary of State for the Home Department* [2001] 3 All ER 433.

The enforcement of rights is made more effective by virtue of the fact that a court or tribunal called upon to do so, must interpret primary legislation and subordinate legislation 'in a way which is compatible with the Convention rights': s3(1). This duty applies whether the legislation in question was enacted before or after the coming into force of the Human Rights Act 1998. The extent to which the courts are prepared to resort to 'creative' interpretations of domestic statutes to achieve compliance is vividly illustrated by the House of Lords' decision in *R v A* [2001] 3 All ER 1 – see in particular the speech of Lord Steyn.

Although the courts are not be able to disapply legislation that conflicts with the Convention rights, where an irreconcilable issue of compatibility arises before the House of Lords, the Judicial Committee of the Privy Council, the Courts-Martial Appeal Court, or the High Court or the Court of Appeal, that court is empowered to grant a declaration of incompatibility. The granting of such a declaration should trigger action by the relevant minister to amend the offending law to ensure compliance.

In conclusion it is fair to say that in some respects the incorporation of the ECHR into domestic law was unnecessary – there is evidence of the judges being willing to develop the common law so as to offer similar guarantees. Incorporation has, however, enabled a root and branch reassessment of individual rights within the unwritten constitution, and has helped spark the development of a more human rights conscious culture amongst both legislators and the judiciary. This cannot but be a good thing.

Chapter 11

Public Order

11.1   **Introduction**

11.2   **Key points**

11.3   **Key cases and statutes**

11.4   **Questions and suggested solutions**

11.1 Introduction

English law provides for numerous restrictions on the individual's freedom to assemble and associate with others. The purpose of these restrictions is to ensure that public expressions of dissent and protest take place within legal parameters, thus ensuring a balance between the interests of protesters and others who wish to go about their day-to-day business without let or hindrance. Inevitably the imposition of such restrictions can create tensions between those who prioritise public order on the one hand and those who fear excessive state controls on the other.

The demonstration, protest march and public meeting are important political weapons that can result in government policy being changed, for example the abolition of the Poll Tax, demonstrations relating to the banning of fox hunting and the petrol price protests. One of the priorities of government is to maintain public order, and a balance has to be drawn between the right to protest and the existence of legal controls to prevent the breakdown of public order. Historically governments have reacted to threats to social order by introducing measures that restrict the scope of protest action. In the United Kingdom, in the latter part of the twentieth century, public order problems have been raised by violence on football terraces, serious disorder in urban areas, terrorist activities and the actions of 'new age' travellers and 'eco-warriors'. Key developments have included the Police and Criminal Evidence Act 1984, the Public Order Act 1986 and the Criminal Justice and Public Order Act 1994. These Acts taken together represent a significant step towards the codification of the law on public order but there are other very significant measures, and various important common law rulings. The Human Rights Act 1998, incorporating as it does the European Convention on Human Rights, establishes for the first time a positive legal right to demonstrate, although this is subject to certain limitations as set out below.

11.2 Key points

The Human Rights Act 1998

The Human Rights Act 1998 incorporates aspects of the European Convention on Human Rights into domestic law, including art 11, which provides:

'(1) Everyone has the right to freedom of peaceful assembly and to freedom of association with others, including the right to form and to join trade unions for the protection of his interests.

(2) No restrictions shall be placed on the exercise of these rights other than such as are prescribed by law and are necessary in a democratic society in the interests of national security or public safety, for the prevention of disorder or crime, for the protection of health or morals or for the protection of the rights and freedoms of others. This Article shall not prevent the imposition of lawful restrictions on the exercise of these rights by members of the armed forces, of the police or of the administration of the State.'

The Act came fully into force in October 2000.

Statutory powers restricting the right of public protest

Obstruction of the police

Under the Police Act 1996 s89(1) any person who assaults a police constable in the execution of his duty or (under s89(2)) resists or wilfully obstructs a police constable in the course of his duty is guilty of an offence. Policing inevitably involves the exercise of discretion. In the context of public order the issue is the extent to which the police can lawfully intervene. See *Duncan* v *Jones* [1936] 1 KB 218; *Piddington* v *Bates* [1960] 3 All ER 660.

Obstruction of the highway

Under the Highways Act 1980 a person is guilty of an offence if he wilfully obstructs the free passage of the highway. To initiate a meeting which results in such an obstruction can result in conviction, even in circumstances where the highway was not completely blocked: see *Arrowsmith* v *Jenkins* [1963] 2 QB 561; *Hirst and Agu* v *Chief Constable for West Yorkshire* [1987] Crim LR 330. *Director of Public Prosecutions* v *Jones* [1999] 2 All ER 257 confirms that use of the highway for the purpose of peaceful non-obstructive protest can be lawful use.

Public Order Act 1986

The Public Order Act 1986 provides a framework of controls that apply to processions and demonstrations and enacts a range of offences to deal with conduct of varying seriousness.

a) Public order offences

The Public Order Act 1986 abolishes the common law offences of riot, rout, unlawful assembly and affray. It also abolishes the statutory offence of threatening behaviour under the Public Order Act 1936. These it replaces with an expanded range of public order offences – riot, violent disorder, affray, threatening behaviour and disorderly conduct.

Section 1 – riot. The offence of riot is retained for the most serious public order offences.

i) Twelve or more persons must be present together and the difficult concept of common purpose is retained. This is to underline the seriousness of violent behaviour when committed collectively.

ii) A person of reasonable firmness must, as a result of the incident, fear for his personal safety. This hypothetical person need not actually be present at the scene at the time of the riot.

iii) Each of the persons present using unlawful violence is guilty of an offence. Unlawful violence is defined in s8.

iv) The consent of the DPP is necessary for a prosecution with underlying policy implications.

Section 2 – violent disorder. The offence of violent disorder is intended to deal with a range of situations from major public disorder to minor group disturbances, eg football hooliganism. It is a lesser offence than riot.

i) Note the similarities with riot, ie the use or threat of unlawful violence and the fact that a person of reasonable firmness present at the scene should fear for his personal safety (although again this hypothetical person need not actually be present): see *R v Hebron* [1989] Crim LR 839.

ii) The number of persons present need only be three.

iii) The consent of the DPP is not necessary for a prosecution.

Section 3 – affray. This redefined offence is directed at those who use or threaten violence towards others as individuals.

i) A person of reasonable firmness must fear for their personal safety.

ii) The offence anticipates the following sort of conduct – fighting outside pubs or football grounds and also on private premises: see *R v Davison* [1992] Crim LR 31.

iii) The jury should be directed to consider what the effect of the appellant's actions would have been on a putative third person, ie the bystander of reasonable firmness. Although there need not actually be any third person present for the offence to be made out, such a direction was necessary because the offence of affray was enacted for the protection of the innocent bystander, as opposed to the person at whom the violence was aimed: see *R v Sanchez* (1996) The Times 6 March. *I v Director of Public Prosecutions* [2001] 2 All ER 583 confirms that a person should not be charged with affray unless he uses or threatens unlawful violence towards another person actually present at the scene and his conduct is such as would cause fear to a notional bystander of reasonable firmness.

Section 4 – threatening behaviour. This section replaces s5 of the Public Order Act 1936.

i) The concept of threatening abusive or insulting words or behaviour is retained and words can be verbal or in writing.

ii) There must be an intention to provoke unlawful violence or a person must believe that unlawful violence will be used against him: see *R v Horseferry Road Magistrates Court, ex parte Siadatan* [1990] Crim LR 598.

iii) Much of the old case law will continue to be relevant: see *Brutus v Cozens* [1973] AC 854; *Jordan v Burgoyne* [1963] 2 All ER 225.

iv) Section 154 of the Criminal Justice and Public Order Act 1994 adds a s4A to the Public Order Act 1986. An offence is committed where a defendant, with intent to cause a person harassment, alarm or distress (a) uses threatening, abusive or insulting words or behaviour, or disorderly behaviour, or (b) displays any writing, sign or other visible representation which is threatening, abusive or insulting, thereby causing that person, or another person, harassment, alarm or distress.

Section 5 – this section introduces a new offence of causing harassment, alarm or distress.

i) The offence applies to disorderly behaviour and a person who sees or hears the conduct must be likely to be caused harassment, alarm or distress. The objective here is to protect the vulnerable.

ii) 'Disorderly behaviour', not being defined in the Act, is to be given its ordinary and everyday meaning and whether it was made out is also a question of fact for the court at first instance. In general terms, the expression does not require proof of threatening, abusive or insulting behaviour as these were matters dealt with elsewhere in the 1986 Act: see *Chambers and Edwards v Director of Public Prosecutions* [1995] Crim LR 896.

iii) Defences are: that the accused had no reason to believe that any such person was present; that the conduct was reasonable; and that the accused was inside a dwelling and had no reason to believe anyone outside could see or hear them.

Sections 17–23 – racial hatred. The sections deal with a variety of circumstances in which racial hatred is likely to be stirred up.

i) As with s4, conduct must be threatening, abusive or insulting. The consequence must be the stirring up of racial hatred.

ii) The same interpretative conditions will apply to 'threatening', or 'abusive' or 'insulting' as with s4: see *Jordan* v *Burgoyne* [1963] 2 QB 744. Racial hatred is defined in s17. See too *Mandla* v *Lee* [1983] 2 AC 548.

iii) Section 155 of the Criminal Justice and Public Order Act 1994 makes publishing or distributing racially offensive material (s19 Public Order Act 1986) an arrestable offence.

iv) The Crime and Disorder Act 1998 adds a number of racially aggravated versions of public order offences under the Public Order Act 1986 Act, specifically s4 (causing fear or provocation of violence), s4A (intentional harassment, alarm or distress) and s5 (harassment, alarm or distress). For these purposes an offence is racially aggravated if (under s28 of the 1998 Act):

'(a) at the time of committing the offence, or immediately before or after doing so, the offender demonstrates towards the victim of the offence hostility based on the victim's membership of, or association with members of, a racial group; or
(b) the offence is motivated (wholly or partly) by hostility towards members of a racial group based on their membership of that group.'

b) Processions and demonstrations

A more comprehensive legal framework is laid down by the Public Order Act 1986 for the control of public processions and public meetings.

Section 11 – this section requires advance notice to be given to the police of public processions. By and large this section is intended to cover planned marches, including commemorative marches and excluding instances where it is not practicable to give notice, ie a spontaneous march.

Section 12 – authorises a senior police officer to impose conditions as to time, place or route on a public procession. There must be belief that serious public disorder or damage to property will result or that the objective is intimidation.

Section 13 – authorises the chief constable to apply to the council for an order prohibiting all marches for three months.

i) The ban is a blanket ban and not aimed at specific groups. Clearly the chief constable must believe that serious public disorder would result in the event that the march was allowed to proceed.

ii) The ban is subject to the consent of the Home Secretary.

iii) The ban is subject to judicial review: *Kent* v *Metropolitan Police Commissioner* (1981) The Times 15 May.

Section 14 provides that a senior police officer may impose conditions in relation to public assemblies. Sections 70 and 71 of the Criminal Justice and Public Order Act 1994 insert new sections into s14 Public Order Act 1986 concerning the regulation of assemblies in progress. A chief constable can apply to the local authority for an order banning a trespassory assembly on the grounds that it may give rise either to serious disruption to the life of the community, or where the land or a building or monument on it is of historical, architectural, archaeological or scientific importance and significant damage to the land, building or monument may occur. These provisions cover places to which the public has no, or limited, rights of access. The ban is for up to four days and needs the consent of the Secretary of State.

Public assemblies are defined in s16, and the conditions on public assemblies are virtually the same as for public processions. In *Director of Public Prosecutions* v *Jones* [1999] 2 All ER 257 it was held that an assembly on the highway is not necessarily trespassory in nature – much depends upon the purpose for which the highway is being used. The House of Lords accepted, by a majority, that a peaceful, non-obstructive assembly of 20 or more persons on the public highway, might not exceed the public's right of access to the highway so as to constitute a trespassory assembly within the terms of s14A.

Public Order Act 1936

Section 1 of the Act makes it an offence to wear a uniform signifying membership of a political organisation: see *O'Moran* v *DPP* [1975] QB 364.

Picketing

Pickets can be in breach of both the civil and criminal law. Generally there is no 'right' to picket because it will not be a reasonable use of the highway unless for passing and re-passing. However, under s220 of the Trade Union and Labour Relations (Consolidation) Act 1992, picketing is lawful if it is in contemplation or furtherance of a trade dispute and at or near the strikers' own workplace for the purpose only of peacefully obtaining or communicating information or peacefully persuading any person to work or to abstain from working. This provision provides pickets with immunity in respect of civil actions for trespass or for inducing breach of contract. It follows from this that picketing someone else's place of work is illegal and the employer can obtain an injunction to stop it. In addition pickets find themselves in breach of the Public Order Act 1986 (as above).

Criminal Justice and Public Order Act 1994

a) Removing trespassers

Section 61 repeals s39 of the Public Order Act 1986 and gives police new powers to remove trespassers on land. Trespass was already criminalised by s39 of the 1986 Act, but it proved difficult to enforce. Section 61 is more tightly drawn and covers cases where permission to be on land has been withdrawn, reduces the number of vehicles required for a dispersal order to be made from 12 to six, extends definition of 'land' to include common land, and gives police powers to confiscate vehicles not willingly removed.

b) Aggravated trespass

Section 68 – a person commits an offence if he trespasses on land in the open air and, in relation to any lawful activity which people there assembled are doing or are about to engage in, does anything that is intended by him to have the effect of:

i) intimidating those persons so as to deter them from engaging in that activity; or

ii) obstructing that activity; or

iii) disrupting that activity.

c) Squatters

Sections 75 and 76 – lawful owners and occupiers of property now have access to quicker and effective remedies against squatters. They can go to court immediately and apply for an interim possession order. If granted, squatters will have 24 hours to leave premises. Failure to do so will be an offence.

d) Unauthorised campers

Section 77 – local authorities now have the power, where people are for the time being residing in a vehicle or vehicles on a highway or any unoccupied land, or on any occupied land without the occupier's consent, to give a direction that those persons must leave, taking vehicles and property with them. Failure to comply is a criminal offence. Note that s80(1) repeals a provision in the Caravan Sites Act 1968 which required local authorities to provide sites for gypsies. They are still empowered to do so, but are no longer required to.

e) Raves

Sections 63–67 – a rave is defined as a gathering in open air of 100 or more persons (whether or not they are trespassers), at which amplified music is played during the night which, by reason of its loudness and time at which it is played, is likely to cause serious distress to inhabitants of the locality. If a police officer reasonably believes that two or more people are planning a rave and that ten or more are waiting for it to begin or attending such a gathering, dispersal orders may be made requiring them to leave. Powers of entry and seizure of vehicles and sound equipment are given. Police officers are also empowered to turn people within a five-mile radius away before sufficient numbers gather.

Protection from Harassment Act 1997

Under this Act it is a criminal offence to use words or behaviour, on more than one occasion, which puts the victim in fear of violence, either intentionally or in circumstances where a reasonable person would have realised this would be the effect. The maximum penalty upon conviction is five years' imprisonment or an unlimited fine. The Act also provides for a lesser offence of using words or behaviour, on more than one occasion, which could cause the victim to be harassed, alarmed or distressed, either intentionally, or in circumstances where a reasonable person would have realised this would be the effect. The maximum penalty upon conviction is six months' imprisonment or a £5,000 fine. In respect of both offences there is a defence to the effect that the defendant was acting in the interests of national security; to prevent or detect crime; or was otherwise authorised by statute. The lesser offence is also be subject to a defence that the defendant had acted reasonably and necessarily in pursuit of a business trade or profession or other lawful activity. Both offences are 'arrestable' in the sense that police have powers of arrest without warrant as outlined in s24 of the Police and Criminal Evidence Act 1984.

Common law

Breach of the peace

Section 40 of the Public Order Act 1986 specifically retains the common law powers to deal with or prevent a breach of the peace, and s17(5) and (6) of the Police and Criminal Evidence Act 1984 preserve common law powers of entry to deal with breaches of the peace. A precise definition of breach of the peace is difficult to give, but it must involve an element of actual or apprehended violence to person or property. It could further be defined as arising when a person causes harm to, or appears likely to do so, persons or property or acts in a manner the natural consequence of which is to provoke others to violence. A police officer who has either witnessed a breach of the peace, or who has reasonable grounds for believing that a breach of the peace is about to occur, can arrest an offender without warrant: see *R* v *Howell* [1982] QB 416; *R* v *Chief Constable of Devon and Cornwall, ex parte CEGB* [1982] QB 458; *Moss* v *McLachlan* (1985) 149 JP 167. In *Duncan* v *Jones* [1936] 1 KB 218 the power was used to effectively prevent a public meeting. In *Moss* v *McLachlan* (1985) 149 JP 167 flying pickets were turned back on the basis that a breach of the peace was imminent. In *Steel and Others* v *United Kingdom* (1998) The Times 1 October the European Court of Human Rights held that arrest and detention for breach of the peace could amount to a breach of art 10 of the European Convention on Human Rights where those arrested where engaged in peaceful protests. Breach of the peace itself was held to satisfy the test requiring any restriction on Convention rights to be 'prescribed by law' (ie it was a sufficiently certain and ascertainable legal concept in domestic law).

Entry into meetings

The police have the right to be present in public places where there are fears of public disorder. They also have the right to enter private premises where there are reasons to believe a breach of the peace is imminent as a result of a private meeting being held there: see *Thomas* v *Sawkins* [1935] 2 KB 249. Similarly, there is a power to enter private premises to deal with 'domestic' disputes: see *McLeod* v *Commissioner of the Metropolitan Police* [1994] 4 All ER 553.

11.3 Key cases and statutes

- *Director of Public Prosecutions* v *Jones* [1999] 2 All ER 257
  Identifies lawful use of highway for the purpose of peaceful protest

- *Hirst and Agu* v *Chief Constable for West Yorkshire* [1987] Crim LR 330
  Use of highway for protest

- *I* v *Director of Public Prosecutions* [2001] 2 All ER 583
  Sets out elements of affray

- *Kent* v *Metropolitan Police Commissioner* (1981) The Times 15 May.
  Public order bans subject to judicial review

- *R* v *Howell* [1982] QB 416
  Defines breach of the peace

- *Steel and Others* v *United Kingdom* (1998) The Times 1 October
  Peaceful protest should not be regarded as breach of the peace

- *Thomas* v *Sawkins* [1935] 2 KB 249
  Right to enter private meetings

- Crime and Disorder Act 1998 – racially aggravated versions of public order offences under the Public Order Act 1986

- Criminal Justice and Public Order Act 1994 – powers to remove trespassers and deal with other forms of unlawful land occupation

- Highways Act 1980 – offences of obstruction

- Human Rights Act 1998 – incorporates art 11

- Police Act 1996, s89(1) – assault on a police constable in the execution of his duty

- Police and Criminal Evidence Act 1984, s17(5) and (6) – preserves common law powers of entry to deal with breaches of the peace

- Public Order Act 1936 – prohibits uniforms signifying membership of a political organisation

- Public Order Act 1986 – basis of modern public order law

11.4 Questions and suggested solutions

QUESTION ONE

Article 11 of the European Convention on Human Rights provides that 'Everyone has the right to peaceful assembly'. How is this human right guaranteed in English Law?

University of London LLB Examination
(for External Students) Constitutional Law June 1996 Q5

General Comment

This is a question that requires a good working knowledge of the provisions of both the European Convention on Human Rights and the Human Rights Act 1998. Thought should be given to the powers domestic courts have in reviewing administrative decisions relating to public order and the power of interpretation under the 1998 Act. A few examples of restriction imposed in domestic law will suffice as the emphasis is on how compliance with the European Convention on Human Rights is achieved.

Skeleton Solution

The issue of 'rights' in English law – s14 Public Order Act 1986 – Criminal Justice and Public Order Act 1994: trespass, trespassory assemblies, 'raves' – common law powers to control assemblies – Highways Act 1980 – conclusion.

Suggested Solution

Traditionally, by which is meant pre-October 2000, English law has not recognised any positive right to demonstrate or take part in public political protest. The approach in the past was always to work on the basis of negative rights. Citizens could demonstrate and meet together subject to the myriad common law and statutory limitations imposed on them.

In legal terms there has been a revolution. Article 11 of the European Convention on Human Rights (ECHR) provides that everyone has the right to freedom of peaceful assembly and to freedom of association with others. The Human Rights Act 1998 incorporated the European Convention on Human Rights into domestic law. The effect of this is that public bodies, such as police constables, government ministers, local authorities and the courts themselves, are now under an enforceable legal duty not to act in a way that is contrary to the right given under art 11. If administrative action is alleged to be in breach of art 11 the 'victim' of the alleged breach can apply to the court for judicial review. In reviewing the impugned action the court will not be confined to the traditional domestic grounds of *Wednesbury* ultra vires (*Associated Provincial Picture Houses Ltd v Wednesbury Corporation* [1948] 1 KB 223) – a more robust approach will be taken that requires more by way of justification from the public body that the interference with the Convention right was really justified: see *R (Daly) v Secretary of State for the Home Department* [2001] 3 All ER 433.

If it is a legislative provision in domestic law that is impugned as being incompatible with art 11 the court will exercise the powers of interpretation provided by the 1998 Act. Under s2(1) any court or tribunal determining a question arising in connection with a Convention right must take into account: any judgment, decision, declaration or advisory opinion of the European Court of Human Rights. Further, under s3(1) of the 1998 Act, a court or tribunal called upon to do so, must interpret primary legislation and subordinate legislation 'in a way which is compatible with the Convention rights.'

Thus the entire cannon of domestic law must now be looked at afresh should a dispute arise as to the extent to which it is compatible with the ECHR.

With this in mind it is perhaps appropriate to briefly summarise some of the key restraints on the freedom to protest found in domestic law. The Public Order Act (POA) 1986 is of key significance here, providing for the imposition of restrictions and bans on assemblies and processions. If, for example, a senior police officer reasonably believes that an assembly will result in serious public disorder, serious damage to property or serious disruption to the life of the community, or the purpose is the intimidation of others, he may impose conditions on the organisers relating to the duration of the assembly and the maximum number of people who may make up the meeting: s14 POA 1986. What constitutes the reasonable belief of the senior police officer (presumably the senior police officer present) as to these factors is not defined in the Act – but as noted above reliance on a belief that is merely reasonable in the *Wednesbury* sense would no longer be appropriate. The test would now be one of proportionality, as Convention rights are in play (see below).

Restrictions are also imposed by measures such as the Criminal Justice and Public Order Act (CJPOA) 1994. This Act was passed in response to a number of public order issues ranging from 'New Age Travellers' to 'rave' parties on disused airfields. Associated with these groups and events is the issue of trespass and trespassory assembly. The POA 1986 attempted to deal with some of these issues by providing a senior police officer (ie the most senior present) with powers to direct trespassers to leave land: s39 POA 1986. These could only be invoked if the police officer believed that two or more persons had entered the land as trespassers with a common purpose of residing there, that they had not heeded reasonable steps, by the occupier, to leave and that they had caused damage to the property on the land or that they had used threatening, abusive or insulting words or behaviour towards the occupier or his agent. The police officer could also direct the trespassers to leave the land if they brought 12 or more vehicles on the land: s39(1)(b).

In addition, English law has extensive common law powers that in effect curtail an assembly. The test is whether there will be a breach of the peace or a reasonable likelihood of breach of the peace at the gathering, rather than what is the intention of the organisers or those attempting to reach the assembly. In *O'Kelly* v *Harvey* (1883) 15 Cox CC 435, for instance, a meeting of the Land League was ordered to be dispersed by the local justice of the peace as it was in danger of being broken up by Orangemen members of a Protestant organisation hostile to the aspirations of the Land League. The reasoning of this nineteenth-century precedent has been utilised by the police in preventing individuals from attending a gathering whose purpose is per se lawful. In *Moss* v *McLachlan* [1985] IRLR 76 the Divisional Court held that the police had reasonable grounds for apprehending a breach of the peace as imminent when they stopped a group of striking miners from going to attend a mass picket. The miners were arrested for obstruction of the police. It is not necessary in such a situation to argue that the meeting is unlawful, but rather whether the natural consequence of the meeting will be a breach of the peace. If, however, the natural consequence of an assembly is not to provoke violence then it would appear that it is legitimate to proceed. *R v Morpeth Ward Justices, ex parte Ward and Others* [1992] Crim LR 497 appears to indicate that individuals may protest at a meeting but not in a manner likely to provoke violence. Such reasoning is an echo of *Beatty v Gillbanks* (1882) 9 QB 308 in which the court emphasised that so long as the participants at a gathering were 'quiet and reasonable' then the unlawful actions of the other participants were not deemed to be the 'natural consequences' of the event.

Even before the coming into force of the Human Rights Act 1998 the courts were beginning to show themselves more willing to develop domestic law in a manner consistent with the requirements of the ECHR: see for example *Director of Public Prosecutions* v *Jones* [1999] 2 All ER 257. Now that the Act is in force restrictions such as those above have to be set against art 11(2), which sets out the basis on which such restrictions can be imposed. It provides that no restrictions may be placed on the exercise of art 11(1) rights other than such as are: prescribed by law; and are necessary in a democratic society in the interests of national security or public safety, for the prevention of disorder or crime, for the protection of health or morals or for the protection of the rights and freedoms of others.

Even if these requirements are met, the restriction must still be shown to be a proportionate response to the problem posed by the individual's activity. Hence in *Steel and Others v United Kingdom* (1998) The Times 1 October the European Court of Human Rights held that arrest and detention for breach of the peace could amount to a breach of art 10 of the ECHR where those arrested where engaged in peaceful protests. Although the offence of breach of the peace itself was held to satisfy the ' prescribed by law' test, and it was aimed at maintaining public order, the use of breach of the peace powers against protestors who were not blocking the highway and who were not preventing others from going about their lawful business could not be seen as a proportionate response. This approach to art 11(2) would also be applied to any decision to ban or restrict a public march.

In conclusion, therefore, it can be said that even if domestic law does not entirely tally with the requirements of art 11 of the ECHR, procedures are now in place whereby individuals can take effective legal proceedings to rectify the matter before domestic courts.

QUESTION TWO

What difference, if any, has the Public Order Act 1986 made to English law?

University of London LLB Examination
(for External Students) Constitutional Law June 1987 Q8

General Comment

A relatively straightforward question concerning the Public Order Act 1986. Students should know the changes introduced by this Act and compare the new provisions with those existing at common law and under the Public Order Act 1936. The extent to which rights have been augmented by the Human Rights Act 1998 should also be addressed.

Skeleton Solution

Introduction – general provisions of the Public Order Act 1986 – abolition of common law riot, rout, unlawful assembly and affray – introduction of statutory riot, violent disorder and affray – provisions relating to processions: ss12 and 13 – provisions relating to assemblies: s14 – provisions relating to racial hatred – causing fear or provocation of violence – causing harassment, alarm or distress – the Human Rights Act 1998.

Suggested Solution

The Public Order Act 1986 was passed on 7 November 1986. Some provisions of the Act came into force on 1 January 1987. Most of the rest of the Act came into force on 1 April 1987. The Act firstly repeals certain provisions of the Public Order Act 1936. Second, it abolishes the common law offences of riot, rout, unlawful assembly and affray. Third, it introduces new statutory offences to replace some of the common law offences abolished or statutory offences repealed. Fourth, it amends or repeals other statutory provisions including those concerning racial hatred. Fifth, it introduces new powers in relation to offences committed at or in connection with football matches. Sixth, it introduces miscellaneous provisions in relation to tampering with goods on sale and also mass trespass.

One of the main differences made to the law under the new Act is that the ancient common law offences of riot, rout, unlawful assembly and affray have been abolished and replaced by three statutory offences: riot, violent disorder and affray. The basis of these offences is no longer breach of the peace but fear for personal safety on the part of a person of reasonable firmness present at the scene.

As regards the Public Order Act 1936 this is largely repealed. Section 3 has been repealed and replaced by a new provision of greater scope and effect and has been extended to certain public assemblies. As was already the case under the old 1936 Act, s12 of the 1986 Act gives the police the power to impose conditions on certain processions and under s13 the chief officer of police may in certain circumstances prohibit processions in his district with the consent of his local authority and the Home Secretary. The major difference under the new Act however is that now the organisers of public processions must give advance notice in writing to the police not less than six clear days before the date of any procession which is intended to demonstrate support for or opposition to the views or actions of any person or body of persons; or publicises a cause or campaign; or which marks or commemorates an event.

Section 14 of the 1986 Act (as amended by ss70 and 71 of the Criminal Justice and

Public Order Act 1994) provides that a senior police officer may impose conditions in relation to public assemblies if, having regard to the time or place at which and the circumstances in which any public assembly is being held or is intended to be held, he reasonably believes that: it may result in serious public disorder, serious damage to property or serious disruption to the life of the community; or the purpose of the persons organising it is the intimidation of others with a view to compelling them not to do an act they have a right to do, or to do an act they have a right not to do.

The section states that he may give directions imposing on the persons organising or taking part in the assembly such conditions as to the place at which the assembly may be (or continue to be) held, its maximum duration, or the maximum number of persons who may constitute it, as appears to him necessary to prevent such disorder, damage, disruption or intimidation. Section 16 defines 'public assembly' as an assembly of 20 or more persons in a public place that is wholly or partly open to the air. Events such as the 'invasion' of Stonehenge during the summer solstice led the government to conclude that the 1986 Act was lacking in terms of the powers vested in the police to deal with static demonstrations. Hence, under ss14A, B and C (added by the 1994 Act), a chief officer of police is empowered to apply to the relevant local authority for an order prohibiting trespassory assemblies on land to which the public does not normally have a right of access, provided that there are grounds to reasonably believe that the owner of the land has not granted permission for the assembly and that the trespassory assembly may result in either serious disruption to the life of the community, or significant damage to land or buildings of historical, archaeological or scientific importance.

It is an offence to organise or participate in any such trespassory assembly in the knowledge that a banning order has been granted. *DPP* v *Jones* [1999] 2 All ER 257 confirms however, that peaceful non-obstructive gatherings are not necessarily trespassory assemblies, provided the use of the highway can be regarded as reasonable.

Under s14C a police constable has the power to intercept and stop those reasonably believed to be proceeding to a trespassory assembly, and direct them not to proceed to the assembly. Disobedience to an order under this provision is a summary offence in relation to which a constable may exercise a power of arrest without a warrant.

Section 5A of the 1936 Act dealing with racial hatred has been restructured and amended to produce six new offences. Section 17 of the 1986 Act defines racial hatred as hatred against a group of persons in Great Britain defined by reference to colour, race, nationality (including citizenship) or ethnic or national origins. All six offences created by the Act require the consent of the Attorney-General to institute proceedings. All of these offences concern conduct which is threatening, abusive or insulting and which is intended or which is likely, having regard to all the circumstances, to stir up racial hatred. They are: (i) using such words or behaviour or displaying such materials; (ii) publishing or distributing such materials; (iii) presenting or directing a public play which involves such words or behaviour; (iv) distributing, showing or playing a recording of such visual images or sounds; (v) certain participation in a broadcast or cable programme service which includes such images or sounds; and (vi) possessing such material or recordings with a view to its being displayed, published, distributed, broadcast or included in a cable broadcast service.

Section 5 of the 1936 Act has also been repealed, and replaced by two new offences. Section 4 of the 1986 Act creates the offence of causing fear or provocation of violence. A person is guilty of an offence if he uses towards another person threatening, abusive or insulting words or behaviour, or distributes or displays to another person any writing, sign or other visible representation which is threatening, abusive or insulting, with intent to cause that person to believe that immediate unlawful violence will be used against him or another by any person, or to provoke the immediate use of unlawful violence by that person or another, or whereby that person is likely to believe that such violence will be used or it is likely that such violence will be provoked.

Section 5 of the 1986 Act creates the controversial offence of causing harassment, alarm or distress. A person is guilty of an offence if he uses threatening, abusive or insulting words or behaviour, or disorderly behaviour, or displays any writing, sign or other visible representation which is threatening, abusive or insulting, within the hearing or sight of a person likely to be caused harassment, alarm or distress thereby. Section 5 provides for three specific defences. First, that the defendant had no reason to believe that there was anyone within hearing or sight of his or her conduct who was likely to be harassed, alarmed or distressed; second, that he or she was inside a dwelling and had no reason to believe that the conduct would have been seen or heard by anyone outside; third, that his or her conduct was reasonable.

Following the enactment of s154 of the Criminal Justice and Public Order Act 1994 a further offence of causing intentional harassment alarm or distress has been created by adding a s4A to the 1986 Act. Under s4A a person will be guilty of the offence if he, with intent to cause another harassment, alarm, or distress, uses threatening, abusive or insulting words or behaviour or disorderly behaviour, or displays any writing, sign or other visible representation which is threatening, abusive or insulting, thereby causing another person harassment, alarm or distress. The offence can be committed in a public or private places, except where both parties are in private dwellings. A constable may arrest without a warrant anyone he reasonably suspects to be guilty of committing the offence. The offence is likely to be charged in cases of racial harassment, although it is clearly not limited to such activities. The offence is effectively an aggravated form of the offence created by s5 of the 1986 Act, ie causing harassment, alarm or distress, and shares many of its features. The Crime and Disorder Act 1998 also introduced racially motivated versions of the offences under ss4 and 5.

The 1986 Act also creates several miscellaneous offences. Under s30 a court by or before which a person is convicted of an offence connected with football may make an exclusion order prohibiting him from entering premises to attend a prescribed football match. Section 38 creates various offences connected with contamination of or interference with goods.

A further area in which the 1986 Act has been found wanting is in relation to so-called 'mass trespass'. Originally dealt with by s39 of the Public Order Act 1986, the matter is now dealt with by ss61 and 62 of the Criminal Justice and Public Order Act 1994. The provisions, which seem to be specifically targeted at the activities of persons leading a nomadic lifestyle ('new age travellers', etc), state that a police constable is empowered to order the removal of trespassers (ie two or more persons) from land where he reasonably believes that: (i) they are present with the common purpose of residing there for any period; and (ii) reasonable steps have been taken by or on behalf of the occupier to ask them to leave; and either (iii) any of the persons has caused damage to the land or property on the land or used threatening or abusive or insulting words or behaviour towards the occupier, his family or agents; or (iv) the trespassers have between them six or more vehicles (a reduction from 12 under the 1986 Act) on the land. For these purposes 'land' does not include land forming part of a highway other than footpaths, bridleways, byways or cycle tracks. Subject to certain statutory defences, failure to comply with a constable's direction under this section is an offence in relation to which a person can be arrested without a warrant, and in relation to which a constable has the power to seize vehicles involved. A person removed from land under these provisions is prohibited from returning for the following three months.

The enactment of the Human Rights Act 1998 ensures that all of the above restrictions on assemblies have to be looked at in the context of art 11(2) of the European Convention on Human Rights. This means that no restrictions may be placed on the exercise of art 11(1) rights other than such as are: prescribed by law; and are necessary in a democratic society in the interests of national security or public safety, for the prevention of disorder or crime, for the protection of health or morals or for the protection of the rights and freedoms of others. Clearly assemblies can be banned or restricted on these grounds, but any such ban must be proportionate to the aim it seeks to achieve. Hence the 1986 Act must now be read in the context of the European Convention on Human Rights.

QUESTION THREE

'The Public Order Act 1986 represents a failure on the part of Parliament to rationalise the law. Public order law remains a miscellany of disparate rules.'

Discuss.

University of London LLB Examination
(for External Students) Constitutional Law June 1991 Q4

General Comment

A question that requires a good knowledge of the central measures in the Public Order Act 1986, and also a knowledge of the related common law provisions. The theme of the solution is to pick out the salient provisions of the 1986 Act, and demonstrate the extent to which they overlap with other statutory and common law provisions.

Skeleton Solution

Assemblies, Public Order Act 1986, other statutes, common law – processions, Public Order Act 1986, other statutes, common law – examples of other pieces of legislation and common law powers – explain need for reform.

Suggested Solution

It is well known that under English law individuals are free to meet together in public in such groups and for such purposes as they see fit, subject only to the limitations imposed by the law. There is no right to march or demonstrate, but instead a variety of limitations imposed by common law and statute.

The Public Order Act 1986 (hereinafter referred to as the 1986 Act) represents an attempt to clarify certain points of law relating to public order, and to consolidate and update the law on a number of issues, but as the quotation under consideration suggests, it has only been partially successful in this respect. The problem remains that the term 'public order law' is necessarily vague. To ascertain the law relating to meetings both public and private, and marches on the highway, one still has to consult a variety of pieces of legislation, and some confusing and contradictory statements at common law.

Consider the law relating to public assemblies. Section 14 of the 1986 Act (as amended by ss70 and 71 of the Criminal Justice and Public Order Act 1994) provides that a senior police officer may impose conditions in relation to public assemblies if, having regard to the time or place at which and the circumstances in which any public assembly is being held or is intended to be held, he reasonably believes that: it may result in serious public disorder, serious damage to property or serious disruption to the life of the community; or the purpose of the persons organising it is the intimidation of others with a view to compelling them not to do an act they have a right to do, or to do an act they have a right not to do. The section states that he may give directions imposing on the persons organising or taking part in the assembly such conditions as to the place at which the assembly may be (or continue to be) held, its maximum duration, or the maximum number of persons who may constitute it, as appears to him necessary to prevent such disorder, damage, disruption or intimidation. Section 16 defines 'public assembly' as an assembly of 20 or more persons in a public place that is wholly or partly open to the air. Events such as the 'invasion' of Stonehenge during the summer solstice led the government to conclude that the 1986 Act was lacking in terms of the powers vested in the police to deal with static demonstrations.

Hence, under ss14A, B and C (added by the 1994 Act), a chief officer of police is empowered to apply to the relevant local authority for an order prohibiting trespassory assemblies on land to which the public does not normally have a right of access, provided that there are grounds to reasonably believe that the owner of the land has not granted permission for the assembly and that the trespassory assembly may result in either serious disruption to the life of the community, or significant damage to land or buildings of historical, archaeological or scientific importance. It is an offence to organise or participate in any such trespassory assembly in the knowledge that a banning order has been granted. The Crime and Disorder Act 1998 also introduced racially motivated versions of the offences under ss4 and 5. Under s14C a police constable has the power to intercept and stop those reasonably believed to be proceeding to a trespassory assembly, and direct them not to proceed to the assembly. Disobedience to an order under this provision is a summary offence in relation to which a constable may exercise a power of arrest without a warrant.

This may be thought to be a comprehensive measure governing such gatherings. But one would still have to have regard to other measures if the meeting takes place on the highway: see s137(1) Highways Act 1980, under which it is a criminal offence wilfully to obstruct the free passage along a highway. If the highway is obstructed then a constable can arrest those causing the obstruction. Obstruction, in this context, is a very flexible term. Special provisions apply to meetings in certain public places such as Hyde Park Corner or Trafalgar Square, which are Crown property. For any meeting to take place the permission of the relevant Secretary of State is needed, and he can if he wishes impose restrictions on any meeting for which permission has been granted.

The 1986 Act also seeks to regulate the use of the highway for processions. Advance notice of public processions must be given in certain circumstances. Section 11 provides that proposals to hold a public procession must be notified to the police if it is a procession intended to demonstrate support for or opposition to the views or actions of any person or body of persons; or publicise a cause or campaign; or mark or commemorate an event. Written notice must be given to the police not less than six clear days before the date of the procession, or as soon as is practicable. The organisers commit an offence if they fail to satisfy these requirements or, if in general, the conduct of the procession differs from that indicated in the notice. The powers provided by the Act are directed to preventing serious public disorder rather than dealing with it when it has occurred. The framework of control has two stages. Marches can be allowed subject to conditions (s12) or banned outright: s13.

These provisions are tolerably clear in their scope and effect, but again they are not comprehensive. Other legislation needs to be consulted in certain cases. For example, Under s52 of the Metropolitan Police Act 1839 the Commissioner of Police of the Metropolis may make regulations for preventing obstruction of the streets within the vicinity of Parliament. Any contravention of those regulations is a criminal offence. The police also have the power to stop potential disorderly processions by bringing the possible demonstrators before the magistrates before the demonstration. They may then be bound over to keep the peace. Should they refuse to be bound over then they can be imprisoned for up to six months.

Those partaking in a procession along the highway could be dealt with under the common law if the procession goes beyond what is a reasonable use of the highway, since it may constitute a public nuisance. This offence is rare but it was used in the case of *R v Clarke (No 2)* [1964] 2 QB 315.

There remains the question of the offences that may be committed once disorder breaks out during a public meeting during a procession. The 1986 Act creates a range of new offences that can be used in such situations.

Section 1 redefines the offence of riot. Section 2 creates a new offence of violent disorder. Section 3 redefines the offence of affray. Section 4 largely replaces s5 of the Public Order Act 1936 with the new offence of causing fear or provocation of violence. Finally s5 introduces the controversial offence of causing harassment, alarm or distress.

All of these new offences co-exist, however, with long established offences such as breach of the peace, an offence drawn in such broad terms it allows the police the power to arrest in situations where the legality of their actions may be unclear.

A brief list will give a flavour of the other disparate offences touching upon 'public order law'. The Unlawful Drilling Act 1819, which prohibits assemblies for the purpose of training or drilling in the use of arms or practising military exercises without lawful authority. The Public Meeting Act 1908, makes it an offence to endeavour to break up a public meeting by acting in a disorderly manner for the purpose of preventing the transaction of the business for which the meeting was called together. The Representation of the People Act 1983 s97 makes it an offence to cause a disturbance at an election meeting. The Police Act 1996 s89(1) makes it an offence to assault a police officer in the execution of his duty. Section 89(2) makes it an offence to wilfully obstruct the police in the execution of their duty.

Finally, the Criminal Justice and Public Order Act 1994 adds further offences relating to the removal of trespassers, further powers to ban trespassory assemblies and powers to deal with squatters and 'raves'.

Not only does the 1986 Act co-exist alongside myriad other related offences, the Act itself was used by Parliament as an opportunity to enact measures which in some cases have only a tenuous link with public order. For example s38 creates various offences connected with contamination of or interference with goods.

In short it is submitted that the whole of the law relating to public order should be looked at again with a view to greater consolidation and rationalisation.

It is fair to say that public order law in the United Kingdom remains a mixture of disparate legislative provisions and common law rules, but the enactment of the Human Rights Act 1998 has ensured that any restrictions imposed by statute or common law must now be subject to a more vigorous scrutiny by the courts, given that the rights provided by art 11 of the European Convention on Human Rights have been given statutory force.

QUESTION FOUR

The PRO organisation arranges a procession through the streets of London. They do not ask anyone for permission. The ANTI organisation arranges a counter demonstration, again without seeking official permission. When the two marches converge on the Strand, violence breaks out. Nobody in the PRO march uses force except in self-defence. A police constable orders the PRO marchers to stop their procession and to disperse. They continue to march and are arrested. Pleased with their success the ANTI marchers disperse and make their way home. A dozen of them decide to have some 'fun' on the Underground platform. They surround an old lady and begin to chant 'euthanasia, euthanasia'. She is alarmed by this and collapses. The ANTI marchers later discover that she was of an unusually weak disposition and had previously suffered heart attacks. But at the time they panic and run away. One of them is intent on escape and has no intent of causing further trouble. The others take the opportunity of lashing out violently at passers-by.

Which offences, if any, have been committed against the Public Order Act 1986?

Written by the Editor

General Comment

A question that demands a comprehensive knowledge of public order offences but a well-prepared student should have no problem if application is logical and thorough. Clearly a good grasp of the Public Order Act 1986 is essential.

Skeleton Solution

Introduction – effect of the Public Order Act 1986 – powers of the police to impose conditions on processions: s12 – common law powers to prevent a breach of peace – s1: riot – s2: violent disorder – s3: affray – s4: provoking violence – s5: disorderly conduct – analyse and apply facts to above sections of the Act.

Suggested Solution

Regarding the problem for consideration, the PRO organisation has arranged a procession through the streets of London and has not asked for permission. While there is no requirement under the law that permission has to be obtained to hold a procession, under s11 of the Public Order Act 1986 the organisers of public processions must give advance notice in writing to the police not less than six clear days before the date of any procession which is intended to demonstrate support for or opposition to the views or actions of any person or body of persons; or publicise a cause or campaign; or which marks or commemorates an event. In not giving such notice the procession organisers therefore commit an offence. The same will be true of the organisers of the ANTI procession.

When the two groups converge violence, instigated by the ANTI marchers, breaks out and a police constable orders the PRO marchers to stop their procession and disperse. It is of course a fundamental principle of our law that one cannot be stopped from doing what one is lawfully entitled to do merely because others act unlawfully: *Beatty v Gillbanks* (1862) 9 QBD 308. However, s12 of the 1986 Act gives the police the power to impose conditions on certain processions if a senior police officer, having regard to the time or place at which and the circumstances in which, any public procession is being held or is intended to be held, reasonably believes that it may result in serious public disorder, serious damage to property or serious disruption to the life of the community, or the purpose of the persons organising it is the intimidation of others with a view to compelling them not to do an act they have a right to do, or to do an act they have a right not to do. Further, under s13 the chief officer of police may in certain circumstances prohibit processions in his district.

While the power therefore exists under the Public Order Act for the police to impose conditions on, and even in some circumstances ban, a lawful procession, it is questionable whether the conditions for so doing apply in this particular case. If they do, conditions can be imposed by the most senior police officer at the scene, arguably a constable in uniform: see s12(2). Under s12(7) a constable may arrest without warrant anyone he reasonably suspects to be committing an offence under s12. At common law a police officer has the power to take such steps as are reasonably necessary to prevent a breach of the peace and in so doing is acting in the execution of his duty so that a failure to obey would be an offence under s89(3) Police Act 1996, and if a breach of the peace is occurring or threatened there is a common law right to arrest preserved by the Police and Criminal Evidence Act 1984.

As regards the violence that takes place in the Strand and the actions of the ANTI marchers on the Underground platform, various offences under the Public Order Act 1986 may have been committed.

The basis of these offences is fear for personal safety on the part of a person of reasonable firmness present at the scene. Section 1 redefines the offence of riot. Where 12 or more persons who are present together use or threaten unlawful violence and the conduct of them (taken together) is such as would cause a person of reasonable firmness present at the scene to fear for his personal safety, each of the persons using or threatening unlawful violence for the common purpose is guilty of riot.

The s2 offence of violent disorder has similarities with riot but the three persons (rather than 12) need not be acting for a common purpose. Note *R v Hebron* [1989] Crim LR 839 which established that mere threats suffice to support a conviction.

Section 3 defines the offence of affray. A person is guilty of affray if he uses or threatens unlawful violence towards another and his conduct is such as would cause a person of reasonable firmness present at the scene to fear for his personal safety.

Section 4 of the 1986 Act creates the offence of causing fear or provocation of violence. A person is guilty of an offence if he uses towards another person threatening, abusive or insulting words or behaviour, or distributes or displays to another person any writing, sign or other visible representation which is threatening, abusive or insulting, with intent to cause that person to believe that immediate unlawful violence will be used against him or another by any person, or to provoke the immediate use of unlawful violence by that person or another, or whereby that person is likely to believe that such violence will be used or it is likely that such violence will be provoked. As the House of Lords made clear in *I* v *Director of Public Prosecutions* [2001] 2 All ER 583, a person should not be charged with affray unless he uses or threatens unlawful violence towards another person actually present at the scene and his conduct is such as would cause fear to a notional bystander of reasonable firmness.

Section 5 of the 1986 Act creates the controversial offence of causing harassment, alarm or distress. A person is guilty of an offence if he uses threatening, abusive or insulting words or behaviour, or disorderly behaviour, or displays any writing, sign or other visible representation which is threatening, abusive or insulting, within the hearing or sight of a person likely to be caused harassment, alarm or distress thereby. Section 5 provides for three specific defences. First, that the defendant had no reason to believe that there was anyone within hearing or sight of his or her conduct who was likely to be harassed, alarmed or distressed; second, that he or she was inside a dwelling and had no reason to believe that the conduct would have been seen or heard by anyone outside; third, that his or her conduct was reasonable. Additionally, the demonstrators may have committed an offence contrary to s4A to the 1986 Act (added by s154 of the Criminal Justice and Public Order Act) of intentionally causing harassment, alarm or distress. The offence can be committed in a public or private place, except where both parties are in private dwellings. A constable may arrest without a warrant anyone he reasonably suspects to be guilty of committing the offence.

From the facts given in the problem it appears that the actions of the ANTI organisation in the Strand could amount to riot, violent disorder and affray since it appears that the violence was instigated by them. However, the PRO organisation acting only in self defence do not seem to fall within the definitions of ss1 and 2 since they acted only in self defence, ie no unlawful violence.

When the ANTI demonstrators gather on the underground platform it seems they simply surround the old lady and chant 'euthanasia, euthanasia'. From the facts given it would seem doubtful whether it would be possible to establish 'use or threats of unlawful violence' so as to sustain charges under ss1, 2 and 3 and s4 also depends upon the threat of 'immediate unlawful violence'. It would therefore seem that the actions in respect of the old lady would have to be prosecuted under s5, causing harassment, alarm or distress. The words 'euthanasia, euthanasia' could be classified as threatening and since an old lady has been singled out for the treatment none of the defences seem appropriate. It will of course be no defence that the ANTI group was not aware of her unusually weak disposition. In *Jordan* v *Burgoyne* [1963] 2 QB 744, a case dealing with similar provisions in the old s5 Public Order Act 1936, it was made clear that the person using threatening, abusive or insulting words cannot look at their effect on a hypothetical reasonable audience but must take note of the effect on the actual audience addressed.

The ANTI demonstrators then disperse, one on his own, leaving 11 who commit acts of violence on passers by. Since there are then only 11 people no offence of riot can be established but violent disorder and affray charges are available, under ss2 and 3 of the 1986 Act respectively.

QUESTION FIVE

To what extent do British citizens enjoy the right to freedom of peaceful assembly under existing domestic law?

University of London LLB Examination
(for External Students) Constitutional Law June 1998 Q6

General Comment

This is a potentially wide-ranging question and the student should direct his/her attention to the area of assemblies and not be diverted into discussing other areas of public order such as processions. The main statutes to be familiar with are the relevant sections of the Public Order Act 1986 and the Criminal Justice and Public Order Act 1994. In addition, candidates should be aware of the available common law powers to curb an assembly, as well as any statutes that might be utilised for this purpose.

Skeleton Solution

The issue of 'rights' in English law – s14 Public Order Act 1986 – Criminal Justice and Public Order Act 1994 – trespass – trespassory assemblies – Highways Act 1980 – common law powers – breach of the peace.

Suggested Solution

Traditionally English law has not recognised any positive right to peaceful assembly. Dicey (*Law of the Constitution* (10th edn, 1959)) regarded rights as residual. This meant that the individual was permitted to do something provided it was not forbidden. A starting point for the examination of the modern law relating to peaceful assembly would now have to be the European Convention on Human Rights, art 11 of which provides that 'Everyone has the right to freedom of peaceful assembly and to freedom of association with others.' Article 11(2) does provide for restrictions to be placed on the exercise of these rights, provided they are prescribed by law and are 'necessary in a democratic society in the interests of national security or public safety, for the prevention of disorder or crime, for the protection of health or morals or for the protection of the rights and freedoms of others.'

With the Human Rights Act 1998 fully in force it is unlawful, under s6(1), for any public authority to act in a manner that is incompatible with any Convention rights protected by the 1998 Act (such as art 11), and that the courts will have regard to those rights in interpreting domestic legislation, whether past before or after incorporation.

As art 11(2) anticipates, restrictions upon the right of peaceful assembly have been imposed under domestic law – the vast majority of them being created by statute.

Section 52 of the Metropolitan Police Act 1839 empowers the Commissioner of Police of the Metropolis to make regulations for preventing obstruction of the streets within the vicinity of Parliament. The constitutional importance of ensuring that MPs are able to attend the House in order to vote is self-evident.

More significantly s14 of the Public Order Act (POA) 1986 (as amended by s70 and s71 of the Criminal Justice and Public Order Act (CJPOA) 1994) provides that a senior police officer may impose conditions in relation to public assemblies if, having regard to the time or place at which and the circumstances in which any public assembly is being held or is intended to be held, he reasonably believes that: it may result in serious public disorder, serious damage to property or serious disruption to the life of the community; or the purpose of the persons organising it is the intimidation of others with a view to compelling them not to do an act they have a right to do, or to do an act they have a right not to do. The section states that he may give directions imposing on the persons organising or taking part in the assembly such conditions as to the place at which the assembly may be (or continue to be) held, its maximum duration, or the maximum number of persons who may constitute it, as appears to him necessary to prevent such disorder, damage, disruption or intimidation.

Section 16 POA 1986 defines 'public assembly' as an assembly of 20 or more persons in a public place that is wholly or partly open to the air. Under ss14A, B and C (added by the CJPOA 1994) a chief officer of police is empowered to apply to the relevant local authority for an order prohibiting trespassory assemblies on land to which the public does not normally have a right of access, provided that there are grounds to reasonably believe that the owner of the land has not granted permission for the assembly and that the trespassory assembly may result in either serious disruption to the life of the community, or significant damage to land or buildings of historical, archaeological or scientific importance. It is an offence to organise or participate in any such trespassory assembly in the knowledge that a banning order has been granted. Under 14C a police constable has the power to intercept and stop those reasonably believed to be proceeding to a trespassory assembly, and direct them not to proceed to the assembly. Disobedience to an order under this provision is a summary offence in relation to which a constable may exercise a power of arrest without a warrant.

The extent of these powers was tested in *DPP v Jones* [1999] 2 All ER 257, a case concerning an order granted pursuant to s14A(2) of the 1986 Act prohibiting the holding of any trespassory assembly within a four-mile radius of the Stonehenge site. The House of Lords had to consider whether an assembly could be trespassory in nature, notwithstanding that it was peaceful and did not obstruct the highway. By a majority their Lordships held that the use of the highway for peaceful purposes, such as assembly, did not automatically exceeded the public's right of reasonable use. Lord Irvine observed that, provided the activities of those forming the assembly were reasonable, did not involve the commission of a public or private nuisance, and did not amount to an obstruction of the highway unreasonably impeding the primary right of the general public to pass and repass, there would be no trespass. This holds true whether the assembly is premeditated or spontaneous.

The decision is significant in that it arguable represents a shift in emphasis from the notion of negative rights (ie freedom to do as one pleases subject to the limitations imposed by the law) towards a concept of positive rights. Such a change is perhaps not surprising given the impact of the Human Rights Act 1998.

Much will depend on the perceived purpose of those engaging in the peaceful assembly. If they are genuinely seeking to draw attention to a grievance and they have no intention of remaining on the land for an unreasonable length of time the court, following the above decision, should regard the activity as lawful. Where, however, the action amounts to a so-called mass trespass (such as might occur when people gather on land for a 'spontaneous' music festival) the authorities will invoke ss61 and 62 CJPOA 1994. Under these provisions a police constable is empowered to order the removal of trespassers (ie two or more persons) from land where he reasonably believes that: (i) they are present with the common purpose of residing there for any period; and (ii) reasonable steps have been taken by or on behalf of the occupier to ask them to leave; and either (iii) any of the persons has caused damage to the land or property on the land or used threatening or abusive or insulting words or behaviour towards the occupier, his family or agents; or (iv) the trespassers have between them six or more vehicles (a reduction from 12 under the 1986 Act) on the land. Section 68 CJPOA 1994, primarily aimed at the activities of groups such as hunt saboteurs, animal rights protesters attempting to prevent the transport of live animals, or demonstrators attempting to disrupt road building programmes, provides the police with the power to deal with those committing aggravated trespass on open land. Aggravated trespass arises where a person is present on land (excluding highways other than footpaths, bridleways, byways or cycle tracks) without the owner's permission, and he commits acts intended to intimidate others present on the land so as to deter them from engaging in any lawful activity, or intended to obstruct or disrupt such activities.

Under s137(1) of the Highways Act 1980 it is a criminal offence for any person to wilfully to obstruct the free passage along a highway without lawful authority or reasonable excuse. Such an obstruction could arise where a group gathers together as an assembly. Lord Clyde in *DPP v Jones* (above) accepted that there was a general common law right of assembly, but did not accept that this necessarily extended to the highway. What was reasonable was linked to what was in the public interest. He regarded standing in the street to sing hymns or Christmas carols as a legitimate use of the highway, provided it was for a reasonable period and without any unreasonable obstruction to traffic.

In *Hirst and Agu* v *Chief Constable of West Yorkshire* (1986) 85 Cr App Rep 143 Glidewell LJ explained that for the defence of lawful excuse to arise under s137(1) the activity in question must of itself be inherently lawful. If it is not the question of reasonable excuse does not arise. Lord Hutton in *DPP* v *Jones* (above) was also of the view that the law as to trespass on the highway should conform with the law relating to wilful obstruction of the highway under s137 of the Highways Act 1980 – ie that a peaceful assembly on the highway may be a reasonable use of the highway, noting in particular that the public's right to use the highway should be extended 'in accordance with the enlarged notions of people in a country becoming more populous and highly civilised', provided those rights were not extended in a manner that was inconsistent with the maintenance of 'the paramount idea that the right of the public [in relation to the highway] … was that of passage.'

Picketing by strikers is another form of peaceful assembly that is recognised at law. Although there is no general 'right' to picket (in the sense that it would constitute an unreasonable use of the highway) s220 of the Trade Union and Labour Relations (Consolidation) Act 1992 makes picketing is lawful if it is in contemplation or furtherance of a trade dispute and at or near the strikers' own workplace for the purpose only of peacefully obtaining or communicating information or peacefully persuading any person to work or to abstain from working. This section provides pickets with immunity in respect of civil actions for trespass or for inducing breach of contract, but does not provide immunity from prosecution for other criminal offences (such as those related to public order) that might be committed.

In addition to these statutory restrictions on the right of peaceful assembly one should not overlook the limitations imposed by the common law powers to take steps to deal with a breach of the peace or apprehended breach of the peace. The test is whether there will be a breach of the peace or a reasonable likelihood of breach of the peace at the gathering. The intention of the organisers is not decisive. In *O'Kelly* v *Harvey* (1883) 15 Cox CC 435, for instance, a meeting of the Land League was ordered to be dispersed by the local justice of the peace as it was in danger of being broken up by Orangemen members of a Protestant organisation hostile to the aspirations of the Land League. This should now be considered, however, in the light of *Steel and Others* v *United Kingdom* (1998) The Times 1 October, where the European Court of Human Rights held that if an assembly was entirely peaceful there would be no basis for those involved being arrested for breach of the peace – to do so could amount to a violation of art 5(1).

Chapter 12

Freedom of Expression

12.1 Introduction

12.2 Key points

12.3 Key cases

12.4 Questions and suggested solutions

12.1 Introduction

Prior to the enactment of the Human Rights Act 1998 English law relied on the principle that, as far as freedom of expression was concerned, what was not prohibited was permitted. The common law and legislature, between them, attempted to strike a balance between the right of their individual to express his opinions, and the right of the individual to be protected from the worst excesses of those views. There was also the balance to be struck between the public interest in the state security and maintenance of public order. As a result English law exhibits a wide range of specific offences to provide remedies to either individuals or the state when views expressed go beyond what is considered tolerable. The area includes such diverse topics as theatre censorship and state security, contempt of court, obscene publications and the right to privacy. The positive right of free expression has been introduced by the Human Rights Act 1998 in the United Kingdom with the incorporation of the European Convention on Human Rights, in particular art 10.

12.2 Key points

The protection of the state

Sedition

This common law offence is now largely of historical interest as other offences have largely superseded the need to prosecute for sedition.

The element of incitement to violence has been stressed: *R v Caunt* (1948) 64 LQR 203.

Incitement to disaffection

It is an offence to undermine the loyalty of:

a) a police officer: s53 Police Act 1964; or

b) a member of the armed forces: Incitement to Disaffection Act 1934. See *R v Arrowsmith* [1975] QB 678.

Incitement to racial hatred

a) Threats, abuse and insults which are likely to result in unlawful violence are criminal: Public Order Act 1986, s4.

b) Threats, abuse or insults which are intended or are likely to stir up racial hatred are specifically dealt with by ss17–23 Public Order Act 1986. The offences are unlikely to be committed by those who use reasoned argument: *Jordan v Burgoyne* [1963] 2 QB 744.

Note the meaning of racial group – a group of persons defined by reference to colour, race, nationality or ethnic or national origins: *Mandla v Dowell Lee* [1983] 2 AC 548.

Blasphemy

a) Blasphemy is a common law offence committed through the vilification of Christ, the Christian religion, the Bible, or any subject sacred to Christians.

b) In *R v Lemon* [1979] AC 617 it was held that there was no need for an intention to blaspheme, publication was enough. Publication need not necessarily lead to a breach of the peace.

c) In *R v Bow Street Magistrates, ex parte Choudbury* (1990) The Times 9 April the Divisional Court refused an application for judicial review of the magistrates' refusal to issue a summons for blasphemy in respect of the Salman Rushdie book *Satanic Verses*.

d) The Law Commission Working Paper: *Offences against Religion and Public Worship* (No 79) based its conclusions on the need to promote free speech, the fact that most serious instances of blasphemy could now be prosecuted under other public order offences, the inappropriateness of giving special protection to Christianity in what was now a multi-faith society, and the unfairness that could result from the imposition of strict liability.

e) The United Kingdom's blasphemy laws were, indirectly, relied upon by the European Court of Human Rights as justifying the British Board of Film Classification's refusal to grant a certificate to a video entitled Visions of Ecstasy: see *Wingrove v United Kingdom* Case 19/1995 (1996) The Times 5 December.

Criminal libel

Criminal libel covers cases of libel where there is considered to be some threat to the preservation of the peace. Prosecutions are rare and only with the order of a High Court judge: *Goldsmith v Pressdram Ltd* [1976] 3 WLR 191.

Freedom of communication and information

a) Government has a duty to preserve the security of the state. National security includes not only measures intended to protect the state from espionage but also all matters that are considered subversive. Governments are often seen as using the cloak of national security to 'gag' the communication of information that should be in the public domain.

b) What is 'national security'?

It is not clear exactly what is included in the concept of national security. Courts often accept the word of governments. National security interests have been invoked in a variety of instances, such as: defence of the realm and the prosecution of war (*The Zamora* [1916] 2 AC 77); the disposition of the armed forces (*Chandler v DPP* [1964] AC 763); nuclear weapons (*Secretary of State for Defence v Guardian Newspapers* [1984] 1 All ER 453); and the activities of intelligence services (*Attorney-General v Guardian Newspapers (No 2)* [1988] 3 All ER 545).

c) Official Secrets Acts

Section 1 of the Official Secrets Act 1911 creates offences of espionage. It is not restricted to spying but includes acts of sabotage: *Chandler v DPP* [1964] AC 763.

Section 2 created some 2,000 offences directed at the misuse of information. It was criticised for being used to keep policy making free of outside scrutiny.

In 1989, s2 was repealed by the Official Secrets Act 1989. The Act creates specific categories of information that is sensitive and should be controlled. These are: security and intelligence; defence; international relations; and criminal investigations. The disclosure must be 'damaging'. This concept operates differently in respect of each of the four categories. There is no public interest defence or a defence of prior publication.

R v Shayler (2002) The Times 22 March confirms that there is no public interest defence permitting disclosure of information by serving or former members of the Security Services. Disclosures will only be permitted where they have been authorised by ministers or senior civil servants. This restriction on free speech was held by the House of Lords to be compatible with art 10 of the European Convention on Human Rights. Although these restrictions did interfere with the right to free expression enjoyed by members of the security services, they were clearly prescribed by law (ie laid down in legislation), had been imposed for purposes consistent with art 10(2) (maintenance of national security), and did not go further than was required to achieve those aims (ie the restrictions were a proportionate response to the threat posed by members of the security services divulging classified information). The House of Lords regarded it as significant that any refusal to authorise disclosure would itself be subject to judicial review.

d) 'D' Notices

A form of extra legal censorship which depends on co-operation between governments and the press with the objective of achieving a ban on the publication of matters which are considered likely to jeopardise national security.

Regulation of Investigatory Powers Act 2000

This major piece of legislation replaces the Interception of Communications Act 1985 and introduces additional safeguards in respect of covert surveillance. In doing so it complements provisions of the Police Act 1997 and the Intelligence Services Act 1984. Interception of communications is permitted if: the sender and receiver consent to the interception; the sender consents to the interception and interception is authorised under Pt II of the 2000 Act (which deals with authorised surveillance operations); the interception is conducted under specific provisions relating to prisons, or international mutual assistance agreements; and the interception is pursuant to a warrant issued under s5. In granting a warrant s5 provides that the Secretary of State must believe that it is necessary to do so on one of the following grounds: the interests of national security; preventing or detecting serious crime; or of safeguarding the economic well-being of the United Kingdom. In any event the conduct authorised by the warrant must be proportionate to what is sought to be achieved by that conduct.

Part IV of the 2000 Act sets out the framework for oversight of the operation of the authorisations machinery and the functions of the intelligence services. The Interception of Communications Commissioner, a senior judicial figure, replaces the Commissioner appointed under the 1985 Act. He will review the Secretary of State's role regarding the granting of intercept warrants and the operation of the regime for acquiring communications data.

Breach of confidence

An equitable doctrine to ensure that a person should not take unfair advantage of confidences obtained: *Argyll v Argyll* [1967] Ch 302; *Attorney-General v Jonathan Cape* [1976] QB 752.

It is worth noting in this context because of the attempt made by the government in the 'Spycatcher' affair to assert that members of the security services owe a lifelong duty of confidentiality to the Crown: *Attorney-General v Guardian Newspapers (No 2)* [1988] 3 All ER 545.

It seems that the courts are more willing to consider the issue of 'the public interest' and not to depend on the government's view: *Lord Advocate v Scotsman Publications* [1990] 1 AC 812.

The Human Rights Act 1998 has provided the stimulus for significant development of the doctrine of breach of confidence as a means of protecting individuals from the excesses of the tabloid press. Although newspapers are not private bodies, and thus not bound by the 1998 Act, the courts as public bodies are under a duty to develop the common law so as to ensure that rights, such as the art 8 right to privacy, are protected under domestic law. The result is that the courts have shown themselves sympathetic to the development of breach of confidence as a way of developing a quasi-right to privacy at common law. Significant developments in this respect have been the decisions in *Douglas v Hello! Ltd* [2001] 2 All ER 289 (duty of confidence could arise simply by agreeing to attend a wedding and not take photographs) and *Venables v News Group Newspapers Ltd* [2001] 1 All ER 908 (perpetual injunction granted to prevent disclosure of new identities). The key point is that a duty of confidence can arise notwithstanding the absence of any express or implied agreement between the parties that the material would not be disclosed.

Obscene publications

a) The trade in pornography is lucrative and the state seeks to limit publication to limit 'depravity'. There are statutory and common law offences.

b) Obscene Publications Act 1959

An obscene article is one where the effect 'if taken as a whole, would tend to deprave and corrupt persons who are likely having regard to all the circumstances to read, see or hear the matter contained or embodied in it': s1.

i) Article is defined widely and includes pictures, books and film negatives.

ii) The definition of obscene requires the jury to consider whether the article has a tendency to deprave and corrupt and this has caused inconsistency. It is not limited to sexual matters: *John Calder (Publishers) v Powell* [1965] 1 QB 509; *Director of Public Prosecutions v A and BC Chewing Gum* [1968] 1 QB 159.

iii) Policing the trade in pornography is difficult – 'an attempt to eradicate the ineradicable' (Robert Mark, ex Chief Commissioner for the Metropolis, in *Policing a Perplexed Society* (1977)). See *R v Metropolitan Police Commissioner, ex parte Blackburn (No 3)* [1973] QB 241.

iv) Section 3 confers search, seizure and forfeiture powers.

v) Section 4 makes it a defence if the material is 'for the public good on the grounds that it is in the interests of science, literature, art or learning'. Whether publication is for the public good is for the jury to decide.

See *Attorney-General's Reference (No 3 of 1977)* [1978] 3 All ER 1166; *R v Penguin Books* [1961] Crim LR 176.

c) The Obscene Publications Act 1964 allows the police to seize material if the material was 'in possession for gain' thus it can be effective – material can be seized – before publication.

d) Other legislation

This includes Customs Consolidation Act 1876, the Children and Young Persons (Harmful Publications) Act 1955, the Post Office Act 1953 and the Protection of Children Act 1978.

e) Common law offences

i) Conspiracy to corrupt public morals: *Shaw* v *DPP* [1962] AC 220.

ii) Conspiracy to outrage public decency: *Knuller* v *DPP* [1973] AC 435.

f) Cinema and theatre

There are general controls over films (Cinemas Act 1985 and Video Recordings Act 1984) and over live performances (Theatres Act 1968).

Contempt of court

a) Civil contempts

The breach of or disobedience to an order of the court: *Harman* v *Secretary of State for the Home Department* [1982] 2 WLR 338.

b) Criminal contempts

The objective here is to ensure both the fairness of a trial and also that the judiciary is accorded respect.

c) Contempt of Court Act 1981

The Act clarified the position regarding newspaper publication of matters of public interest that could prejudice the outcome of court proceedings by the following reforms.

See also *Attorney-General* v *Times Newspapers Ltd* [1974] AC 273, a case that went to the European Court of Human Rights.

i) It is an offence 'to interfere with the course of justice in particular legal proceedings regardless of intent' where the proceedings in question are active: s1.

ii) There is no offence if there was no reason to suspect that proceedings are active (s3) or that publication is a discussion in good faith of public affairs: *Attorney-General* v *English* [1982] 2 WLR 278.

iii) Section 10 gives limited protection to journalists of their sources unless disclosure is necessary in the interests of justice, national security or for the prevention of disorder or crime: *Secretary of State for Defence* v *Guardian Newspapers Ltd* [1984] 2 WLR 268.

iv) The prevention of crime exception in s10 encompasses the prevention of crime in general: *Re an Inquiry under the Company Securities (Insider Dealing) Act 1985* [1988] AC 660.

Censorship

a) Theatres are subject to the laws on obscenity, defamation and incitement to racial hatred.

b) Cinemas are licensed by the local authority, which attaches conditions, and recommendations of the British Board of Film Censors are usually followed.

c) Broadcasting

Both the BBC and IBA are under a duty to provide programmes which comply with good taste and decency and to preserve political impartiality. This last point has sometimes caused political controversy with governments.

Defamation

a) Defamation is a tort, in respect of which damages can be obtained, that can take one of two forms: if transitory in nature, such as the spoken word or gestures, it is referred to as slander; if in a more permanent form, such as the printed word, or a broadcast, it is referred to as libel. The essence of the tort is that, as a result of things said, done or published by the defendant, the plaintiff has suffered the hatred, ridicule and contempt of others such that would tend to lower him in the estimation of right-thinking members of society.

b) Defences at common law include: justification, ie that the impugned statement is essentially true; 'fair comment', provided the defendant was expressing his view of a matter of public interest, was not motivated by malice, and that the statement did not contain any significant factual errors; absolute privilege, which attaches to statements made during proceedings in Parliament and statements made during judicial proceedings. Absolute privilege also extends to fair and accurate reports of proceedings in public before any court in the United Kingdom, the European Court of Justice and the European Court of Human Rights: see further s14 Defamation Act 1996. Qualified privilege is a defence to defamation in respect of statements made by a defendant in the course of his performing a legal, social or moral duty, where the statements are directed to another person who has a corresponding interest in receiving the material, and where the defendant is not motivated by malice, ie he believes the statement to be accurate.

In *Reynolds* v *Times Newspapers Ltd and Others* [1999] 4 All ER 609 the House of Lords held that journalists could not rely on qualified privilege simply because they were commenting on political matters. Assuming the absence of malice, there were a number of factors that would have a bearing on the availability of the defence including: the seriousness of the allegation; the extent to which the material was in a matter of public interest; the source of the information; the steps taken to verify the information; the status of the information; the urgency of the matter; whether the plaintiff had been invited to comment; whether the article indicated the plaintiff's view of the allegation; the strength of the assertion of fact; and the timing of the publication.

c) The defence of qualified privilege is also available to those who publish fair and accurate reports of proceedings in Parliament; for the scope of this defence: see now s15 of the Defamation Act 1996.

d) Section 1 of the Defamation Act 1996 provides that a person has a defence if he shows that: he was not the author, editor or publisher of the statement complained of; he took reasonable care in relation to its publication; he did not know, and had no reason to believe, that what he did caused or contributed to the publication of a defamatory statement.

e) The 1996 Act also creates a new defence based upon the defendant's offer to make amends. The defence replaces the defence of unintentional defamation created under s4 of the Defamation Act 1952. The defendant must be prepared to make a suitable correction of the statement complained of and a sufficient apology to the aggrieved party; to publish the correction and apology in a manner that is reasonable and practicable in the circumstances; and to pay to the aggrieved party such compensation (if any), and such costs, as may be agreed or determined to be payable. An offer to make amends cannot be made if a defence to the action has already been served.

f) Changes introduced in the Courts and Legal Services Act 1990 empowered the Court of Appeal to overturn 'excessive' awards: see further *John* v *MGN Ltd* (1995) The Times 14 December. Section 8 of the Defamation Act 1996 introduces a new summary procedure for the disposal of defamation actions where there is either 'no realistic prospect of success' for the plaintiff, or no defence.

Prior restraint

A person whose interests are likely to be affected by the publication of material or the Attorney-General in his role as guardian of the public interest can apply to the court for an injunction restraining such publication. The injunction is interim until such time as a full hearing of the issues can take place: see *Attorney-General* v *Guardian Newspapers (No 1)* [1987] 3 All ER 316; *Attorney-General* v *Newspaper Publishing plc* [1987] 3 All ER 276. Note that some prior constraints are extra-legal, eg D notices.

The positive right to freedom of expression

The Human Rights Act 1998 brings certain provisions of the European Convention on Human Rights into domestic law, including art 10, which provides:

'(1) Everyone has the right to freedom of expression. This right shall include freedom to hold opinions and to receive and impart information and ideas without interference by public authority and regardless of frontiers. This article shall not prevent states from requiring the licensing of broadcasting, television and cinema enterprises.

(2) The exercise of these freedoms, since it carries with it duties and responsibilities, may be subject to such formalities, conditions, restrictions or penalties as are prescribed by law and are necessary in a democratic society, in the interests of national security, territorial integrity or public safety, for the prevention of disorder or crime, for the protection of health or morals, for the protection of the reputation or rights of others, for preventing the disclosure of information received in confidence, or for maintaining the authority and impartiality of the judiciary.'

Under the Human Rights Act 1998 the courts are required to interpret domestic legislation so as to ensure compliance with art 10 in so far as this is possible. It will also become unlawful for any public authority to act in a way that is inconsistent with the Convention rights. Section 12 of the 1998 Act provides in particular that the courts must have regard to the importance of the Convention right to freedom of expression.

12.3 Key cases

- *Attorney-General* v *Newspaper Publishing plc* [1997] 1 WLR 926
  No contempt of court in publishing restricted documents unless the administration of justice in the relevant proceedings has been wholly frustrated or rendered utterly futile

- *Goldsmith* v *Bhoyrul* [1997] 4 All ER 268
  Political party cannot be defamed

- *Reynolds* v *Times Newspapers Ltd and Others* [1998] 3 All ER 961
  Defamation – implied criticism of politician – whether statements attracting qualified privilege where they were concerned with public conduct of affairs of state

12.4 Questions and suggested solutions

QUESTION ONE

'Viewed as a liberalising measure, the Official Secrets Act 1989 is something of a disappointment.'

Discuss this view, by reference to the aims and provisions of the Act.

University of London LLB Examination
(for External Students) Constitutional Law June 1995 Q6

General Comment

This question requires detailed knowledge of the terms and the scope of the Official Secrets Act 1989 and the role it played in reforming the 1911 Act. Where the candidate is comfortable with the subject-matter, the structure of the Act should determine the structure of the answer.

Skeleton Solution

Aim of the 1911 Act – aim of the 1989 Act – categories of person criminalised – categories of act criminalised – absence of a public interest defence.

Suggested Solution

The predecessor of the Official Secrets Act 1989 Act, the Official Secrets Act 1911 was introduced to protect the interests of the state against espionage and other activities which might be useful to an enemy and therefore injurious to state security; and to guard against the unauthorised disclosure of information held by servants of the state in their official capacity, whether or not the information had any direct reference to state security as such. The 1911 Act was widely regarded as being far too wide in its application.

The 1989 Act grew out of the Franks Committee Report (Cmnd 5104 (1972)), which recommended protection of: classified information relating to defence matters and internal security which would cause injury to the nation; information relating to the prosecution of criminal offences; information which had been entrusted to government by individual concerns for tax or social security purposes; and Cabinet documents. The Committee recommended that protection of Official Secrets and information should be by criminal sanctions only where the circumstances required it.

Further reforms were considered in a White Paper published in 1978, and again in the White Paper of June 1988 (Cm 408) that led to the 1989 Act. The 1988 White Paper observed that the most obvious areas in which the public interest needed to be protected were those where the protection of the nation from attack from outside or from within was involved. It argued that any new legislation in this area would have to protect information relating to defence (including civil preparedness) and information relating to security and intelligence. It went on to hold that the reforming legislation should make a distinction between disclosures by members and former members of the security and intelligence services and disclosures by other persons – with greater restrictions on the former as compared to the latter.

As a consequence the 1989 Act liberalised the law by repealing s2 of the 1911 Act, but introduced sanctions against unauthorised disclosure of a narrower range of information. Section 1 of the 1989 Act protects from disclosure information relating to security and intelligence, but distinguishes between disclosures without lawful authority by security and intelligence staff on the one hand, and civil servants and government contractors on the other hand. It is an offence for any person to disclose any information obtained in the course of employment in the intelligence services without first obtaining the appropriate authorisation.

Unauthorised disclosure by civil servants and government contractors is unlawful where it is 'damaging' to the defence of the nation or international affairs. Sections 2 and 3 make it an offence for a civil servant or government contractor to disclose damaging information in this way. In the case of disclosures made in the area of defence, the material is considered to be damaging where it restricts the capability of the armed forces to carry out their tasks. Disclosure is considered to be damaging with reference either to defence or international affairs where it endangers the interests of the United Kingdom abroad, or where it endangers the safety of British citizens abroad.

Under s4 of the 1989 Act it is an offence for a civil servant or government contractor to disclose any information where it results in the commission of an offence or facilitates an escape from custody or impedes the prevention or detection of criminal offences. It is similarly an offence to disclose information relating to the obtaining of information as a result of any phone-tapping operation or interference with private property where the latter is permitted by the Security Services Act 1989 and the Regulation of Investigatory Powers Act 2000. Therefore, information obtained without a warrant can be disclosed lawfully under s4 but not under s1 of the 1989 Act.

In all circumstances the offence is committed where the information is disclosed without lawful authority. This is similar to s2 of the 1911 Act, which provided that the offence was committed where the disclosure was unauthorised. There is, however, great difficulty in identifying those cases where a Crown agent or employee is permitted to disclose information. There is also difficulty here with reference to disclosures by Cabinet ministers or senior ministers. Under s7 of the Act a disclosure is authorised where it is made in accordance with the official duty of the minister or civil servant in question. An offence may be committed only by the official disclosing the information or where a third party discloses that information and reports it (for example, a newspaper or radio station).

It is no longer an offence to receive information protected against disclosure. However, under s5 of the 1989 Act it is an offence for the recipient to disclose the information without lawful authority knowing or having reasonable cause to believe that it is protected from disclosure. Therefore, it would be an offence were a newspaper to publish protected information under the Act where that information had been leaked without authorisation. In this circumstance there is no public interest defence because the government rejected the inclusion of such a defence in the Act. The newspaper would be liable only if the disclosure were damaging and was made in the knowledge (or having reasonable cause to believe) that it was damaging.

It is this aspect of the 1989 Act that undermines some of the liberalising effect of much of the Act. The failure to provide for leaking in the public interest maintains the culture of official secrecy that many sought to have removed with the introduction of the 1989 Act. In the United Kingdom the constitutional position is far less advanced than in the United States in refusing to hold that there should be a public interest defence in making disclosures which fall foul of the Official Secrets Act 1989.

The Human Rights Act 1998 has not had the impact in this area that some might have hoped. Section 1 of the 1989 Act clearly restricts the rights to free expression granted to all by virtue of art 10 of the European Convention on Human Rights. Certain restrictions are envisaged by art 10(2), however, which provides that the right may be subject to such formalities, conditions, restrictions or penalties as are: prescribed by law; and necessary in a democratic society, in the interests of national security. In *R v Shayler* (2002) The Times 22 March the House of Lords, confirming that there was no implied public interest defence in s1 of the 1989 Act permitting security service members to disclose information because they felt the public ought to have it, held that s1 was consistent with art 10(2). The restrictions were clearly prescribed by law (ie laid down in legislation) and had been imposed for purposes consistent with art 10(2) (maintenance of national security). Crucially the restrictions were not seen as going further than was required to achieve those aims (ie the restrictions were a proportionate response to the threat posed by members of the security services divulging classified information). The House of Lords also regarded it as significant that any refusal to authorise disclosure would itself be subject to judicial review, and it was noted that where Convention rights were engaged, judicial review would subject the administration to more vigorous scrutiny: see *R (Daly) v Secretary of State for the Home Department* [2001] 3 All ER 433.

QUESTION TWO

To what extent does the law successfully balance competing interests in the area of press freedom?

Written by the Editor

General Comment

A straightforward question requiring students to review the law on civil and criminal law restraints on press freedom.

Skeleton Solution

Introduction nature of freedom of speech in the United Kingdom remedies available – prior restraint an evaluation of the effect of prior restraint on the media – defamation – breach of confidence its use particularly by government – Official Secrets Act 1989 – contempt of court – the individual and the press remedies and contrasts with the above.

Suggested Solution

Freedom of speech is fundamental to a free society. It is protected by art 10 of the European Convention on Human Rights now incorporated into domestic law by the Human Rights Act 1998. The position in the United Kingdom is that individual members of the state are free to express views and opinions that are not against the numerous laws that restrict freedom of speech and to this extent the law attempts to balance competing rights. The press has a fundamental role to perform in informing the public, not least on government activities. However, individuals have a right not to be offended or abused and the state has a right to prevent the publication of sensitive material that could, for example, jeopardise national security. There is an inherent conflict here and some of the ways in which the law deals with that conflict in relation to press freedom will now be examined. The major restrictions on press freedom are to be found in the laws on defamation, breach of confidence and contempt of court.

It is important at the outset to draw a distinction between prior restraint and subsequent penalties. Blackstone (in his *Commentaries* (1765)) emphasised the importance in a free society of laying no prior restraints on publications, namely 'every free man has an undoubted right to lay what sentiments he pleases before the public; to forbid this is to destroy the freedom of the press', and his sentiments were included in the first amendment to the American constitution. It is arguable that prior restraint has become relatively easy to obtain in Britain either by the person whose interests are affected or by the Attorney-General as 'guardian' of the public interest. The injunction is interim and the applicant has to show that he has an arguable case, and that the balance of convenience is against publishing and damages are not an adequate remedy. That balance of convenience is normally in favour of a ban and some writers (see G Robertson, *Freedom, the Individual and the Law*) argue that this can amount to political interference with free speech. In *Attorney-General v BBC* (1987) The Times 18 December the government was successful in getting an interim injunction against a series entitled *My Country Right or Wrong* on the grounds that ex-employees of the security services might have breached confidences during interviews.

Injunctions can also be granted to protect commercial interests when the courts balance the public's right to information against the private interest in ensuring that discussion should be prevented. In this context the private interest will be to protect trade secrets whilst the public interest may relate to the effect for example of a drug: *Schering Chemicals v Falkman Ltd* [1982] QB 1. An injunction once granted binds third parties: *Attorney-General v Observer Newspapers Ltd* [1988] 1 All ER 385. Whilst the nature of the injunction is limited to the period until trial, it may well be that the information may by then be no longer important.

The press will always be mindful of the restrictions imposed by the law of defamation. The essence of this tort is that, as a result of things said, done, or published by the defendant, the plaintiff has suffered the hatred, ridicule, contempt of others such that would tend to lower him in the estimation of right thinking members of society. Key defences where comment is made on the activities of those in the public eye are that the impugned statement is essentially true; 'fair comment', provided the defendant was expressing his view of a matter of public interest, was not motivated by malice, and that the statement did not contain any significant factual errors; absolute privilege which attaches to statements made during proceedings in Parliament and statements made during judicial proceedings; and qualified privilege – where statements are made by a defendant in the course of his performing a legal, social or moral duty.

The latter defence was considered in *Reynolds v Times Newspapers Ltd and Others* [1999] 4 All ER 609. The defendant newspaper published an article about the resignation of the plaintiff, Albert Reynolds, formerly the Prime Minister of Ireland. The article was critical of the plaintiff's alleged involvement in the appointment of a former Irish

Attorney General to the post of President of the Court. The gist of the criticisms was that the plaintiff had knowingly misled the Irish Parliament. The plaintiff brought an action for defamation and the defendant newspaper sought to rely on the defence of qualified privilege at common law. Lord Nicholls confirmed that the purpose of the defence of qualified privilege was to ensure that there should be uninhibited communication between two particular parties where such communication was in the public interest. He acknowledged the important role played by the press in keeping the public informed. It performed, he said, vital functions both as 'bloodhound' and 'watchdog'. He also expressed the view that, in respect of political discussion, the courts should be slow to conclude that the public had no 'right to know'. Any residual doubts regarding whether or not material should be made public should normally be resolved in favour of disclosure. He rejected, however, the contention that there could be a defence of qualified privilege based simply on the fact that the subject matter complained of constituted political information. A proper balance could be struck between press freedom and the protection of an individual's reputation by granting political reporting qualified privilege provided certain factors were satisfied.

Assuming there was no malice in the reporting of these matters the courts would consider factors such as: the seriousness of the allegation; the extent to which the material was in a matter of public interest; the source of the information; the steps taken to verify the information; the status of the information; the urgency of the matter; whether the plaintiff had been invited to comment; whether the article indicated the plaintiff's view of the allegation; the strength of the assertion of fact; and the timing of the publication. In theory 'responsible' journalists, ie those that check their sources and behave ethically, should benefit from the decision in that they can expect their work to attract qualified privilege, but much will depend on the view of the judge presiding over any consequent libel action.

The Press may also be prohibited from publishing material where the courts hold that it is protected from disclosure by the doctrine of breach of confidence. Traditionally this protection has been granted to information is given in circumstances of confidence, such as intimate communications between husband and wife (*Duke of Argyll* v *Duchess of Argyll* [1967] Ch 302), trade secrets (*Lion Laboratories* v *Evans* [1985] QB 526) or employment. A confidence ceases to be a confidence once it is in the public domain. The Human Rights Act 1998 has thrown this issue into stark relief. On the one hand the press can claim a right to freedom of expression under art 10 of the Convention. On the other hand individuals will claim a right to privacy under art 8. Matters are further complicated by the fact that newspapers are not under any duty to abide by the Convention, as they are not public bodies. Section 12 of the 1998 Act attempts to deal with this potential conflict by providing that the courts must have particular regard to the importance of the Convention right to freedom of expression – but it is not clear how this is really of assistance. Ultimately the United Kingdom courts are bound by the jurisprudence of the European Court of Human Rights as regards the 'hierarchy' of rights (ie whether freedom of expression outweighs the right to privacy). If domestic courts restrict the scope of Convention rights in a manner that is contrary to the rulings of the European Court of Human Rights, the way lies open to have the matter determined at Strasbourg with the prospect of the United Kingdom being found in breach of its Convention rights, notwithstanding incorporation.

For the time being the courts have made some inroads on Press freedom by extending the doctrine of breach of confidence to situations where there is no contractual or quasi-contractual relationship between the parties: see for example *Douglas* v *Hello! Ltd* [2001] 2 All ER 289 (duty of confidence could arise simply by agreeing to attend a wedding and not take photographs) and *Venables* v *News Group Newspapers Ltd* [2001] 1 All ER 908 (perpetual injunction granted to prevent disclosure of new identifies). In determining whether or not material should be protected in this way the courts will have to assess the extent to which the litigant's right to privacy under art 8 is engaged: see *A* v *B plc and Another* (2002) The Times 13 March (newspaper allowed to publish information provided by the mistress of a married professional footballer detailing their sexual relationship).

Governments are concerned to limit information which is of a sensitive nature in terms of national security but also may be inclined to prevent publication where information is simply politically embarrassing. The use of the discredited s2 of the Official Secrets Act 1911 provides evidence of the preoccupation of governments with secrecy. In *R* v *Aitken* [1974] Crim LR 639 the government prosecuted under s2 for the publication of information already in the public domain, and in the celebrated case of *R* v *Ponting* [1985] Crim LR 318 the jury found not guilty a civil servant who had leaked information to an opposition MP which revealed that the government was attempting to deceive Parliament. Section 2 of the Act has been repealed by the Official Secrets Act 1989. Journalists and editors can be imprisoned if they encourage civil servants to make disclosures or publish such disclosures. During the debate, attention focused on whether there should be a public interest defence, but amendments to the Bill were successfully resisted. Under s5 members of the press can be successfully prosecuted if they publish information which they know is protected by the Act and they had reason to believe the publication would be damaging to the interests of the United Kingdom. If information is published from former or serving members of the security service the offence is one of strict liability. It is notable that the court in *Attorney-General* v *Guardian Newspapers (No 2)* [1988] 3 WLR 776 accepted the principle of a public interest defence in breach of confidence actions which the government was anxious not to see in the Official Secrets Act 1989.

It is essential that court proceedings are not disrupted and justice is not impeded through press comment on cases in progress. In *Attorney-General* v *News Group Newspapers Ltd* [1987] QB 1 an injunction to restrain further publication of allegedly defamatory material was refused because the trial was some months away and a substantial risk to proceedings would not result. Clearly if the Press was to publish details of a person's previous convictions shortly before trial, or publish a picture of someone involved in identification evidence, there would be contempt. The Contempt of Court Act 1981 legislation, enacted in the wake of the decision of the European

Court of Human Rights in *Sunday Times* v *United Kingdom* (1979) 2 EHRR 245 sought to provide a clear logical basis for the operation of the rules on contempt. For liability to arise there must be a 'substantial risk' to proceedings: see s2. Under s5, media comment, made in good faith, where the risk to legal proceedings is incidental, should not result in liability: see *Attorney-General* v *English* [1983] 1 AC 116. Section 10 of the Act provides for the protection of journalistic sources unless it is established to the satisfaction of the court that disclosure is necessary in the interests of justice or national security or for the prevention of disorder or crime. The courts have tended to order disclosure however eg *Secretary of State for Defence* v *Guardian Newspapers Ltd* [1984] 2 WLR 268, and more recently in *X* v *Morgan Grampian (Publishers) Ltd* [1991] 1 AC 1.

While there are many remedies available to the government to restrict press freedom, the protections available to individuals are more limited. The action of defamation can be brought but the expense involved is often prohibitive. The private interests of individuals and the lack of a comprehensive law on privacy in this country all too often leave the individual with no remedy: *Re X (A Minor)* [1975] 2 WLR 335. The Press Complaints Commission considers complaints against newspapers but in practice has little effect against newspapers that invade privacy in the interests of sensationalism.

QUESTION THREE

'The security of the state is one of the most important functions of government.' To what extent does the law relating to national security reflect this importance?

University of London LLB Examination
(for External Students) Constitutional Law June 1991 Q8

General Comment

There is no 'right way' to tackle a question of this nature since its terms are open to such wide interpretation. Establish what you mean by the term national security law and proceed to cite relevant statutory and common law examples.

Skeleton Solution

Explain difficulties of interpretation – relate leading judicial review cases – note judicial reluctance to question ministers' views – cite various statutory provisions concerned with national security.

Suggested Solution

The question refers to 'the law relating to national security', and asks to what extent that law reflects the importance of the government's role in maintaining state security. An initial difficulty in answering such a question lies in ascertaining the area of law the question is referring to. Clearly national security is not a recognised discrete area of law such as contract or criminal law. If anything it is a concept that cuts across many different areas of law that is used to justify, action or inaction on the part of the government of the day.

In proceedings for judicial review of administrative action the courts have, on occasion, refused to interfere with the decision of a minister on the ground that he has cited 'acting in the interests of national security' to justify his actions.

R v *Secretary of State for the Home Department, ex parte Hosenball* [1977] 1 WLR 766 concerned a challenge to the actions of the Secretary of State himself in refusing to give information about the reasons for making a deportation order against an alien. The Divisional Court and the Court of Appeal refused to grant an order of certiorari because the refusal had been based on grounds of national security. Note that if the refusal of reasons had occurred in what Lord Denning MR called an 'ordinary case', that is, one in which national security was not involved, the position would have been different. He stated:

> '… if the body concerned, whether it be a minister or advisers, has acted unfairly, then the courts can review their proceedings so as to ensure, as far as may be, that justice is done.'

Similarly, in *Council of Civil Service Unions* v *Minister for the Civil Service* [1985] AC 374, where the House of Lords had to consider a challenge to the validity of the Prime Minister's oral direction prohibiting civil servants employed at GCHQ from membership of a trade union, Lord Fraser stated that:

> '… whatever their source, powers which are defined, either by reference to their object or by reference to procedure for their exercise, or in some other way, and whether the definition is expressed or implied, are in my opinion normally subject to judicial control to ensure that they are not exceeded. By "normally" I mean provided that considerations of national security do not require otherwise.'

In that particular case, the House of Lords held that, had it not been for the issue of national security, (ie the need for the Prime Minister to pre-empt potentially damaging industrial action by unilaterally banning union membership), her actions would have been in breach of natural justice on the ground of her failure to consult the civil servants on an issue relating to their terms and conditions of employment.

The courts have always been careful to maintain the view that they will not accept an argument based on national security as being sufficient in itself to oust their jurisdiction, but in practice they have rarely if ever, rejected it. Some of the dicta in *Chandler* v *DPP* [1964] AC 763 are instructive on this point. The House of Lords considered the appeal by CND members who claimed that they had not been planning to act in a manner prejudicial to the interests of the State by preventing planes carrying nuclear warheads from taking off. Lord Reid, questioning who was to determine what is and is not prejudicial to the interests of the State, did not subscribe to the view that the government or a minister must always or even as a general rule have the last word. In his opinion it was clear that the disposition and armament of the armed forces was, and for centuries had been, within the exclusive discretion of the Crown, and that no one could seek a legal remedy on the ground that such discretion has been wrongly exercised.

Lord Devlin, agreeing, observed that there was no rule of the common law that questions of national security were to be determined according to what the Crown thought necessary or expedient. He emphasised that as individuals could exaggerate their interests, so could the Crown. On the whole, however, given the political nature of many decisions affecting national security, the judiciary cannot be criticised for deferring to the Crown's assertions where there is room for doubt.

Various statutes also recognise the importance of ministers acting in the interests of national security.

In relation to broadcasting the Home Secretary can prevent television and radio programmes from being broadcast on the ground that damage would be done to national security; see also the operation of the 'D' Notice committee (Defence, Press and Broadcasting Committee).

A further obvious example is provided by the Official Secrets Act 1989. Section 1 imposes a stringent duty on members or retired members of the security and intelligence services and those notified that they are subject to the section. It provides that such a person commits an offence if without lawful authority he discloses any information or document he has received in the course of such work or while such notification is in force. The House of Lords, in *R v Shayler* (2002) The Times 22 March, has confirmed that there is no public interest defence permitting disclosure of information by serving or former members of the Security Services. Disclosures will only be permitted where they have been authorised by ministers or senior civil servants. This is on the basis that it cannot be left up to individual Crown servants to determine when classified information should be made public.

Certain modern statutes expressly refer to the concept of 'national security'. For example, s1(2) of the Security Service Act 1989 provides that the functions of the Security Services include the protection of 'national security' in particular 'protection against threats from espionage, terrorism and sabotage, the activities of agents of foreign powers and from actions intended to overthrow or undermine parliamentary democracy by political, industrial or violent means.'

Similarly, s10 of the Contempt of Court Act 1981 provides:

> 'No court may require a person to disclose, nor is any person guilty of contempt of court for refusing to disclose, the source of information contained in a publication for which he is responsible, unless it be established to the satisfaction of the court that disclosure is necessary in the interests of justice or national security or for the prevention of disorder or crime.'

The effect of this provision was considered in *Secretary of State for Defence v Guardian Newspapers Ltd* [1984] 2 WLR 268, which concerned the refusal of *The Guardian* newspaper to reveal the source of leaked documents concerning the arrival of Cruise missiles at RAF Greenham Common. Regarding the construction of s10 of the 1981 Act, the House of Lords held that the disclosure of the document was needed in order to identify the servant of the Crown who in breach of his statutory duty had copied the document and supplied a copy to *The Guardian*. The real issue was that it had in its employment a servant or servants who had access to classified information and who were prepared, for reasons which seemed good to them, to betray the trust which was reposed in them. On that basis it was fully established that the exceptions to s10 applied, and that the Crown was entitled to discovery as an aid to pursuing its rights against its servant.

QUESTION FOUR

'When the security of the State is under threat the individual's right to freedom of expression must give way to the greater interests of society as a whole.'

Discuss in the light of recent changes in the law.

Adapted from University of London LLB Examination
(for External Students) Constitutional Law June 1990 Q6

General Comment

A relatively straight forward question requiring students to assess the balance between state security and the individual's right to freedom of expression. Care should be taken to set out the human rights context within which this debate will now be conducted.

Skeleton Solution

Introduction – general principles regarding free speech and scrutiny of governmental action – impact of the Human Rights Act 1998 – examination of key constraints at common law and under statute – compliance with European Convention on Human Rights – conclusion.

Suggested Solution

In the modern world, threats to the security of some or all of the nation, may come in a large variety of forms, often considerably different from those experienced in the past. Principally, the development of systems that allow a complex society to function smoothly also make it vulnerable. From the terrorist's bomb on a plane to security considerations in defence establishments, lawmakers have been forced, by the circumstances of recent years, to curtail the freedoms that individuals have come to expect.

The right to freedom of expression is now enshrined in statute in the domestic law of the United Kingdom by virtue of the Human Rights Act 1998. The Act incorporates art 10 of the European Convention on Human Rights, which provides that everyone has the right to freedom of expression, the right extending to the freedom to hold opinions and to receive and impart information and ideas without interference by public authority. The House of Lords in the course of its decision in *R v Shayler* (2002) The Times 22 March noted the importance of this right as regards the public discussion of political matters and the actions of governments. Lord Bingham emphasised the point that although modern democratic government means government of the people by the people for the people, there could be no government by the people if they were ignorant of the issues to be resolved. He felt that the business of government was a participatory process which meant that facts had to be made known and issues publicly ventilated. Referring to the fact that politicians and other members of the executive might be guilty of 'error, incompetence, misbehaviour, dereliction of duty, even dishonesty and malpractice' that they might not want made public, he observed that 'publicity is a powerful disinfectant.' He went on to acknowledge that where abuses occur the public might be entitled to know about them, and accepted that the role of the press in exposing abuses and miscarriages of justice was a potent one.

Notwithstanding the existence of a statutory right to freedom of expression, and a common law recognition of the importance of a free exchange of knowledge within a democratic society, some restrictions are inevitable if the balance between freedom and state security is to be maintained. Article 10(2) of the European Convention on Human Rights recognises this where it provides that the exercise of these freedoms carries with it duties and responsibilities. It specifically envisages restrictions being imposed to maintain national security.

The two major restraints on freedom of expression in the interests of national security are those imposed by statute, principally under the Official Secrets Act 1989, and those imposed at common law under the doctrine of breach of confidence.

The 1989 Act, enacted to liberalise the law in this area, distinguishes between different classes of disclosure – members and former members of the intelligence and security services on the one hand and past and present Crown servants and government contractors on the other. The Act distinguishes between different kinds of information. Section 1 deals with security and intelligence information. Successive sections deal with information relating to defence, international relations and crime.

Members and former members of the intelligence and security services are prohibited from passing on any details of information obtained whilst employed as by the security services without first obtaining authorisation from the relevant civil servant or minister as the case might be. If unauthorised disclosure is made by members and former members of the intelligence and security services an offence may be committed, even though no actual damage is proved to have been caused by the disclosure. For other classes of Crown servant the proof of damage must be established. *R v Shayler* (above) clearly establishes that members and former members of the intelligence and security services are not entitled to rely on any residual public interest defence to justify unauthorised disclosure. Neither did the House of Lords regard it as realistic that there might be any defence based on the common law concept of necessity or duress of circumstance.

Breach of confidence is a much wider restraint in the sense that the Crown could apply to the court for an order prohibiting any person or body from disclosing information given in confidence. This issue was brought into the public view by the litigation surrounding the publication of the memoirs of a former member of MI5, Peter Wright. The Attorney-General was granted an injunction to prevent the publication of extracts from these memoirs by *The Observer* newspaper, even though the nature of the revelations in the extracts was becoming well known. The basis for the injunction was not so much that confidentiality had to be maintained, but more that no disclosure had been authorised by the government. Ultimately case reached the House of Lords: *Attorney-General* v *Guardian Newspapers (No 1)* [1987] 3 All ER 316. By a majority of three to two it was held that, pending a trial of the main issue, the interim injunction would remain. Lord Brandon thought the maintenance of the injunction might serve to deter further disclosures, whilst Lord Ackner, referring to the fact that the Attorney-General had been unable to prevent publication in the United States, felt that to lift the injunction now would be seen as surrendering to the American constitutional right to free speech. By the time the matter came to trial, international publication of *Spycatcher* had become much more widespread and it was held in *Attorney-General* v *Observer Newspapers (No 2)* [1988] 3 WLR 776 that no final injunction to restrain a breach of confidence would be granted unless it could be shown to be in the public interest to do so. Where the information had already been published abroad, little further damage would be prevented by an injunction.

If material enters the public domain, therefore, it is now very unlikely that the courts will be willing to grant it any further protection from re-publication by way of an injunction. In *Attorney-General* v *Times Newspapers Ltd* (2001) The Times 31 January the court confirmed that it would not be appropriate to grant an injunction in terms that required editors to seek clearance from the Attorney-General before deciding whether or not to publish. The decision was one for the editor to take, mindful of the consequences of any misjudgment on his part.

How is the balance to be struck, therefore, between protecting the right to free speech and maintaining the security of the state? Article 10(2) of the European Convention on Human Rights provides the key here. It provides that the right to free speech may be curtailed by a signatory state provided three conditions are met: the restriction must be 'prescribed by law'; the restriction must seek to achieve the aims identified in art 10(2); and the restriction must go no further than is necessary to achieve the aims identified in art 10(2) – ie it must not be a disproportionate interference with the right provided in art 10(1).

Regarding the restrictions imposed under the Official Secrets Act 1989, there seems little doubt that they satisfy the first two conditions – they are clearly provided for in the statute and seek to achieve a permitted aim, that of the protection of national security. The difficult issue is whether or not the restrictions are a disproportionate interference with the right to free speech. It should be noted that the prohibitions imposed under s1 of the 1989 Act apply even though the information is in the public domain.

Addressing these issues in *R* v *Shayler* (above) the House of Lords adopted the view that s1 was consistent with art 10. Not only was there an internal authorisation process that could permit disclosure, the refusal of authorisation was challengeable by way of judicial review. A refusal of authorisation for disclosure would not merely be subject to review on the grounds of reasonableness. As *R (Daly)* v *Secretary of State for the Home Department* [2001] 3 All ER 433 makes clear, where Convention rights are in play and the courts are considering the issue of proportionality judges are required to assess the balance which the decision-maker has struck, not merely whether it is within the range of rational or reasonable decisions. Attention will be directed to the relative weight accorded to interests and considerations.

Where the prohibition on publication arises from the common law doctrine of breach of confidence the courts will employ the same analysis, but there may be more debate as to whether the doctrine has been established with sufficient certainty in domestic law for it to pass the 'prescribed by law' test.

In conclusion, therefore, domestic law is at something of a crossroads on this issue. Old restrictions remain in place, but these are now to be examined through the prism of the growing human rights culture. This offers the best hope that executive excesses will be kept in check.

QUESTION FIVE

Critically assess the extent to which the incorporation of the European Convention on Human Rights has led to the development of a right to privacy in domestic law.

Written by the Editor

General Comment

Recent case law developments have brought the issue of privacy very much to the forefront. This question requires an explanation of the impact of the Human Rights Act 1998, along with an examination of how the right to privacy has been developed regarding the actions of public and private bodies.

Skeleton Solution

Consider pre-incorporation position – what does the European Convention on Human Rights provide? – consider the framework of the 1998 Act – look at the impact on public bodies and provide examples – consider the development of breach of confidence as the private law equivalent of art 8.

Suggested Solution

Although the United Kingdom was instrumental in the development of the European Convention on Human Rights (ECHR) over 50 years ago, it was not until October 2000 that the rights provided for in that Convention were finally incorporated into domestic law. To what extent is it true to say that prior to that date domestic law failed to recognise any such right?

Certainly in *Malone v Metropolitan Police Commissioner* [1979] Ch 344 the court refused to accept that there was any actionable right to privacy in domestic law, simply because the ECHR was, at the time, an international treaty that had not been incorporated into domestic law. Hence it could not be used as the basis of an action in the courts. To the extent that there was any right to privacy it was protected by other means, such as through actions for breach of confidence, or even trespass to property.

How has the Human Rights Act 1998 changed all this? The Act incorporates art 8 of the ECHR, which provides that: 'Everyone has the right to respect for his private and family life, his home and his correspondence' (art 8(1)); and that 'There shall be no interference by a public authority with the exercise of this right except such as is in accordance with the law and is necessary in a democratic society in the interests of national security, public safety or the economic well-being of the country, for the prevention of disorder or crime, for the protection of health or morals, or for the protection of the rights and freedoms of others': art 8(2).

Section 2(1) of the 1998 Act makes it clear that any court or tribunal determining a question arising in connection with a Convention right must take into account any judgment, decision, declaration or advisory opinion of the European Court of Human Rights. Further, s3(1) of the 1998 Act provides that a court or tribunal called upon to do so, must interpret primary legislation and subordinate legislation 'in a way which is compatible with the Convention rights.'

The 1998 Act places public bodies under a duty not to act in a way that is contrary to the rights protected by the ECHR, hence an individual can bring an application for judicial review against a public body if he or she feels that the body in question has violated the right enshrined in art 8. In such a case the court will have to determine the following questions: has there been an interference with the right to privacy by the public body?; is the basis for the interference prescribed by law? (ie is there an identifiable legal basis for the public body's actions?); does the interference seek to achieve one of the legitimate aims listed in art 8(2)?; if so, does the interference with the right to privacy exceed what is required in order to achieve the legitimate aims listed in art 8(2) – ie is the interference disproportionate?

There are a number of examples of cases where the art 8 right has been invoked against public bodies.

Regulations made pursuant to the Representation of the People Act 1983 required electoral registration officers to supply copies of the register to those wishing to purchase them for marketing purposes. The applicant in *R (Robertson) v Wakefield MDC* (2001) The Times 27 November successfully challenged its practice on the basis that, whilst he was under a legal duty to register to vote (it being a criminal offence to fail to do so), he did not want his details released to commercial organisations without his consent. The court accepted that, given modern marketing techniques, the selling of personal details to direct marketing organisations did raise a potential threat to privacy under art 8 of the Convention. In *R (Daly)* v *Secretary of State for the Home Department* [2001] 3 All ER 433 the House of Lords held that a policy of excluding prisoners (regardless of status) from their cells whilst the cells were searched was a breach of art 8 as it went further than was necessary in securing the legitimate aim of ensuring that prisoners were not secreting prohibited articles. A particular aspect of the policy that the House of Lords found unacceptable was the checking of correspondence between prisoner and lawyer to ensure that legal professional privilege was not being abused.

By contrast in *R* v *Ashworth Special Hospital Authority and Another, ex parte N* (2001) The Times 26 June the policy of recording and listening to a random 10 per cent of non-high risk patients' telephone calls at Ashworth Hospital was held to be permitted within art 8(2). The court was satisfied that, although the measures adopted did interfere with the applicant's right to privacy: (i) there was cogent compelling evidence that patients were likely, unless prevented, to abuse the use of telephones so as to give rise to security risks to themselves, other patients, staff and the public; (ii) random monitoring would achieve a legitimate security aim; (iii) random monitoring interfered with the right under art 8 no more than was necessary to achieve the permitted purpose; (iv) the Secretary of State had established a compelling need for it proportionate to that aim; and (vi) the measure adopted was within the margin of appreciation permitted in respect of art 8, tailored to the aim to be achieved, and not excessive having regard to the extent and consequences of the security risks and the established degree of manipulation possible.

Much of the concern regarding privacy has arisen not in relation to actions of administrative agencies, but in relation to the activities of the Press, particularly tabloid newspapers publishing intimate details of the private lives of persons in the public eye. The problem here is that newspapers are clearly not public bodies, hence not bound by the Human Rights Act 1998. The response of the courts has been to follow the lead given by the 1998 Act and to regard themselves as public bodies under a duty to enforce the ECHR – the so-called horizontal effect. The way this has been done is by the courts developing the common law doctrine of breach of confidence so that it follows the contours of art 8, even though art 8 is not directly applicable in litigation between private parties. In *Douglas* v *Hello! Ltd* [2001] 2 All ER 289 the Court of Appeal agreed to extend the concept of breach of confidence so that private parties would be bound, in certain circumstances, to act in conformity with Convention rights, such as the right to privacy. The interesting development here is that a duty to abide by confidentiality (and thereby respect the privacy of another party) was not seen as being limited to those situations where there had been an express or implied agreement to maintain confidentiality.

Drawing the boundaries has proved to be difficult, however. This was shown by the dilemma facing the court in *A* v *B plc and Another* (2002) The Times 13 March. A Premier League footballer had had a number of affairs with young women. He was a married man and wanted to prevent these women from publishing details of their liaisons with him in national newspapers. Rejecting the request to restrain publication the court held that whilst permanent or stable relationships might give rise to a duty of confidence, it was unlikely that transient liaisons would do so where one of the parties did not want the details to remain confidential. Figures in the public eye were entitled to enjoy a private life, but equally they should expect their actions to attract closer scrutiny than might otherwise be the case. Even where the material concerned was effectively 'kiss and tell' gossip any interference with the right to publish had to be justified on a balancing of the competing interests. It is significant, however, that Lord Woolf CJ expressed the view that there was no need for the courts to recognise a new tort of interference with privacy as in most cases an action for breach of confidence, as now developed, would provide the necessary protection.

Old Bailey Press

The Old Bailey Press integrated student law library is tailor-made to help you at every stage of your studies from the preliminaries of each subject through to the final examination. The series of Textbooks, Revision WorkBooks, 150 Leading Cases and Cracknell's Statutes are interrelated to provide you with a comprehensive set of study materials.

You can buy Old Bailey Press books from your University Bookshop, your local Bookshop, direct using this form, or you can order a free catalogue of our titles from the address shown overleaf.

The following subjects each have a Textbook, 150 Leading Cases/Casebook, Revision WorkBook and Cracknell's Statutes unless otherwise stated.

Administrative Law
Commercial Law
Company Law
Conflict of Laws
Constitutional Law
Conveyancing (Textbook and 150 Leading Cases)
Criminal Law
Criminology (Textbook and Sourcebook)
Employment Law (Textbook and Cracknell's Statutes)
English and European Legal Systems
Equity and Trusts
Evidence
Family Law
Jurisprudence: The Philosophy of Law (Textbook, Sourcebook and
    Revision WorkBook)
Land: The Law of Real Property
Law of International Trade
Law of the European Union
Legal Skills and System
    (Textbook)
Obligations: Contract Law
Obligations: The Law of Tort
Public International Law
Revenue Law (Textbook,
    Revision WorkBook and
    Cracknell's Statutes)
Succession

Mail order prices:	
Textbook	£14.95
150 Leading Cases	£11.95
Revision WorkBook	£9.95
Cracknell's Statutes	£11.95
Suggested Solutions 1998–1999	£6.95
Suggested Solutions 1999–2000	£6.95
Suggested Solutions 2000–2001	£6.95
Law Update 2002	£9.95
Law Update 2003	£10.95

Please note details and prices are subject to alteration.

To complete your order, please fill in the form below:

Module	Books required	Quantity	Price	Cost
		Postage		
		TOTAL		

For Europe, add 15% postage and packing (£20 maximum).
For the rest of the world, add 40% for airmail.

ORDERING

By telephone to Mail Order at 020 7381 7407, with your credit card to hand.

By fax to 020 7386 0952 (giving your credit card details).

Website: www.oldbaileypress.co.uk

By post to: Mail Order, Old Bailey Press at Holborn College, Woolwich Road, Charlton, London, SE7 8LN.

When ordering by post, please enclose full payment by cheque or banker's draft, or complete the credit card details below. You may also order a free catalogue of our complete range of titles from this address.

We aim to despatch your books within 3 working days of receiving your order.

Name

Address

Postcode   Telephone

Total value of order, including postage: £

I enclose a cheque/banker's draft for the above sum, or

charge my   ☐ Access/Mastercard   ☐ Visa   ☐ American Express
Card number

☐☐☐☐ ☐☐☐☐ ☐☐☐☐ ☐☐☐☐

Expiry date   ☐☐☐☐

Signature: ....Date: ....